HEART OF AN
AFRICAN HUNTER

HEART OF AN AFRICAN HUNTER

Stories of the Big Five and the Tiny Ten

Peter H. Flack

Safari Press Inc.
P. O. Box 3095, Long Beach, CA 90803

Flack, Peter H.

Second edition

Safari Press Inc.

1999, Long Beach, California

ISBN 1-57157-115-9

Library of Congress Catalog Card Number: 98-60866

10 9 8 7 6 5 4 3 2

Readers wishing to receive the Safari Press catalog, featuring many fine books on big-game hunting, wingshooting, and sporting firearms, should write to Safari Press Inc., P.O. Box 3095, Long Beach, CA 90803, USA. Tel: (714)894-9080 or visit our Web site at www.safaripress.com.

TABLE OF CONTENTS

FOREWORD

I knew of Peter Hamilton Flack long before I met him in the flesh, having both been regular contributors for a number of years to *Magnum*, South Africa's only gun and hunting magazine. I always looked first for Peter's stories when my monthly copy of *Magnum* arrived, and always with a slight twinge (or is it green tinge) of jealousy. I had spent a lifetime as a professional hunter, first hunting crocodiles for their skins, then cropping large quotas of big game when I held the game-management rights over more than one million acres in old Rhodesia, and finally taking clients on safari in both Rhodesia and Botswana as a professional hunter. Peter, on the other hand, was a sport hunter, hunting only in his spare time. Surely I should have been the one to have interesting, varied, and exciting things to write about. This was not the case. Peter hunted so persistently, ranged so widely in his search for new hunting grounds, and took so many different species under so many diverse conditions in other continents, that I have to concede he held the edge.

Peter has taken every legal species of South African game, and every legal species of southern African game except for less than ten of the rarer species, which he is still seeking. But what of the other side of the man whom we are introducing here, a side that must also interest the potential reader of this book.

After his military training, which he completed as a second lieutenant in 1966, Peter received a BA and an LLB at the University of Cape Town, a DCLS at Cambridge University, and an H Dip Tax at the University of Witwatersrand. From there he joined the law firm of Webber Wentzel in Johannesburg. After four years he was transferred by them to their American branch, Casey Lane and Mittendorf in New York, where he passed the New York bar examination and was admitted as an attorney and counselor-at-law. From there he became partner and director of Bowman Gilfillan and Blacklock, Inc., one of the biggest law firms in South Africa.

Ever searching for a new challenge, he left law and turned to business. Within a year he was appointed executive chairman of both Fralex Limited and Fraser Alexander Limited, mining contracting companies quoted on the Johannesburg Stock Exchange. Ten years later he resigned to joined Randgold and Exploration Company Limited, a South African gold mining company, and two years later listed its African gold mining arm on the London Stock Exchange. Peter held the position of executive chairman of both companies until his retirement in 1998 at the ripe old age of fifty.

Of all Peter's executive positions, the one of most interest to me was his appointment as chairman of Karoo Safaris (Proprietary) Limited. In 1992, Peter purchased a rundown domestic stock farm in the Karoo adjoining that of his longtime friend, Louis Marais. They game fenced their farms into a single unit and began to assiduously pursue a strategy of creating the biggest and best private-plains game nature reserve in the country. Since then Peter and Louis have been joined by four of their friends and together they have added a further twelve farms to create the Agtersneeuberg Nature Reserve, proclaimed as such by the East

Cape Parliament. This single block of land, without internal fences, houses twenty-three species of antelope, measures close to eighty thousand acres, and is the largest private nature reserve in South Africa. It was here that I first met Peter when given an assignment by *Magnum* magazine to write a feature on the reserve, which I visited at Peter's invitation. Everywhere I saw the hand of the perfectionist, as well as the proof of an exceptional organizing ability—the same talent for organization that took Peter to the pinnacle of management in top-flight South African businesses.

This same retired business genius has no intention of becoming a gentleman of leisure. Peter is already well ahead with his second book on African hunting, a book with a difference, and one that I am proud to have been asked to contribute to, and he has plans for a third. But for now, if you would please turn the page and begin to read what he has written, you will see for yourself that I have not deceived you. Peter is indeed as good at stringing words together to create interesting, informative, and genuinely true hunting narratives as he has been at everything else.

Brian Marsh
Durban
South Africa

INTRODUCTION

It all started once I bought a halfway decent camera. No more dark blobs against murky backgrounds. You could actually make out the animals and recognize people and places. From there it was but a short step to photograph albums, then annotating the pictures, then keeping a hunting diary to ensure I had the photos in the correct chronological order and that my comments beneath them were accurate.

Over time, the comments became more extensive and the albums began to consist of a page of print opposite a page of pictures. Then my hunting companions began asking me to make copies of my albums for them, and someone—I can't for the life of me remember who—suggested I send off an account of one of the hunts to a magazine.

I reached an agreement with my secretary to type my article after hours on condition that we share the proceeds, if any, if the story was published. I seem to remember that, by draft sixteen, we called it a day and posted it off to three hunting magazines, starting with *Safari*, which I still rate the best pure hunting magazine, and then *Magnum* and *Petersen's Hunting*. To my amazement, both the first two accepted my story, "Croc Around the Rock." I was as excited as a boy with his first airgun. While *Safari* couldn't give me a publication date, *Magnum* could and so I chose the South African magazine. The unadulterated pleasure of seeing my story in print has never left me, and I have never become blasé at knowing hunters read and enjoy my articles.

Writing about hunts and hunting has become part and parcel of my passion (my wife says obsession) for wildlife, conservation, and hunting. The stories I write and the videos I film and edit somehow fix the game and the hunts more firmly in my memory and extend the pleasure, the excitement, and the lessons learned.

I may not have any of my hunting trophies from my early hunting days. I may not even have any photographs of some of the best trophies I took, of the extraordinary places I visited, of the many warm and wonderful people I met, but my stories have helped me relive those moments. By asking old friends and family members to correct or verify my memory of past events, I have been amazed at how much I have been able to recall.

The stories cover my hunting life in Africa from the age of nine to my current age, which, as I write, is just three months short of my fiftieth birthday. Over this forty-year period, I have hunted in eight African countries (South Africa, Namibia, Botswana, Zimbabwe, Mozambique, Tanzania, Ethiopia, and the Central African Republic) with twenty-four different professional hunters on close to one hundred hunts with a variety of hunting companions. The most constant have been Derek Carstens, Louis Marais, John Oosthuizen, Phil Pascal, Curt Goetz, and G. T. Ferreira. I have taken every available game animal in South Africa and every one available in southern Africa except Damara dik-dik and black-faced impala from Namibia, black lechwe and Cookson wildebeest from Zambia, and Nyasa wildebeest and suni from Tanzania.

This book contains twenty-five articles. Some have appeared in magazines, and I would like to sincerely thank Ron Anger, editor of *Magnum*, (the best all-round hunting magazine, in my opinion) in particular, for permission to reprint those articles of mine that he has had the temerity to publish. They form the bulk of the stories that appear in this book. I have used my original titles, even though the stories appeared with different titles when published in *Magnum*. I have also rewritten some, edited and added to others, and included a few that have never seen the light of day.

I have written them from my heart and as honestly as I am able. I have not tried to hide my many mistakes and failures. I have tried to "tell it as it is," warts and all, in the hope that anyone reading the articles will not only be able to identify with my stories but be able to learn from my mistakes.

This is my first book—I commend it to you in fear and trepidation. I hope it will not be my last. I also hope you will enjoy reading it as much as I have enjoyed writing it. Lastly, I hope that the little bit of experience and wisdom I have acquired over forty years of hunting and share with you in these stories will add a new dimension to your hunting life.

PELEA CAPREOLUS
A Vaal Rhebok by Any Other Name

My mom, God bless her, is of Afrikaans stock on my grandma's side. Her relatives arrived in South Africa some two hundred years ago. My dad, one of nature's true gentlemen, is a *rooinek* (red neck), Afrikaans slang for an Englishman. Born in Zimbabwe, he had no real wish or ability to speak my mom's native tongue. She, in turn, was worried that I would grow up a barbarian in our English-speaking home, with no understanding of her language or culture.

So, at the age of nine, I found myself sitting on the hard, green, leather seats of the South African Railway's milk train to Swellendam en route to Afrikaner farming friends near Bredasdorp. I was going to spend my June holidays with them. A package of cheese sandwiches in wax paper, a plastic bottle of milk, and an apple in a brown paper bag were next to me on the seat. Across from me sat a suntanned giant of a man into whose care my mother had tearfully entrusted me. He wore a white, open-necked shirt, with the collar spread flat over the lapels of his blazer. I remember a lot of gray—gray hat, gray slacks—and black shoes. I also remember the crinkles at the corners of his eyes, and his big hands, with the nails thick and jagged and not altogether clean, neatly peeling my apple with a black Joseph Rogers penknife (immediately the stuff of future birthday present dreams), in one long coil of green skin. He called me "Son" as he stowed his lunch—a battered, brown, tin box with a round top and twine wrapped around the handle—under the seat.

"The Old Trout," as I affectionately call my mother, still teases me about the call I made to her that night on the party line from the farm. "Please speak Afrikaans, Mom," I am told I said. "I don't understand English that well anymore!" *Oom* Kleinman (literally, Uncle Small Man) was a grizzled old man with a smoker's cough and seemed as old and wise as Moses. His wife was a warm, loving, homey woman who always cooked stewed fruit with the inevitable mutton stew, rice, and potatoes. What were they to do with this hyperactive little hooligan? Their youngest child was in his twenties and the only one left at home. A dark, saturnine, silent, surly whip of a man, he lived in an outside room, drove a razzy car, and scared the living day-lights out of me. Still does, come to think of it.

They gave me a .22 rifle and entrusted me to the care of Hendrik, one of the farm labourers. I was always being entrusted in those days. I think I was the most entrusted little spiky-haired, blond thug in the whole of the Western Cape. Fat lot of good it did Hendrik. I was way ahead of him when I came over the false crest of a kopje (hill). If nine-year-olds are as fit as Olympic athletes, I would have won a medal in those days. Hendrik must have thought I was the reincarnation of his worst nightmare. I didn't understand him. I didn't listen to him even when I did. He would have dearly loved to belt the "white" off me, to use a phrase coined by Bill Cosby. When the shot went off, I can only imagine that he must have thought that I'd killed myself be-cause, when he arrived on the scene, he was bug-eyed, breath-less, and sweating something terrible.

He relaxed when he saw the vaal rhebok at my feet, para-lyzed but breathing. Watching Hendrik cut its throat was the most fascinatingly revolting thing I had ever seen, only to be surpassed shortly thereafter when he gralloched the animal.

Hendrik's relief at finding me up and about and the buck down and dying probably lent a degree of enthusiasm to his praise that otherwise would have been absent. Hendrik's version of the story made me into a regular little hero in the district. I was trotted around to the neighbours and the tale recounted endlessly. Aunt Anna even bought me a sheath knife. I felt terribly guilty, particularly when my silence was interpreted as modesty. It wasn't until I was married that I told the real story.

According to Hendrik, I had seen the flick of an ear from the foot of the kopje. I slithered up the side of the bush-strewn hill like a veritable sniper, skillfully using the cover like a veteran. As I disappeared from view, I came within range and shot a big vaal rhebok ram in the back of the head with my .22. End of story. Not bad for a nine-year-old—and a *stadsjapie* (city dweller) at that! Certainly a lot better than the eleven-year-old *boertjie* (little farmer/Afrikaner) on the neighbouring farm who had inflicted a *boudskoot* (Texas heart shot) on a buck and a gash under his eye with his father's .303.

The truth is substantially different. In my clamber up the kopje, I saw a leopard lurking in the kloof (ravine) and loaded the .22. When my overactive imagination was distracted by a different daydream, I forgot to unload the rifle or put the safety on. As I climbed over the rocks edging the false crest of the hill, I turned to the left around a clump of haphazardly strewn rocks and came face-to-rear, so to speak, with a small herd of vaal rhebok walking slowly away from me at a distance of some fifty metres. I got such a fright I almost leapt out of my skin. The rifle went off and the herd went bouncing and skittering down the slope and out of sight. I walked forward, trying to collect myself and to see where they had gone when I virtually tripped over the ram.

It took me almost twenty years to tell the true story, and twelve or so more before I shot my second vaal rhebok. In the interim, I graduated from the little nine-year-old who was only too happy to be given the opportunity to hunt anything to a gangly, spotty teenager who didn't care what he shot, provided it was a lot, then on to a young trophy hunter, a big-game hunter, a father teaching a young son, a budding and inept photographer, and finally to an enthusiastic and barely educated conservationist and occasional culler and hunter of whatever.

I am an average shot and an average hunter at best. I know it. My friends know it. And I know that they know it. But I am a lucky hunter, in more senses than one. I enjoy good health. I have the resources to hunt regularly. Most importantly, I have a family and friends who encourage and share my hunting with me. Partly because I don't want to disappoint them, partly because I don't enjoy making a clot of myself, and mostly because I hate hurting animals, I practice a great deal.

I normally take a break from hunting from October to March, although I keep up mild physical exercise such as daily Canadian Air Force exercises. Depending on my hunting program for the next year, I start running and cycling in earnest around October or November. Shooting practice starts in January with an old Brno .22. Don't laugh, but I start using it with a silencer and subsonic rounds, off a dead rest at 50 metres and carry on from there. By the time I move up to 100 metres, switch to normal ammunition, and shoot from standing, kneeling, sitting, and lying positions, I have fired about 250 rounds.

It amazes me each year at how poorly I start shooting and how much I improve as the weeks roll by. My original group with the .22 at 50 metres is often more than an inch square. Within a couple of weeks, it covers the area of my thumbnail and is within an inch at 100 metres—off a rest, of course. What is it? Carelessness as the season moves on? Casualness? Forgetting some of the basics? The result of continual heavy caliber use? The break from October to January? I don't know. What I do know is that the practice is essential for me.

Pelea capreolus

From the .22 I move on to the 7x57mm, then the 7mm Remington Magnum, then my favourite .375 Brno, and then fewer and fewer shots with the .416, .460, and .475, respectively. By March or April, my shooting is respectable, by my standards at any rate, and just as important, my mind is right. I know my rifles are sighted in and functioning properly. I know, within the limitations I set for myself, that I can use them adequately.

I believe that this practice, combined with the limitations I have referred to, helped me become a lucky hunter. At any rate, my practicing helps to create a very limited reputation as a reliable hunter, at least in the Karoo where I have hunted for the last fifteen years with Louis Marais of Karoo Safaris.

For those who don't know this little bundle of gray, furry joy—*Pelea capreolus*, the symbol of the East Cape Game Management Association—I can do no better than quote the description of the vaal rhebok in the *SCI Record Book of Trophy Animals*:

> The vaal rhebok is a small, graceful antelope with a long slender neck and a soft, thick, woolly, gray coat. Underparts are white. The end of the nose is very large, rounded and glandular. The ears are long, narrow and pointed. There are no bare, glandular patches below the ears. The tail is short and bushy, white underneath. The horns (males only) are straight, vertical, parallel, ringed in the basal half, and extraordinarily slim for their length. Females are similar to males but are slightly smaller and without horns. Behavior: Gregarious, living in family groups of up to a dozen—occasionally as many as thirty— usually led by a master male. Young males form bachelor groups, while very old males are often solitary. Males are highly territorial and aggressive, often killing each other during the breeding season. The young (one to two) are usually born November to December. Life span in the wild is eight to ten years. Both diurnal and nocturnal. Entirely a

grazer. Drinks water daily. Very wary and alert, with a herd member usually acting as a sentinel while the others feed or rest. Alarm call is a sharp cough or snort. Eyesight, hearing, and sense of smell are excellent. A swift runner and an accomplished leaper, clearing barriers easily. Males are extremely aggressive, being reputed to attack and kill mountain reedbuck and the smaller predators, and even occasionally domestic sheep and goats (but this is disputed). Vaal rhebok are not generally considered edible because of the presence of bot fly larvae under the skin. Habitat: Rocky hills, mountain slopes, and grassy plateaus. The vaal rhebok utilizes a more open and exposed habitat than the mountain reedbuck. Lives at elevations of 5,500 feet (1,675m) and higher, but seldom lower.

James Mellon, in his book *African Hunter* (my bible on hunting in Africa), only discusses hunting four species in South Africa on the basis that they occur almost nowhere else. These are the vaal rhebok, which he states, from the standpoint of hunting difficulty, is the top trophy; the white-tailed gnu (or black wildebeest); the blesbok; and the bontebok. Pictures of these animals along with nyala and white rhinoceros are the only photographs that appear in that chapter. The clear implication is that better examples of other species can be obtained in other countries, certainly at the time the book was written, which was in 1975. Fortunately, the changes that he perceived were beginning to occur in game management in our country have become a reality, and I believe he would write a substantially different chapter on South Africa today.

Some five years ago, one of Louis's neighbours by the name of Danie paid me a great compliment and offered to let me hunt one of his prize animals—vaal rhebok—on his farm in the high, cold mountains of the Eastern Cape. We arrived at Danie's farm, Grootvlei, as dawn broke on a cold, gray, blustery winter's morning. Danie, two of his sons, and a collection of farm hands and horses were already waiting. The clingle of metal bits, the stamp and snort of a horse, the low rumble of talk, breath pluming in the cold air, hot, unsweetened, strong black coffee and slices of dried sweet bread called *beskuit* (rusks). Just the beginnings of a bite of anticipation in the pit of the stomach. Magic! How else in your forties do you get to feel like a five-year-old at Christmas?

We walk down through the spotless farmyard toward a coppice of leafless poplar trees, silver gray, still, and stiff, like Russian soldiers standing guard in Red Square. We set up my inch-by-inch target, which I tape to a cardboard box, at 100 metres. The first three shots from my customized .243 Brno almost cut one another in a neat triangle about an inch above the white blob of the bull. Out of the corner of my eye, I see a couple of knowing nods and glances being exchanged. Louis had put in some powerful propaganda spade work to convince Danie that I was not just another bonehead from Johannesburg with more mouth than skill. Thus far, I had at least vindicated his sterling work on my behalf, and I overheard a muttered *grootwild jagter van Johannesburg* (big-game hunter from Johannesburg) spoken with an unaccustomed degree of respect. These hardy folk have seen dozens of South African and overseas hunters arrive with their hot magnums, impossibly expensive highpower scopes, roaring like lions about their prowess only to depart like meek little lambs, cowed by the challenge of hunting these bleak Scottish-like hills and mountains.

I, too, felt reassured by my performance on the range, which to tell the truth, exceeded my expectations. I do not usually use the .243, much preferring my 7mm Remington Magnum. I had been persuaded by the locals, however, that a .243 was all I needed in the Karoo. The ammunition is much less expensive, and on culling, more comfortable over a long day's shooting. And so I brought it. I would still have brought my 7mm Remington Magnum on the hunt except two of my friends who had joined me on the trip had developed an over-powering urge to hunt black wildebeest while we were away for the day. Louis had refused to let them hunt this hardy and underrated animal with their culling calibers. My 7mm was commandeered because, as they said, a vaal rhebok was hardly larger than a rabbit and a .243 ample!

I agreed. Besides, I had shot well in the culling exercise over the two previous days and Louis's walk-in cold room was full to the brim with forty-nine springbok and blesbok, of which my share was almost half. I was on a roll. Nothing could go wrong. . . .

Up and up we rode. Checking first this valley and then that. Glassing from this crest and then to that. I was thankful for my two down jackets, one a waistcoat and the other full-length plus a hood. It was bitter. By midmorning when we stopped for a smoke, we had seen plenty of mountain reedbuck but few vaal rhebok and then only at a distance, alert on a sky-line or rocketing away, white tails bobbing.

We decided to proceed on foot. No sooner had we descended to the bottom of a half-bowl-like formation, surrounded by moun-tain tops, than Louis tugged my arm. Crouching, he pulled me down to a kneeling position as he gestured up to the right. Around the edge of the cliff I could see three ewes proceeding cautiously, looking back over their shoulders. They had not seen us and I laid down, simultaneously extending the legs of the Harris bipod attached to the front swivel of the .243.

Louis shook me again, *"Daar kom 'n ram nou!"* (There's a ram!) I looked up, searching for the ram. *"Hy's 'n moerse ram, Peter, jy moet hom vat!"* (He's a hell of a ram, Peter, you must take him!) Ah, there he was. Even moving, the animals were difficult to make out against the gray-green background of rock, *renosterbos* (rhinoceros bush), and *suurpol* (sour grass). Cradling the stock, I looked through the scope. The ram was a beauty, his long, elegant horns extending way past the tips of his alert, 6-inch ears as he picked his way daintily after the advancing ewes.

They were going to cross in front of me, 250 to 300 yards away. "*Wag*" (Wait), said Louis, echoing my own thoughts. Cautiously they kept on coming. I was rock steady, the cross hairs of the scope tracking the left shoulder of the ram. When he was directly opposite me, he stopped. *Dead,* I thought, as I gently squeezed the trigger. The animals froze into a still life as the shot reverberated around the basin. Before the sound died away, the next round was in the chamber. I checked carefully through the scope. Except for his head, which was now looking back over his rump, the ram had not moved. No, there was no grass or bush in the way of the bullet; the shot was clear. Three shots later, I degenerated into a hot, sweaty, confused mess. All the rams were standing pretty much where they had been when I first fired. I wanted to stand up and chase them away. I wanted the ground to open up and engulf me. I was *ge-rattle* (rattled), as they say here. I did not begin to understand what was happening.

Sighted in an inch high at 100 metres, the ammunition I was using grouped 9 inches down at 300 metres, the distance I estimated between myself and the ram. I was dead steady, although becoming less so. I was aiming behind the shoulder with the horizontal cross hairs resting along the animal's back. It made no sense. I turned to Louis. "Give me your rifle," I hissed. Pulling his .270 tightly into my shoulder, I battled to find the ram in the scope. Louis is much shorter than I and so is the stock of the .270 compared with the .243. What a nightmare! Black holes floated around the scope. The ewes were leaving. They had had enough. The ram must run!

At last, by resting the barrel of the .270 across the stock of the .243, I managed to steady myself. Pulling my head back and up, I could hold the ram in the scope. It was now facing me at a slight angle to my right. The trigger pull took an eternity as I tried to hold steady in line with the left front leg. *Boom!* "*Jy het hom!*" (You've got him!), yelled Louis, scrambling to his feet and grabbing for his .270. I stood up shakily, reduced to a quivering wreck in less than a minute by this tiny animal. My knees were like rubber as I stepped off the 338 paces to the animal. I looked down at the ram. He was still alive but only just. As with my first ram, I had to ask someone else to deliver the *coup de grace.* I couldn't. "*Groot wildjagter se voet!*" (Big-game hunter's backside!)

It was the worst moment of my hunting life. I had frightened and hurt a beautiful animal. I had embarrassed Louis and made an idiot of myself. No one, not least the kindly Danie and his sons, knew what to say. If I could, I would have dug a large hole, climbed in, and buried myself. Pride comes before a fall, they say. How true!

I remembered the smug thoughts of the last two days as I had silently examined some of the animals shot by my companions. Some of these had been badly shot, and, as a result, the venison that we were after had been spoiled or ruined. I recalled my superiority in the lift of an eyebrow to Louis, the brief shake of a head. Well, I didn't feel so *windgat* (hotshot) now.

What could I do but apologize, and profusely at that. It was a long, silent drive home. The next morning I was out on the range next to Louis's house when I found the problem. After my 7mm Remington Magnum, the .243 was like a toy. I had not been pulling it tightly into my shoulder. This was compounded by the two well-padded down jackets I was wearing. As I squeezed the trigger, the rifle moved ever so slightly farther into my shoulder that in turn, lifted the barrel as it pivoted on the bipod. Over 300 metres, this made a substantial difference. I fired four shots over the back of the buck. With the thick cover on the mountainside, I could not see where the shots fell. When I used Louis's unfamiliar .270, I treated it like my 7mm and mounted it firmly. Even so, that was the last time I fired the .243. Louis sold it for me a few months later.

As for myself, well, as I write this, I can see a magnificent 8 3/4-inch vaal rhebok ram gazing accusingly at me from the wall of my study. A permanent reminder of some very hard lessons. As for Danie, I guess he must have almost forgiven me. Louis says he has asked whether I would like a vaal rhebok full skin. Apparently, there is an excellent ram that regularly visits the lands at Grootvlei. Problem is, he has only one horn, hence I say *almost* forgiven me.

KUDU CAPERS

I stood in the dappled shade of the *haak-en-steek* (hook and stab) thorn trees fringing the foot of the kopje. Through the scope of a borrowed .30-06, I watched a herd of impala precede a group of four kudu bulls plodding along the skyline in the late morning heat and down and out of sight. I estimated the distance between 200 and 250 metres. Leading the biggest bull by a tad, I gently squeezed the trigger. The rifle cracked. The bull dropped in his tracks, and I nearly leapt out of my skin. Aghast, jaw open, eyes popping, blood pressure pounding, I was stunned! *It can't be!* I thought, *it just can't be!*

I sprinted helter-skelter up the hill, refusing to believe what I had just seen. Oh my oath! There it lay. Dead, deceased, departed, gone to the happy hunting grounds in the sky. What to do? Lie—yes, pretend it never happened. Better still—shot by the neighbours. I looked at the borrowed rifle, took it by the barrel and just checked myself from slamming it into the rock at my feet. It wasn't the rifle's fault; it was mine. All my working rifles are Brnos. To fire a Brno, you move the safety toward you. Conversely, to make the rifle safe, you push the safety away from you. My borrowed rifle worked on exactly the opposite basis, and while checking through the scope at the kudu bulls, I ensured that the rifle was on safe and pushed the safety forward. No, I was not poaching. I was hunting on a ranch bordering the Limpopo River in the northern Transvaal with the owner's permission. In fact, he and I parted company only an hour or so ago. I was on an exploratory visit to his game ranch preparatory to booking a ten-day hunt for myself and three friends. It was my turn to do the booking that year, and as such, I was responsible for checking the facilities and making the necessary arrangements with the landowner. The problem was that he happened to be a senior partner in the firm I had just joined. To compound matters, he brought his wife along for the weekend and she had expressly asked me not to shoot any of the kudu. They were her favorite animal.

The closer I got to camp, the slower I walked. Even so, I arrived before my host, and as luck would have it, walked straight into his wife. As she saw me, she gasped and her hand flew to her mouth. "What have you done?" she asked. *How the hell did she find out so fast?* flashed through my mind. All thought of lies, half-lies, and excuses evaporated and all I could do was stammer that, "I have shot a k . . . k . . . k . . ." Before I could get the sentence out of my mouth, she ran toward me, grabbed me by the shoulders and said, "Oh, no, not Kevin!"

To cut a long story short, when I aimed at the kudu, I was holding the rifle loosely, barely tucked into my shoulder. I had absolutely no intention of shooting it and that's the truth. I was merely practicing. Doing what Karamojo Bell of elephant hunting fame recommends. With the shock of the shot going off, I didn't feel the scope tap me on my eyebrow. I had, unknowingly, joined the half-moon club. What I thought was perspiration running down my face was, in fact, blood. By the time I reached camp, my face was a mess. Liz thought that I had a dreadful accident and that her teenage son, Kevin, who was also with us for the weekend, was involved. After we both calmed down, the reality and relief was so great that she quite forgot to tear a strip off me for shooting the kudu. It was a magnificent bull but I did not have the cheek to either measure it or ask for the horns, let alone the cape or some of the meat.

That all took place many years ago during the course of only my second or third hunt in the Transvaal. It was, however, my first kudu "hunt" and the start of a whole series of baffling errors and mistakes regarding kudu.

I can't say that hunting kudu immediately became a passion or an obsession. There was so much in the lowveld that was new and exciting. Slowly, however, the great, gray ghosts grabbed ahold of me. As each hunting season rolled by without a trophy bull, I slowly but surely began to think I was jinxed. Just as slowly and surely, my interest in hunting kudu changed from an occasional pastime to an obsession. Looking back through my diaries, I find the following entries:

1979–Mariental, Namibia. The flip of a coin made it John's turn when we approached the cattle kraal pens on a bitingly cold July dawn. The kraal was on the edge of a dry riverbed along which we had been carefully edging. We barely paid any attention to the kraal, our eyes riveted on the riverine trees and thickets, hoping for the flick of an ear or the glint of the early morning sun's rays on an ivory-tipped horn. Some seventy-five paces from the kraal, as if by some magnetic force, we both flicked a look to our left and stopped instantly, rooted to the spot. A magnificent, majestic, monstrous kudu bull stood in the middle of the kraal, watching us approach with what looked for all the world like kudu curiosity. John fired. The bull gracefully cleared the $5^{1}/_{2}$-foot kraal wall and trotted some eighty paces. John fired again and the bull vanished.

(For many years that remained the biggest bull I had ever seen, and in my mind's eye, I can still see it. So can John!)

1982–Okavango Swamps, Botswana. Trotting to make up time on the buffalo herd that the old cow had led thundering off, taking a couple of trophy bulls with her. Panting. Watching the ground. No twisted ankle wanted now. Breath rasping in my throat. Running shoes quiet. Grass swishing against my bare legs, brown after ten days of hunting. Kudu on the right. Big bull. Right hand down. Flitting through the trees. Trees thickening. Into a clearing. Up against a tree trunk, the bull quartering away. Cupping my hand to form a "v" for the .458. Shaking like a country outhouse on a windy hill. Too late.

1985–Gravelotte, South Africa. Difficult stony ridges. The leaves off the trees are like Kellogg's Rice Krispies underfoot—*snap, crackle,* and *pop!* The bush is gray, dry, dull—waiting for rain. Kudu cows ahead. Gray, eroded folds of rumpled ground leading down to a desiccated dam. Deep footprints imprinted, molded into the gray soil tinged with the black of remaining moisture in the turf. Where is the bull? Where is the bull? A breath of breeze. That fickle midday breeze. A bark, a clatter of pebbles, a breaking branch. There he is. A glimpse. A glance. Good-bye! Back to camp. Derek's beautiful 54-inch bull mocking me from the slaughtering shed but really happy for him.

1989–Matetsi, Zimbabwe. Kudu bulls were aplenty at 48 or 49 inches—nothing special. As if they know it, they stand and stare. The 63-inch set of horns in the skinning shed shot by a previous hunter are aesthetically unappealing, I convince myself. I wouldn't have shot such a bull, given the opportunity. Like hell!

1991–Cabora Bassa, Mozambique. Returning to camp from an aborted lion hunt, drowsing in the front seat of the Land Cruiser, blood sugar low, brain in neutral, backside in overdrive. Magara banging on the roof. Joe pointing. Five huge kudu bulls sprinting for the shelter of the treeline on the flood plain. Hook up and hang on. Wheels churning, dust spewing, teeth-chattering, bone-jarring thuds as we speed to cut them off. "Stop, stop!" I yell at Joe. I knew they were going to beat us. I knew they were going to halt in the safety of the treeline. The Cruiser skidded and juddered to a halt. The fine dust enveloped me as I ran from the Cruiser, plumped down on a ridge out of the dust. Split seconds to play with. The fourth and last bull, the biggest. Huge. Horns twisting into the trees. The fifth bull starting to run past. Tense. No time. Cross hairs wobbling. No good. Too far for the .375. Too little time. Adrenaline level falling back to economy mode.

1993—Venetia Game Reserve, South Africa. I accepted an invitation from a colleague to return to the Limpopo. In fact, he proposed a trip to the new Venetia Game Reserve, a stone's throw from my very first kudu hunt.

Derek is a kudu fanatic and I don't readily know of anyone else who has hunted kudu as frequently or with as much success in recent years. He has reduced the fine art of kudu hunting to nearly a science. He has made a detailed study of their habitat and habits. He has perfected the patience and dead quiet stalk necessary to secure the major trophies that adorn the walls of his home and office. And while I was unable to toughen my feet sufficiently to hunt barefoot like he does, I looked forward to learning from the master.

The first day, as we were returning to camp in the midday heat, we spotted two bulls in the riverine thicket. The smaller of the two was lying down while the larger was quartering away from me and patchily screened by what looked like a thin and ragged shrub of sorts. I lay in the hot sand, extended the legs on the bipod attached to the front swivel of Bertha, my faithful old .375 Brno, and took aim. I was rock steady as I screwed the Zeiss Diavari 1.5–6X variable down to 3X. The bull was dozing some seventy metres away and I carefully aimed to hit the off foreleg. The whine of the cicadas seemed to harmonize with my brain waves. Heat settled over me like an electric blanket on high. The shot exploded a flight of arrow-marked babblers as the bulls rocketed off.

After some forty-five minutes, we were prepared to accept that the bullet must have ricocheted off something of substance in the shrub. Only our persistent belief that I could not have missed kept us searching. And then we found the first drop of blood. By about five o'clock that evening, one of the two trackers said he could go no further, so over our handheld radio, we set up a rendezvous with Derek to fetch the tracker and supply us with some water as none of us had had anything to drink or eat since breakfast. As darkness descended, we had almost caught up to the bull. We twice caught a glimpse of his horns through the thick mopane scrub. With hindsight, our stop for water probably cost us the bull. He was walking steadily, but from the occasional signs on the tall grass, it appeared as if the bullet creased his left shoulder. The blood trail, however, was almost nonexistent, and we only picked up minuscule drips where and when the bull stopped to rest or feed.

It was a miserable, tired, downhearted, forty-five-year-old that sat around the fire that night trying to hold up his end of the conversation. My thoughts kept turning to the kudu.

The next morning, as the light changed from charcoal to gray and the bush started to awaken with the first tentative twitterings and tweets, we waited impatiently to pick up the tracks again. On and on we tracked. Initially we made good time in the sandy soil of the valley, but farther on, the rocky outcrops reduced us to time-consuming circles as we lost the tracks. We ignored an outstanding nyala bull skulking in the shadows of a short acacia, barely gave a passing glance to a family group of eland, and were frankly annoyed when a bunch of donkeys, still dressed in their pyjamas, ran across our front blotting out the tracks.

Midday approached and found us crossing a white, calcrete, barren and stony plain with scattered and stunted mopane trees dotted about as if by random selection. I was reminded of an old picture of Delville Wood. In the distance, an emerald green oasis of trees and bushes shimmered in the mirage, indicating water. My heart leapt as I picked out the horns of one and then two kudu bulls. We dropped to our knees, leopard-crawled behind a fold in the ground and put some cover between ourselves and the bulls. The cover ran out some three hundred metres from the bulls but it was close enough to inspect them carefully through our binoculars. No, neither was our bull. Back to the tracks and then disaster. Some three hundred metres from the large, horseshoe-shaped water hole, the tracks were obliterated by countless hooves of the many different animals that came to drink in the night. Around and around the water hole we patrolled, eyes glued to the ground. Foot by foot in ever widening circles we went, trying to pick up the bull's exit from the dam. Eventually there was nothing for it but to give up.

As best I can remember, it was the first wounded animal I had not found in more than nine years. Not since a "dead" black springbok I was standing next to leapt to its feet and vaulted over the edge of a Karoo cliff, defying the best attempts of myself, my host, and two of his mounted employees, had I lost an animal. With heavy hearts and hanging heads, we plodded back to our rendezvous more than an hour away. I kept on replaying the shot through my mind, furious with myself, at my stupidity for shooting through the shrub despite the fact that I had taken similar shots successfully many times before.

Nothing could cheer me up. I was inconsolable. No more hunting for me this year. Late in the afternoon, I decided to take a drive around the rest of the magnificent 35,000-hectare reserve that was ultimately going to almost double in size. We idled along, stopping to look at sable, gemsbok, impala, and a beautiful, brightly-coloured lilac-breasted roller catching the last of the afternoon sun. As the heat of the day drained away and the colours brightened, we were puttering along the edge of a dry riverbed to our right. From the left, one, two, three . . . eight kudu bulls sauntered across the road. The last bull stopped, satellite dish ears alert, gazing down his regal nose at us poor, lesser mortals. A shiver rippled across his flank. He gave an undignified little twitch and kicked up his heels as a nyala bull trotted out of the bush from behind him, and then he disappeared from view. We drove on past and about a kilometre further on my tracker tapped me on the arm. "Let's go and have a look," he suggested. *What the hell*, I thought as we eased out of the vehicle in the direction of the bulls. Halfway there I came to such a sudden stop that my tracker walked into me. All I could see was this humongous set of horns bobbing slowly through the bush diagonally to my left.

No squeezing the binoculars to try and make the bull beat the minimum trophy standards this time. No "is he, isn't he a good one?" He was a bull of biblical proportions. He was a keeper. A quick, silent sneak brought me to the edge of cover. The bull was walking steadily but slowly away at a distance of some 250 metres. Huge body, huge horns. I took a calculated risk. With his back to me, I tiptoed another thirty to forty metres to a lone sapling barely two inches in diameter. The bull started feeding, stretching to nibble on some leaves at the edge of his reach, his horns splaying down on either side of his body. *Turn*, I willed the bull. I was tempted to make a dash for another mopane tree some thirty metres diagonally to my left. I didn't. Thank heavens. I would have been caught in no-man's-land. The bull turned to its left. My sights quivered over his shoulder, not as steady as I would have liked.

With the shot, the bull swapped ends and disappeared at a gallop into the riverbed. After him we hurtled. Down into the riverbed, slogging through the thick sand, up the bank, through the trees, out into the open. My tracker was following the spoor at a fantastic pace. I was off to the right and looking ahead. There he was! As I raised my rifle, he spun around and battered his way through some thick cover.

Kudu Capers

Three hundred metres later we were almost back where we had started. The light was failing fast. I picked up the bull clearly through the Zeiss, thankful for its tremendous light-gathering powers.

After the excitement and exertion of the last few minutes, I was far from steady. My heart was beating an erratic tattoo on my ribs like a drummer with St. Vitus's Dance. My lungs were heaving. The cross hairs were jitterbugging off, on, and around the kudu's chest. "Please," I heard my tracker whisper behind me. I took a deep breath, let it out, and more in desperation than in certainty, pulled the trigger. The second shot pole-axed the bull as the 270-grain Winchester Power Point entered the base of his muscular, fringed neck.

The recovery operation, photographs, skinning, and capping took us well past midnight. The tape measure eventually stretched to $58^1/_2$ inches around the spiral, 46 inches tip-to-tip and the bull dwarfed Derek's superb $53^1/_2$-inch bull both in body and horn size. The *boma* was a very different place that night. But not for me. Still overshadowed with regret and sadness, I thought of the Friday bull.

SITATUNGA SAGA

I sat on the branch of a wild fig tree, some twelve metres above the ground, on a small island in the middle of the Okavango Swamps. We had been glassing the surrounding papyrus beds for hours. My hunting partner, Derek, who had been in a tree on the opposite side of the island, was standing beneath me beckoning me down. He was bored; I was frustrated. This was my eighth day of hunting that elusive gray swamp fairy, the sitatunga.

As I gestured to him to wait another five minutes, the branch I was sitting on suddenly gave way and down I fell. I knew I was in a lot of trouble but my mind was marvelously clear. In a weird way, things seemed to slow down. I remember a similar sensation when an angry buffalo chased me up a tree. I remember a lioness in thick cover on a riverbank. At any rate, I have a clear recollection of seeing my rifle fall past me to the right and thinking that if I did not catch it, that would be the end of the hunt. I easily caught the rifle firmly in my right hand and in the same movement reached out and grabbed a branch with my left. Fortunately, my ankle caught in a fork of the tree, and quick as lightening, my professional hunter grabbed my leg. Then, slowly and ever so carefully, I began to edge my way back to safety.

When I eventually looked down, the expression of horror on Derek's face told the whole story. Had I completed the fall, I would have been as dead as the proverbial dodo. But, there I was, safe and sound, although starting to shake like a country outhouse on a windy hill as the realization set in. To make matters worse, a breeze had sprung up that started to gently rock the huge tree in which we were sitting. I decided I'd had enough for one day. Once my knees acquired a consistency firmer than newly made jelly, I intended to climb down and start the two-hour journey back to camp at Xunaraga in the heart of Botswana's Okavango Swamps.

Then, from nowhere, he appeared. Out of the papyrus bed that I had been glassing for more than three hours appeared a truly magnificent sitatunga bull, picking his way daintily and noiselessly through the reeds. The stories I've read and heard about sitatungas submerging until only their nostrils were above the water suddenly seemed believable.

"It's a beaut," my pro whispered, awed as I was by the bull. At this distance (some 250 metres) and with the wind blowing, whispering was not necessary but we spoke sotto voce nevertheless. "You must shoot him," he whispered needlessly.

Thoughts of a sitatunga bull I missed on a previous safari flashed through my mind. In this instance we had been poling along quietly in a *mokoro* (dugout canoe) down an old hippo trail. It was early morning and a stiffish breeze was blowing into our faces. The hippo trail opened into a wide lagoon. On the far side of the lagoon, facing away from us at an angle, grazed a sitatunga bull, knee deep in water. We could not get any closer; in fact, we had already reached the point of no return. Any minute now he would turn and see us. The wind was already making him nervous and he would nibble a bit and then jerk his head up sharply, looking from side to side. I could see his mouse-like face quite clearly and remember thinking he looked as if he'd shoved his head into a pencil sharpener.

"You will have to take him from here," whispered the pro. Sitting in the *mokoro*, I was just too low to see over the intervening reeds, and when I stood up, I could not keep the cross hairs on the buck. The wind was rippling the water so that the little *mokoro* was bobbing to a rhythm all of its own. What to do?

I had been hunting sitatunga for a number of days and had begun to realize that everything I heard about their elusiveness was true. We poled to innumerable islands, skirted them, found fresh tracks of sitatunga, climbed trees and spent hour upon hour patiently glassing papyrus beds. All to no avail. Cows we had seen aplenty and one or two young bulls, but nothing worth taking. Apart from this, there were other pressures. My professional hunter had explained in great detail the need for caution in hunting the islands. They were, he said, a refuge for wounded buffalo and elephant carelessly shot by locals, and as the swamp waters rose (which they were in the process of doing, this being April), many snakes took refuge on the islands.

I had already experienced two extremely unpleasant confrontations. The first was an eyeball to eyeball confrontation with a huge water leguan as I climbed a tree to find a good spot to glass the neighbouring papyrus. Originally I thought it was a sleeping python. I was enlightened when he awoke, blinked a beady eye some thirty centimetres from my face, and then tore off through the branches in an ungainly hip-swaying motion that would have been the envy of any hula dancer. For a few seconds, I thought my heart had stopped.

The second episode was even worse. It was midmorning. The sun was warm on my back. The cicadas were buzzing in the background. OK, I confess, I was daydreaming, head down, rifle cradled between my knees. Out of the blue, a thin, olive green snake, about one or two metres long, fell from the reeds across my bare forearms. All I could think of was green mamba! Now I have always prided myself on my quick reflexes, and my overwhelming impulse was to fling the snake from me. My body, however, quite simply would not play ball and there I sat, rooted to the spot, staring at the back of the snake's coffin-shaped head.

After what seemed an eternity, the snake started to ease its way down my bare leg and into the bottom of the *mokoro*. I wanted to tell my pro, who was poling from the front of the boat, that we had a snake on board. My first attempt sounded like the strangled wheeze of a patient on a defective iron lung. My second attempt, though hardly better, was sufficient to make him turn his head. At this stage, the snake was slithering between his legs. All I could do was point. His eyes widened as they followed my finger and he, too, was transfixed as the snake slipped over the gunwales into the water. We looked at one another for a long moment without saying a word. We were a long way from camp and both realized the consequences of a snake bite so far from help. Without a word he turned and continued poling.

Now, with the sitatunga bull in sight, I was standing in the *mokoro* with my rifle barrel weaving all over the place like the Pope blessing the masses at a Vatican rally in St. Peter's Square. I should have climbed out and found a firmer footing in the shallow water, taking one of the punting poles to use as a rifle rest. This was, however, my first hunt in the Okavango and my inexperience told. Taking a deep breath, I lifted the rifle once more, and as I exhaled, eased the cross hairs downward and squeezed the trigger as they passed behind the bull's shoulder. The recoil nearly threw me out of the narrow boat, and I knew I had missed even before I saw the shaking heads. We quartered the area for more than an hour and finally satisfied ourselves that the bull had not been hit.

That was my first trip to the Okavango, and I spent six days looking for sitatunga. Now, somewhat older and definitely wiser, I was trying again. This time with my tried and trusted hunting partner, Derek Carstens.

I could clearly see the thick pelt of the sitatunga through my scope. I was sitting somewhat uncomfortably with my rifle resting on my hand in the fork of a branch. To make matters worse, the branch, the rest of the tree, and I all seemed to be moving in different directions at once. The sitatunga started walking slowly toward a thicket some six metres ahead of him. I could not afford to wait any longer for the breeze to drop. It was now or never. I tried to synchronize the various movements, concentrating on the picture in my scope, and put the cross hairs on his hind quarters. As the movement of the branch took the sights forward, I squeezed the 2½-pound trigger the instant the cross hairs settled on the shoulder.

I looked up slowly as I rocked back from the recoil. "He's down!" I heard. "He's still moving! Shoot him again!" The bull fell into the reeds and water, and from my position, I could not see him. My pro motioned for me to move over to his own precarious position. I was having none of that. I had nearly fallen once already and there was no way the surrounding branches would support my 84 kilogram bulk. I stretched over and handed him my rifle, a customized 7mm Remington Magnum, converted from a 7x64mm Brno by Bill Ritchie.

A shot rang out. That should do it. Probably not necessary but silly to take a chance. "Why don't you stay here and direct Derek and me to the buck?" I was only too pleased to comply. I felt decidedly odd—elated and shaky at the same time. A bit like the feeling after a schoolyard dustup.

I sat patiently while the two of them waded through the water, at times up to their armpits. Like Lord Muck, I yelled instructions and that's when the nightmare began. They couldn't find the sitatunga. Backward and forward they squelched, moving farther and farther away. My heart started to sink. All the fears, so well known by every hunter who has wounded an animal, began to haunt me. Had he slipped away through the reeds? The longer they searched, the more fantastic my thoughts became. Had he been taken by a croc attracted by the blood? There were certainly enough of those long, green, toothy dachshunds about. I shouted to Derek to come back to the original place where I had shot the bull. Just as he reached the spot, he gave a loud yell and leaped into the air, waving his arms and splashing. He had almost stepped on the head of the bull and received an almighty fright in the process.

Much tugging and heaving later, they brought my trophy to me. Then followed the backslapping, laughter, picture taking, and joking. We decided to cape him on the spot. There was probably not enough room in the boat for the whole animal, and in any event, he had a terrible, musky odor not dissimilar to that of a waterbuck. What clinched it, however, was our tracker's unequivocal statement that nobody in their right mind would attempt to cook a sitatunga, let alone eat one.

Our excitement for the day was not over. As we were poling along, discussing the details of the hunt, the wind came up quite strongly. Following a hippo trail, we began to skirt a lagoon shielded from our view by a thin screen of reeds. None of us was paying much attention to our surroundings when our tracker suddenly froze and pointed. Another sitatunga bull just as big as the first! We couldn't believe our eyes.

We went quietly into action, wedging the *mokoro* between the bank and the reeds. Resting his elbows firmly on his knees, my hunting partner took careful aim and squeezed the trigger. The sitatunga reared into the air and started a mad dash across the lagoon, kicking up a mask of spray. As it drew opposite us, it leapt onto a small island. Derek and I fired simultaneously. It wasn't necessary. Shot though the heart, the buck sank to its knees and keeled over.

As we stood on the little island, no bigger than a double bed, waiting for our pro to return with a bigger boat, we relived the day's events and wondered when the last two clients had shot their sitatunga bulls within two hours of one another. Derek's sitatunga measured 25½ inches and mine, marginally bigger at 26 inches. It was the start of a twelve-day hunt in which we successfully bagged buffalo, crocodile, lechwe, tsessebe, reedbuck, and other game. Nothing took precedence, however, over the two sitatunga bulls. Nothing in all our years of hunting had prepared us for what I believe is the most elusive animal in southern Africa. Nothing has a prouder place in my trophy room than that most difficult of all Botswana's antelope.

Bushbuck Bonanza

I am not sure how many hunters can claim that their wives have voluntarily lent them their car to go on a hunting trip—and with an attractive, blonde, twenty-one-year-old woman at that. And yet there I was, cruising down Van Reenen's Pass, the wheels of Jane's car thrumming on the tar, en route from Johannesburg to Weza in Natal. The thought made me smile as I glanced in the rearview mirror and caught Nicky dozing in the back seat. The familiar "let out of gaol/end of term" feeling, coupled with a keen sense of anticipation of the hunt to come, created a heady mixture and I whistled softly to myself, fingers tapping on the steering wheel in time to the tune. Was I happy or what?

Rodney Kretzschmar, Nicky's dad, grinned across at me from the passenger seat. We both felt like a couple of kids with our own private cookie jar. We had been looking forward to our bushbuck hunt at Weza for months, and at last, we were on our way. Our wives were to have joined us, but last minute changes of plan had meant a trip to Switzerland for Lorraine and an all-day seminar for Jane in Johannesburg. Luckily, Nicky agreed to join the two old "bullets" as camp cook, bottle washer, chief photographer, and overall good companion—a role she was well accustomed to and fulfilled with aplomb in the Central African Republic for her fiancé, André Roux, and his safari company.

My thoughts turned to the first South African bushbuck I ever shot. What a performance! It must have been in the early 1980s. Four of us bought a package deal from John Varty of Londolozi. Even at that stage, the Varty brothers were path-finders in the conservation arena, and instead of paying game rangers to cull excess game, they sold these packages to hunters such as ourselves. We each had licenses for buffalo, kudu, impala, and warthog.

We calculated afterward that the four of us brought in more revenue during the week of our hunt than the rest of the Londolozi operation put together. In addition, the landowner on whose farm the game was shot in Sabi Sand (which borders Kruger Park) also benefited. He obtained veld reclamation work equal to the value of the game, free of charge.

Even in those early days I was besot by bushbuck hunting. It is like a bacillus embedded in my bloodstream where no antibiotic can reach. There is something about it that makes me feel alive to the tips of my fingers and the ends of the sparse hairs that fringe my balding dome. The silent, ghostly sneak down a fever-tree-lined riverbank in the gray of dawn. The stopping every one hundred metres or so to glass through the binoculars. The ears attuned to every sound. The eyes searching for a flick of a tail, a sunbeam glinting off a horn, a tan, dainty leg being raised. The sounds of the bush awakening. The clucking of guinea fowl. The zoom of a fly. A breath of breeze against your neck and the heart-stopping abrupt bark of a bushbuck forty metres away. A crash, a thud, and sounds fading into the distance to be overtaken by the pounding of your own heart. *Next time*, you say to yourself . . . *next time*. . . .

So it was that I found myself asking David Varty on the evening of our arrival whether there were any bushbuck available to be culled on Londolozi, and if so, whether I could try for one. I will never forget the withering look David gave me. Maybe it wasn't contemptuous but it was the next best thing. "Sure," he drawled, "we have plenty of bushbuck here and if you find one you may take it. Of course a *stadsjapie* (city dweller) like you will never outwit a bushbuck. In fact, if you manage to shoot one, I will eat any part of the animal you care to offer me, raw," he said, or words to that effect.

The statement fell with a dull thud in the dust at our feet as we stood around the leadwood fire at the bush camp. Eventually, Derek, my hunting companion of many years, filled the lengthening silence. "Do you really mean *any* part?" he asked.

David gave an emphatic nod to accompany his spoken "Yes." It was a real conversation stopper. What could we say? In the end, after scuffling around and a bit of inconsequential chatter, we meandered off to bed each thinking his own thoughts. Mine were locked on to what David had said like a heat-seeking SAM 7 ground-to-air missile. *Stadsjapie* . . . I thought.

Yet, even as I formed these thoughts, they were erased by thoughts of the many bushbuck that ran away from me without ever being seen. I knew their stealth, their legendary caution, their excellent camouflage make them hard to hunt and a trophy well worth working for. As they say: The big ones didn't get that way by accident. I remembered an experienced professional hunter telling me that bushbuck often use a troop of baboons as an early warning system. I remembered watching a bushbuck ram on the shores of Lake Kariba as it emerged from cover. Each step it took was deliberate. The picture of the ram, through my 10X binoculars, with its foreleg poised in the air, its head up and alert and its moist, black nose testing the breeze will remain imprinted on my brain forever. I remembered that bushbuck are, in a word, *tricky*. All these thoughts percolated through my brain in response to David's proposed wager.

But back to the present. A few days after David's challenge, Derek, John, and I were driving along the banks of the Sand River, returning from a long, fruitless morning of buffalo tracking. Out of the corner of his eye, Derek spotted the tips of a set of bushbuck horns wafting through the reeds on an island in the river. While John kept driving, Derek and I bailed out of the moving vehicle and snuck back to the spot.

With patience and a modicum of skill, the bushbuck had to be ours. He was blissfully unaware of our presence and grazing toward a "v" of solid rock. Either he had to climb out on top of the rock or reverse his course. Either way, I would have a 150-metre shot from a dead rest, which should not be a problem for my .30-06 and the 180-grain rounds I was using. Famous last thoughts.

Time drifted. Minutes turned into quarter hours, then half hours. Eventually, however, our original assessment proved correct. The bushbuck ram reversed his course. The .30-06 dropped him in his tracks. The difficult part, however, was still to come—the recovery operation. Leaving Derek on the bank with my .30-06, the tracker and I reluctantly stripped off, forced our way through the dense reeds on the river bank, threw some rocks and dirt clods into the river in the vague hope that this might scare off any lurking green crocodiles and made a dash for it.

At the time, I always brought a handgun on big-game hunts, which I carried in a shoulder holster. For some unknown reason I had developed a deadly fear of being bowled over by something big and hairy, losing my rifle, and being at the mercy of something that either wanted to turn me into strawberry jam or inhale me like a piece of asparagus. Taylor of *African Rifles and Cartridges* fame lends a degree of legitimacy to carrying a sidearm on a hunt, and it certainly made me feel better, even though I only used it once in anger and ineffectually at that (but that's another story.) Old age and long, tiring elephant hunts ultimately cured me of the habit of carrying any extra baggage, but I was younger, fitter, and certainly more foolish in those days.

At any rate, when we emerged from the river, me clutching my *haasboud* (rabbit hind leg) of a revolver (a Ruger .44 Redhawk with a 7-inch barrel, to be precise), I was hot on the heels of my tracker. As we clambered over a flat rock at the water's edge, my feet slipped out from under me. Not wanting to bash the revolver on the rock, I twisted and fell with a thud on my left shoulder. With that, a slim reed penetrated between the side of my eyeball and the eye socket and stuck in the back of my head—or so it felt. Simultaneously, the bushbuck leapt to its feet and charged straight at my tracker. I knelt with the reed sticking out of my head (looking for all the world like a Red Indian victim from the Wild West—or so Derek said later), waving my revolver ineffectually in the air as I was unable to shoot for fear of hitting the tracker. The tracker flung his arms in the air, stood on tip-toe, sucked in his stomach, and did his best imitation of a naked Spanish matador sans cape. The bushbuck stormed past, his horns hooking at the tracker's chest and then he was up, over the ridge and away. Derek fired from the bank—once, twice. Down went the bushbuck, for good this time. What a circus!

After recovering the bushbuck and smuggling it into camp, I headed for the local doctor in Skukuza, the white of my left eye a bright blood-red colour. He cleaned up the eye as best he could while taking advice over the telephone from an eye specialist safely ensconced in Johannesburg. Looking like the South African version of Moshe Dayan, clutching a handful of pain killers and with strict instructions to return to Johannesburg on the next available flight, I headed back to camp. What the good doctor did not know was that I had a very important dinner date that evening and I still had not shot my buffalo.

At camp, I persuaded a waiter to serve a specific "dish" to David as his main course while he presided over dinner for photographic safari guests in the *boma* at the main camp. I thought David was going to suffer irreparable whiplash injuries to his neck when he lifted the lid of the silver serving dish to discover the family jewels of the bushbuck glistening on the china plate. His eyes darted around the *boma* until they came to rest on me standing in the shadows of the entrance. Eat, I mimed—and to his credit, he made a valiant attempt.

Five days later, the joke was on me as they wheeled me into the operating theater to have my badly infected eye attended to. Yes, I had disobeyed the doctor from Skukuza. Yes, I did shoot my first buffalo with John Varty. Yes, the eye acted up. And yes, it does to this day become red and gritty after a hard day's hunting. Another millimetre to the left, the specialist said, and . . .

I could not afford a shoulder mount of my first South African bushbuck, but its 14-inch horns have been hanging on a wooden shield in my study for years. Since then I have collected an excellent Chobe bushbuck (in the top twenty in Rowland Ward) on the banks of the Gwaai River in Zimbabwe and a respectable harnessed bushbuck in the Ubangi concession area in the eastern region of the CAR, a good Masai bushbuck on the slopes of Mount Meru outside Arusha, Tanzania, but not even a sniff of a Menelik bushbuck during the course of a twenty-eight-day hunt in Ethiopia. Although my chances of collecting all eight species of bushbuck (Abyssinian, Arusi, Chobe, harnessed, Masai, Nile, Shoan, and South African) recorded in Rowland Ward are non-existent, I had been looking for a trophy-quality South African bushbuck (*Tragelaphus scriptus sylvaticus*) to add to my collection for some time.

The call from Leon du Casse of Natal Hunters and Game Conservation Association came as an answer to a maiden's prayer. The Association had the rights to cull excess bushbuck and duiker at Weza, the forestry area inland from Port Shepstone, up past Oribi Gorge and Harding. Was I still interested in a bushbuck and duiker hunt? Can a duck swim? Is the Pope a Catholic?

We arrived on a Friday afternoon in June. There, we introduced ourselves to the head forester, Pierre Ackerman, and met our guides for the weekend, Freddie Nhlango and Nelson Malimela (not Mandela as he pointed out with a smile).

Dawn the next day found us sneaking along an overgrown forest path. Quiet as church mice we were and yet we failed to outwit an alert bushbuck ewe. And so it went. A beautiful, mature black ram bounded away before I could even shoulder my rifle. Freddie spooked another, which we stumbled on some sixty metres away, directly downhill from us, our approach masked by a nearby stream. His, "What is that?"

Bushbuck Bonanza

uttered in a strangled, stage whisper as I was examining the bushbuck through my binoculars, galvanized the buck into action. Good-bye, I waved as it disappeared into the forest. Still another spooked as I tried to reach a rest. A frustrating but exhilarating morning. All in all, I'd seen four eminently shootable rams and a similar number of ewes. Rodney's experience was much the same as my own.

We were busy swapping notes on the way back to camp for a well-earned brunch when Nelson spotted an excellent ram sunning itself in a clearing in the valley below. Rodney felt the shot was a touch too far for his 100-year-old Hoff drilling (a pair of 16-gauge barrels over a 9.3x72mm rifle barrel) and kindly offered me the shot. The ram was oblivious to our presence and I had plenty of time to set myself up for the longish 250-metre downhill shot. "Bertha," my faithful old .375 Brno, did the trick and the ram tottered six or seven paces before dropping stone dead, shot through the heart. He was an ancient ram, teeth worn to blackened stubs and blind in one eye but the rest of him, baldish skin and prominent bones, supported a set of 15½ inch lyre-shaped, classic bushbuck horns.

My second ram came later the same day. A silvery stream dribbled through moss and lichen-covered rocks down to our left. Farther to the left lurked the lush, indigenous forest. The afternoon sun dappled the ground beneath our feet, and to our right, the regimented plantation rose up alongside the hill. Freddie and I could both sense that intangible something in the air. This was prime bushbuck territory. This quiet, peaceful, secluded, sunlit glen had to be a favourite place of a big ram. We literally inched our way forward, examining every shadow. I found myself breathing in short, shallow breaths with my mouth open, a sense of anticipation, of excitement fluttering in my stomach. The path wound around to the right. Was that a . . . no.

Then one of the shadows up ahead moved. A bushbuck? Yes! Although facing directly away from me, some one hundred metres away, I could still see that the ram was even larger than the one I shot in the morning. I sank slowly to my knees, intending to shoot from the prone position. I never made it. The ram stopped feeding. His head came up. He lifted a foreleg, listening. I could not believe it. We had not made a sound and I could feel the light breeze on the side of my head. Some sixth sense must have warned him. I rested my left elbow on my knee and took aim. His head swiveled slowly and like a radar dish locked on to me. The ram tensed. I had seconds to make up my mind before the bushbuck emigrated to Transkei. Take the Texas heart shot on offer or wish the buck bon voyage. The cross hairs of my Zeiss 1.5–6X scope were locked on the ram. I was confident the .375 could do the job, and as it turned out, rightly so. The 270-grain Winchester Power Point penetrated nearly the length of the buck, which collapsed, almost gracefully, at the shot.

He was a magnificent, mature black ram in perfect condition. His horns measured a tad under 16 inches, and hopefully, as a full mount, will be around for many years to remind me of a memorable hunt.

The next day, Rodney also took a mature ram. All the animals were carefully measured and samples taken of their heart, liver, and lungs as part of the research project being conducted into the bushbuck in the area.

Altogether, we thoroughly enjoyed our stay, despite having to pay a R200 penalty for not shooting two ewes as we had been required to do as part of the culling operation—time and opportunity not permitting. The hunting lodge was comfortable, clean, and warm. Our guides were friendly, helpful, and capable. The area, with its plantations, indigenous forests, hills, secluded clearings, and valleys, reminded me of parts of Australia. A thoroughly good time was had by all. Yet another excellent example of what the Natal Hunters and Game Conservation Association has been doing for hunting and conservation.

WORLD-CLASS ELAND

My quest for a world-class eland started with a phone call out of the blue. As my memory serves me, it went something like this:

"Hullo. You won't know us, but we've heard of you. You see, the three of us have just begun hunting and we need a hand. We thought you might be prepared to help. What do you say?"

What I said was, "Why?" I listened to tales of woe. Game ranchers who ripped them off. Rifles that wouldn't group. Bullets that blew up. Calibres that mutilated meat. Trophies that shrunk at the taxidermist and . . . and . . .

I tried to duck the issue. "I hunt on my own," I said. "I haven't hunted with anyone other than old, close friends for years," I argued.

"Give us a chance," they replied.

I eventually did.

Our first hunt together was a plains game hunt they had organized in the Orange Free State and occurred on a ranch that was home base to a trucking business. All this created a situation that was quite disconcerting, but the previous weeks of range practice worked and the three came away with what they wanted.

Things improved steadily after that and as we approached the third year of our association, John, the best shot and most serious of the hunters, said he'd like to have a crack at a trophy kudu.

If you gave me a dollar for every kilometre I have walked after kudu, I could comfortably afford to pay for a big-game safari. I have hunted kudu bulls for more years than I care to remember. I have shot bulls there and thereabouts, but never one to meet the exacting standards of Mr. Rowland Ward and associates. Despite my conviction that I was jinxed when it came to kudu, another part of me harboured the view best described by the Afrikaans expression, *"aanhouer wen"* or, "if at first you don't succeed. . . ."

Yes, I have seen big Rowland Ward kudu on a few occasions. I remember a wonderful specimen up in the Chewore Hills while hot on some elephant tracks. We all agreed he would go at least 57 inches. Of course, he stood for ages, broadside, as if cast in bronze. But what do you do? Take the kudu and risk chasing an 80-pounder into Zambia? Not on your Nellie! Although I can tell you I was tempted. I remember the biggest kudu I have ever seen standing amiably in a sheep pen in Marienthal, Namibia. He was only some seventy paces away. He even stopped a second time some 150 paces away from my partner as he missed it for a second time. And then there was that monster near Lethaba in the Kruger National Park but you go to gaol for that kind of thing. And so on and so on . . . all very boring for someone who has not hunted the gray ghost.

In fairness, my lack of success has been compounded by at least two other factors. One, I often hunt alone and find it very difficult to judge kudu horns accurately, and two, once having outwitted a big kudu bull, the final shot becomes the irresistible and natural conclusion to the hunt. In so doing, I am sure I have, from time to time, missed out on other large bulls in the area.

At any rate, after careful research I decided to take the three of them to Emoweni in the bushveld of the Transvaal on the recommendation of two friends, John Oosthuizen and Graham Seegers, who had both visited the area the year before. They told me that it was a big area—classic kudu country that had not been hunted for a number of years. This was confirmed by the resident pro, Cecil Dippenaar, an ex-Malawian professional hunter. Cecil assured me that, if we were prepared to put in the effort, we stood an above average chance of taking the bull I was looking for.

Emoweni also held a good cross section of plains game, which suited the other two members of the threesome who were more interested in venison than trophies. And so we divided into two teams—trophy hunters and meat hunters.

And the meat hunters had a whale of a time. Each evening over a beer they would regale John and me with tales of their successful stalks and shots. We, on the other hand, had not seen a kudu track, let alone the beast itself. Their sympathy changed to friendly banter and then just a touch of needles crept into the conversation. You know the kind—who are the better hunters now?

And then, as it so often does in hunting, Diana, goddess of the hunt, smiled and our luck changed quickly and dramatically. John shot a mature kudu bull as dawn broke over the dry, rock-strewn gully in which the bull had been quietly breakfasting—neck stretched, horns laid down his flanks. He died with a twig tucked between his teeth.

After dropping off the kudu at the skinning shed, we took a route back to camp that took us past a muddy water hole fringed with a latticework of tracks—sharp and faint, big and small, old and new. It was a place I would come to know much better as the hunt wore on.

So there I was, sitting next to a tidy, flickering campfire looking out over a wide valley and some dozen distant hills fading into the evening gray, a glass of amber fluid in my hand. I felt at peace with myself and the world. Cecil and I were idly swapping hunting stories when he suddenly asked me whether I would be interested in shooting a world-record Cape eland. "Not again!" I thought. My estimation of Cecil started to plummet like a chopper minus its main rotor. I had my fill of game ranchers and their tall stories and was suitably cynical. Undaunted by my skeptical look, Cecil continued, "We've just had an American here for ten days hunting this eland. We never caught a glimpse of it, but would you know, the day after he left, I actually saw the eland drinking at the water hole not far from here. He's massive and easily recognizable because of a gimpy front leg. I am telling you, Pete, that if he is not a world record, I will eat the damn eland raw," Cecil stated. Well, I was here to hunt kudu, not eland. Or so I thought.

While I am no Bushman tracker, I could clearly see the elongated track left by the right front hoof of the eland in the damp, khaki-coloured soil at the water's edge. It was almost like a mini waterski. This had to be the bull. Now, I can usually tell whether a track is fresh or old but don't ask me to tell you whether it is one, two, or three hours old. But this track looked like new!

I knew there was a dirt road running along the foothills to the northwest, the general direction in which the eland seemed to be heading. I decided to drive along this road, believing that if the eland had not crossed it, I could hunt back into the wind with a reasonable certainty that the eland was between the hills and the water. Alternatively, if the eland had crossed the road, I could save myself a good few hours walking.

It was one of those crazy bits of luck that everyone who hunts for a long time has—or at least should have if only once. Bouncing down the dirt road about an hour later, I caught a glimpse of a massive gray form off to my right through the bushes. Then the nightmare began. My driver was so busy chatting that it took him much too long to react to my signals and stop the vehicle. He then stopped with a large tree trunk obscuring most of the eland. I knew there was no time for finesse. I could see the bull was tense and ready to run, and as if to bear me out, as we started reversing, he turned on his heels and started that kilometre-eating jog for which eland are famous. I could have wept. Hiding my frustration, disappointment, and irritation as best I could, I motioned the driver to drive up to where the eland had been standing so that I could pick up his tracks and start what I knew was going to be a long day.

As we drove through the bush, out of the corner of my left eye, I became aware of movement in the thick, dry, gray mopane scrub. At first I thought it was a kudu or eland cow as its body was smaller than the bull I had been studying. As the cunning, moth-eaten old bull turned directly away from me, his massive horns were silhouetted and for a split second I knew that I had nearly made a terrible mistake. Much as it goes against the grain, I knew I did not have a second to lose. Standing on the back of the vehicle, I tracked him through my scope as he ran directly away from me. Despite the fact that I was using Bertha, my old .375 Brno loaded with 270-grain Winchester Power Points, I was not prepared to take the shot. As the old bull started to reach the limits of my range for offhand shooting, a little granite kopje to his right saved the day for me. The bull was obliged to veer to his left, exposing his flank, and I made one of my better shots. At some 170 paces, I took the three-quartering shot, aiming for his off-side front leg. The shot went off and the bull collapsed, vanishing in an explosion of dust and dry grass. The shot raked the old bull from the rear-side ribs through to his off-side front leg. As I got to him, he half lifted his venerable old head and then his grizzled muzzle flopped into the dust as his big, soulful eyes glazed over. A deep sadness welled up from deep inside me. I couldn't talk or acknowledge the congratulations. I could only swallow the lump in my throat.

He wasn't old; he was ancient. Big patches of his hide had no hair. I honestly do not think the old man would have survived the winter. He had lost a tremendous amount of condition. His skin hung in folds, like a badly tailored suit, and his gimpy front hoof was filled with maggots. But what a magnificent trophy! His longest horn measured 39¾ inches long and 11½ inches around the base, which according to Rodney Kretzschmar, my taxidermist and our local, official Rowland Ward trophy measurer, made it equal to the largest Cape eland ever shot. The horns were enormously wide at the top—29½ inches from tip to tip. I discussed mounting the bull with Rodney and we decided to mount him the way he must have been in his prime. He stands to the right of my desk in my study and I have preserved his battered, gimpy foot as a penholder.

On the way back to camp, John and I wondered what the others would do when they found out. We looked at one another. A silent understanding passed between us. Over brunch we came in for our now regular session of kidding.

"What if," John asked, "we shoot a kudu and eland before close of play tonight? What would you have to say then?"

"Say? Say? I wouldn't say anything. But I tell you what, I'd eat my flipping hat," answered Gunner.

"I tell you what," I suggested, "I'll bet you R500 each that John and I will be successful. In other words, I'll pay you R500 each if we don't shoot an eland and a kudu. But if we do . . . if we do, you each agree to eat a square inch of whatever part of the animal we give you. What do you say?"

They didn't say anything, but it did take a while for them to stop laughing. They certainly didn't think to ask us if we'd already shot the animals in question.

We still laugh about it. Blatter made a valiant attempt and ate the cube of fillet, but poor old Gunner gagged and choked and spat it out. But we all learnt something from the hunt. The meat hunters learned that hunting is not about competition. John and I learned that you can never discount luck. Luck—when preparation meets opportunity. And I learned what it was like to have a once-in-a-lifetime experience—a world record. Not that it lasted too long. The success of South African game ranching ensured that within two years, my eland was No. 2. Today he barely makes the top twenty.

wry smile was the best I could do after missing this excellent vaal rhebok ram three
mes in a row from about 340 paces before finally dropping it.

Glassing for vaal rhebok on my game ranch in the Karoo.

The one-horned vaal rhebok ram that Danie van Rensburg let me take when I revisited the scene of my previous vaal rhebok fiasco some years later.

Typical vaal rhebok terrain—between 5,000 and 7,000 feet in the Sneeuberge (Snow Mountains).

Danie van Rensburg and me with the one-horned vaal rhebok and a decent mountain reedbuck. Danie made me shoot the reedbuck before the vaal rhebok so I would not repeat my previous effort of three misses in a row.

This superb kudu bull became suspicious shortly after this photo was taken; it turned and ghosted into the thicket never to be seen again. (Photo courtesy of Derek Todd)

Me and kudu (as mentioned in the story)—Venetia, South Africa.

A typical Eastern Cape kudu with tight twisting horns measuring about 46 inches.

Kudu (as mentioned in the story)—Tshipise, South Africa.

Cape Bushbuck—Weza, Natal.

A really good 16¾-inch Chobe bushbuck—shot on the Gwaai River three nanoseconds after my partner, Derek Carstens, turned it down. Carsten subsequently shot a one-horned, 15½-inch ram, but made amends on a later hunt

A representative Masai bushbuck, largest of the bushbuck subspecies. This one was found on the slopes of Mount Meru, Tanzania.

Martin hamming it up for the cameras and pretending to whip Albert (Bert the baggage man) and Antoinne (our second tracker) as they carried my harnessed bushbuck back to the Land Cruiser—Pabou, CAR.

Cape eland herd amongst some of their favourite food, prickly pears—Agtersneeuberg Nature Reserve, Karoo, Eastern Cape.

Young Cape eland bull on full alert—Agtersneeuberg Nature Reserve, Karoo, Eastern Cape

Hoof of Cape eland bull (as mentioned in story).

This lelwel hartebeest won the prize for the best savanna animal at the 1993 trophy competition of the South African Hunters and Game Conservation Association—Pabou, CAR.

Me, Martin (one of the best, if not the best tracker I have ever had the privilege t hunt with), and bongo—CAR.

...merging from rain forest after shooting my bongo.

...ongo—CAR (as mentioned in story).

The dining 'davel at Pabou camp along the Ouarrou River—a pretty and peacef camp and one of only three in this massive 206x196 kilometre concession.

Me and Martin sloshing out of the rain forest after my bongo hunt.

...monster 15½-inch warthog, which unwittingly sealed its own fate by running toward ...e as I hunkered in the tree line along the Baho salt lick.

...estern kob, like the warthog, was also shot before my bongo hunt began—CAR.

...e with giant eland—CAR.

There are a number of subspecies of defassa waterbuck. This good 28-incher is th *West African subspecies, called sing-sing (or* kob defassa, *in French), again shot in th* *week before my bongo hunt began in earnest.*

The best western kob shot in the concession that year—CAR.

CENTRAL AFRICAN ADVENTURE

Once upon a time, long, long ago . . . That's how all good fairy tales begin, and this is a fairy tale—except that I was a participant and it wasn't so long ago.

In fact, the fairy tale began one warm autumn day in May 1992, when I met a twenty-seven-year-old, compact, controlled, and soft-spoken ex-paratrooper named André Roux in the offices of Trans African Taxidermists. Yes, he was a professional hunter and had hunted in the Central African Republic (CAR) for the past three years. What for? Bongo, giant eland, giant forest hog, yellow-backed duiker. . . . As his voice trailed on naming the familiar yet exotic names of the various species, I had a feeling that at last I had found what I had been looking for: I was going to hunt bongo in the CAR with him.

Calls to the references he supplied confirmed my initial impression: He was an excellent, energetic, and ethical hunter. Everyone stressed one more fact—be fit, be prepared, and listen to his advice in this regard. I did. Toward the end of my preparations, I was running more than forty kilometres a week, cycling another forty-five kilometres, and that was apart from my daily dose of Canadian Air Force exercises. My gunsmith, "Silver" Bill Ritchie and his assistant, Vince, built a .416 Rigby for me—Walther barrel, Brno action, and a sturdy stock. No iron sights, of course. André advised against them due to the fact that they hook on the vines, creepers, and grasses that grow in the equatorial rain forests that bongo inhabit. Topping the outfit was a Zeiss 1.5–6X Diavari scope, specifically designed for low light conditions with its fat 32mm tube, which worked so well in Alaska the year before. I put in many hours on the range with the .416, fired dozens of rounds, and was almost as comfortable with it as I was with my normal carry gun, a fifteen-year-old .375 Brno.

It was now April 1993, the start of the rainy season in the CAR and I was ready. In fact, I had been ready for weeks. Like a V8 on grease, revving my motor but going nowhere. I'd had every conceivable inoculation from hepatitis B to rabies to gamma globulin, plus all the usual like tetanus, cholera, and so on—ten in all. My equipment included a few unusual items such as a strong pair of surgical scissors to help cut through the forest undergrowth, a pair of clear-glass spectacles to protect my eyes when walking through the head-high savanna grass, and three separate pairs of footwear, ranging from boots to tennis shoes. As I found out later, I had brought the right footwear for the forest, but not the savanna.

For the rest, my luggage was compact, as we would be hunting out of various fly camps, as well as the main camp on the Bouye River, in the huge 8,600-square-kilometre area that comprised the Oubangui Safari hunting concession. The area was roughly triangular in shape—formed by 206 kilometres of river frontage along the Mbomou River in the south, from Obo via Bande and Ouandu (pronounced "one-do") for 192 kilometres in the east and north and then for about 140 kilometres down to Zemio on the western side.

As the venerable old Cessna dipped its port wing and scrubbed off speed on its final approach to Mboki in the CAR, I experienced a sense of tremendous well being. It was actually happening. I was here at last, my luggage and I both in one piece. After years of reading Stanley, Sutherland, Anderson, Daly, Du Chaillu, Christie, and many others, I was here on the banks of the Mbomou, which feeds the Oubangui, which feeds the mighty Congo River. In the middle, and I do mean the middle, of darkest Africa, some eighty kilometres from the Sudanese border and a stone's throw from Zaire and the vast Ituri Forest.

The countryside was a revelation to me. So beautiful. Hunting in my favourite places—the Zambezi Valley and the Karoo—the winter colours of golden brown and gray and green, all pale and washed out, had become old, familiar friends. Like the smell of dust in the air and fresh buff sign on a cold winter's morning. Here in the CAR, the impossibly bright colours—the lush, fairway greens of the glades, and the dark, glossy greens of the Isoberlinia leaves (favourite food of Derby eland)—joined with the steamy heat and smell of rain about to fall to create a heady mixture.

The first bongo I saw materialized out of nowhere. I gaped at it, looking no doubt like a stunned mullet. It wasn't meant to be there. Apart from three brief smoke breaks, we had been walking solidly for the last ten hours. We still had at least an hour to go to our fly camp at Pabou on the Ouarra River (pronounced "warra"). We had been tracking an eland herd since first light from the Baho salt lick. The second time a wind change spooked them shortly after 1 P.M., they decided to emigrate to Ethiopia and we reluctantly turned for camp some four hours away.

We were plodding along. Even the strong, super-fit Zande trackers—yes, the same tribe that poisoned Sutherland during his elephant hunting stint in the area—were weary. We took a shortcut through a forest along an old elephant track. As it opened into a small glade, we caught the bongo lifting its head from the little stream from which it had been drinking. Drops of water dribbled from its beautiful muzzle, twinkling in the light of a mote-filled sunbeam filtering through the heavy leaf-covered canopy of trees like a stage show spotlight.

To me, bongo, or if you like, *Tragelaphus euryceros euryceros*, are the most magical, mystical, and dramatic of all the animals in Africa. They are shaped like a huge bushbuck with shorter and stubbier legs but coloured like a nyala ewe. What a Rottweiler is to a Doberman pinscher, a bongo is to a bushbuck. A mature adult weighs between 250 and 300 kilograms with magnificent, thick, heavy, spiraled horns shaped like those of a nyala bull. This shy, reclusive inhabitant of the equatorial rain forests is protected both by its environment and its acute senses. From its satellite-dish ears, big, shiny nose, and kudu-like eyes that give it a hair-trigger alarm system to the vines and creepers that make progress in the forests slow, and the beds of leaves, which, when dry, make tracking difficult and noisy, bongo rank with mountain nyala as being the most difficult of all African animals to take. Only about fifteen to twenty are taken each year in the CAR, and on my arrival, I met the departing hunter I was replacing, who was returning empty-handed to America after his third twenty-one-day hunt for bongo. The current edition of Rowland Ward lists about 270 that meet the minimum trophy standard of 27 inches.

And here was my first living and breathing bongo—inadvertently outwitted. The three of us—Martin, André, and I—stood frozen in a weird arabesque, locked into an invisible isosceles triangle with the bongo. Martin was leaning toward me, stretching out a long, sinuous black arm that held my .375 Brno, which he'd been carrying for the past two hours. Time was suspended. Not a sound. Slow motion movement. The rifle slithered into my shoulder, like a tortoise head into its shell. The bright, tan colours of the bongo stood out in bold relief against the dark, waxy, green leaves framing its war-painted head, which was all I could see. *Under the chin,* flitted through my mind and then *funny shaped horns, almost meeting at the tips.* André whispered, "It's a female," breaking the spell. We eventually straightened up. The bongo fled. "You are certainly the first hunter I know who has seen bongo and Lord Derby eland on the same day" said André with a grin. I managed a cardboard replica of a smile, thinking to myself, *fantastic animal, absolutely and unbelievably fantastic, but had this been* my *bongo?*

Central African Adventure

As previously discussed and agreed, we left Pabou the next day for the main camp at Bouye, some four hours away by vehicle. We were now going to hunt bongo and only bongo for the remaining fifteen days of the hunt. We had spent the previous five days hunting a new area in the concession made accessible by a "road" cut in a northerly direction toward Djema. We decided to gamble a week on hunting giant eland in the savanna, and in between I shot an excellent lelwel hartebeest (the butterscotch-coloured larger cousin of our red hartebeest), a good western kob (something like a small red lechwe), and a harnessed bushbuck, the smallest, and to my mind, most delicate and beautiful of all bushbuck. He had a dark, chestnut rump, becoming lighter toward the front with the characteristic dappled white spots on his hindquarters leading into a continuous, uneven, horizontal stripe along his ribs toward his forequarters—hence the "harnessed." Finally, I had taken a Rowland Ward-quality defassa (or sing-sing waterbuck to you and me.) You know the one, without the white circle or ring on its rear.

A stalk through some long grass and then the trees bordering an open *vlei* area revealed a big waterbuck bull grazing and quartering away from us. While André reviewed his original assessment of the animal, I maneuvered into a shooting position. "Don't fiddle around when the time comes to shoot," he warned. "While I'm judging the trophy for you, use the time to get into position." Resting the four fingers of my left hand against the side of a tree, I cradled Bertha, my old, faithful .375, in the "u" formed by my forefinger and thumb. The cross hairs came to rest well behind the foreleg of the waterbuck, some 150 metres away, as I aimed to hit the off-side foreleg. The shot exploded a flock of egrets on the *vlei*. Scattering like shrapnel, some flew over the waterbuck as he bolted into the cover of some palms and thick, scrubby bushes. And that is where we found him. A beautiful, mature bull, darker than our common waterbuck, almost a charcoal gray on his shoulders, fading toward the rear with a teardrop-shaped off white patch running up the back of each rear leg to the rump on either side of the tail. We eventually stretched the tape measure to

28½ inches, well over the minimum 27 inches of Rowland Ward's trophy standard and wended our weary way back to camp.

Altogether our plan worked well. Although we had not found a trophy-quality eland bull of at least 47 inches, I was settling down well and beginning to fit into André's hunting team and routine. Wake-up call was the sound of Jaimis, our camp waiter, softly clapping his hands outside my grass shelter at 3 A.M. Yes, you read correctly. Here it is light enough to track at 5 A.M. and André insisted on being on the spot we had discussed and selected the previous evening as the day dawned.

Usually we chose a saline (salt lick) or open area that we hoped had been visited by eland in the night, in order to pick up tracks. Tracking and walking is everything in the CAR. The area is so large and the game so spread out that it is an exercise in futility to merely plod through the bush in the vague hope of bumping into an animal. I was amazed at the tracking skills of Martin, or Vungueyessi Martin Tito, to give his full name. His air tracking was the best I have seen. Many were the times after crossing a matted, grass-interlocked savanna area, where it had been impossible to see a track on the ground for over half an hour, that we would emerge at a clearing spot on the somewhat dainty tracks (for its size) of the eland bull we had been following. A nibbled leaf here, a bent twig there, and Bob's your auntie.

Martin was ably assisted by Antoinne, our second tracker and the muscle in the team, as well as Albert, "Bert the Baggage Man" as he became known, as he carried the water and a rucksack with our first aid and snakebite kit, rain jackets, camera, and one or two other essentials.

Rain jackets? Yes. We were moving into the rainy season, and thunder showers every other afternoon or evening were the order of the day. The rain is important for bongo hunting. It clears the ground of old tracks and softens the undergrowth, and this allows for quieter walking. The sound of water drip, dripping on leaves in the forest (which continues long after the showers pass) also helped mask our passage as, armed with garden clippers, we snipped a silent path along the bongo tracks.

On day seven, our first full day of bongo hunting, we cut fresh tracks of two bongo bulls, one *une grande male*—a big male, as Martin put it. I was intrigued by the tracks—deep, sharp indentations, as if the bongo was walking on its toes. We followed them down a hill on the edge of a forest, through the forest, and then, suddenly, the gloom gave way unexpectedly to the sunlit opening of a salt lick. These licks appear from time to time like unexpected gifts, relieving the claustrophobic effects of the dense forests where it is seldom possible to see further than twenty-five metres in any direction. The bongo bulls had clearly been visiting the lick on a regular basis as their tracks crisscrossed the area mixing with those of harnessed bushbuck, yellow-backed duiker, and giant forest hog.

Five hours later we were no closer to the bongo and decided to rest my feet, which had become badly blistered (the first time ever) due to continual exposure to water and then long trudges on hard ground and then water again. Back at camp, André used an old paratrooper trick, injecting my blisters with methiolate. It was worth the sharp, burning pain to be able to hunt the following day but ten hours of tracking from one forest, across a stretch of savanna, and into another forest brought us nary a sight of bwana bongo. As the moon was full, we resolved to spend a few nights at the salt lick closest to where we had originally spotted the tracks in the hope of catching at least one of the two bulls on a return visit.

Despite our all-night vigils (or possibly because of them, the wind being extremely variable at that time of year), no bongo put in an appearance. The nights, however, were all action affairs. A rustle, rustle here, a scurry, scurry there, the thud of a falling branch, the blood-curdling screech of a tree hyrax combined with tropical thunderstorms, mosquitoes, and ferocious, Biafran hungry ants to ensure that sleep was, at best, a light and intermittent affair.

During the day we checked other likely forest areas for tracks. The weather was steamy hot and humid, and as the days began tripping by with ever-increasing speed and weariness took its toll, my thoughts kept returning to the "bongo in the bush." Had this been "my" bongo? André's confidence never flagged. "We're going to get him. I've got a good feeling about this hunt," he kept on saying. "You're well prepared and luck occurs when good preparation meets opportunity!"

My forty-fifth birthday came and went. The good wishes and hopes in the birthday cards that Jane and the kids smuggled into my suitcase rejuvenated and motivated me. However, Diana, the goddess of hunting, refused to deliver a fitting bongo for the occasion. We settled for hartebeest steaks with a magnificent, fourteen-year-old bottle of red wine and a superb chocolate cake baked by André's fiancee, Nicole.

Three days later, 15 April 1993 dawned with us at "dead slow ahead." We slithered through the trees bordering a lick where we had previously mixed course salt with the mineralized mud in the hope of attracting the big bongo male that was following the herd of females and young ones that frequented the saline. I caught the flash of a reddish-tan hide through the leaves blocking our view and felt Martin stiffen in front of me and then relax. "*Buffle*" he whispered in French, the universal language of the country. Another of the many, small, red, and aggressive northwestern buffalo of the region. My shoulders drooped with disappointment.

"Let's try the lick where we first spotted bongo tracks and, if we draw a blank, we'll leave for Ouagou (pronounced 'wagoo') this afternoon," suggested André. I had been dreading the trip to Ouagou. Although traces of Anderson's old camp could still be seen there, Ouagou meant an unattractive fly camp on the edge of a small village some three hours away by vehicle, surrounded by forests with thick, secondary growth under foot, making tracking awkward and following worse. At 6 feet 3 inches, as opposed to the uniform 5 feet 7 inches of the rest of the team, a day spent bending, crawling, face in the branches, feet in the vines, left my legs quivering with fatigue, my back aching, and my head pounding. But, there were a lot of bongo that came to feed at the villagers' gardens at the edge of the forest, and if that's what André recommended, that's what we would do.

Scarcely paying attention, I sat at the edge of the salt lick, head between my knees, my .416 cradled in my arms, staring sightlessly at the dark compost between my feet as the others checked for tracks. It took me a moment to realize that the clucking sound was not a crested guinea fowl but Martin. When I looked up, he beckoned me over. As I squelched through the thick, gray, glutinous mud, I could feel my tennis shoes filling with water. *Not again* I thought. But the burning sensation of the methiolate in my blisters faded as he pointed to a huge set of fresh bongo tracks. "*Une grande male. Toute suite,*" he said with an urgency that made me realize that *toute suite* must mean right now. As André joined us, he said, "Look, the water is still muddy in his tracks. These were made only moments ago. If we'd come here first, we might have had him," he added.

"What now?" I asked.

Unselfishly and like a true professional, he summed up the situation. "We haven't had rain for three days. The forest is noisy. You have to track this bull but you and Martin must do it on your own. Every extra person will just reduce your chances of catching up with him that much more."

I could see how much this statement cost him. André loved bongo and eland hunting, and as this was his first season as the new owner of Oubangui Safaris, it was even more important to him that his hunters were successful. Only five hunters had requested bongo this season. A small one had been taken by a hunter, another had given up on the hunt, a third had seen two big males run off on separate occasions when sound and movement, respectively, had spooked them. I was the fourth hunter, with one more to come.

As I walked off into the forest with Martin, I turned at the edge to look back at André, the words forming on my lips to say, "come along." I never spoke them as he waved a hand impatiently at me, shooing me away.

He was right. Martin and I were quiet. I had acquired the knack of walking quietly in the forest. I swapped my boots for tennis shoes and was wearing olive green khakis—long pants, long-sleeved shirt rolled down, and an olive green baseball cap with a short peak. As we twisted and turned through the jungle, it was clear that the bongo was in no hurry. From the salt lick he dawdled down to a clear, cool stream in a calm and serene glade filled with white and red orchids. There he drank and then ambled downstream before climbing up the side of a hill. Tracking became difficult and Martin frequently had to cast around to unravel the fresh track from older ones.

Our extra stillness was nearly our undoing as we surprised a colobus monkey in a tree above us. As the sound of his hoots and the crashing thud he made when jumping to another tree faded, we heard the unmistakable sound of a large animal running through the forest. "*Bangena*," said Martin using the Zande word for bongo and showing me with fore and middle fingers that it was running. *And now?* I thought.

We tracked him out of the forest into a thick, tangled mess of dried reeds and grass. I was convinced we were heading for an action replay of the ten-hour tracking expedition of a few days ago. I started to walk less carefully and stumbled once or twice, my feet hooking in the intertwined grasses. Martin looked at me sternly. "*Dousemente*" (Slowly), he said. The next few hundred metres passed silently and slowly as Martin cautiously air tracked the bongo. The sun hammered down. The usual rolling mass action of sweat bees *toyi-toyied* around my face, trying to occupy every orifice I possessed. We had been on the tracks for two and a half hours.

The bush exploded into life on my right! I wrenched my .416 over my shoulder. I picked up the huge body of the bull in the scope as it tore across the small opening in the front of us. It stopped on a *tickey*. The front half of the bull was totally obscured by a tree and heavy brush. The scope tracked along the

Central African Adventure

bull's hindquarters and stopped where the shoulder had to be. The heavy stock was steady in my hands and the shot went off like silk. The bongo dropped where it stood. My heart pounding, I rechambered and quickly moved forward and to the right. I placed my second shot—a solid—between its shoulder blades. Martin moved up next to me, put his arm around my shoulders, and nearly crushed my ribs. With his left hand holding my shirt front, he pulled me toward the bongo, his eyes wide with excitement and a huge smile across his face.

The magnificence of the bull took my breath away. We stood in silence, heads bowed as the bull's eyes faded. He was enormous, and slowly, as I took in his huge, heavy horns, his magnificent coat, his worn hooves, emotion welled in my chest. As I battled to control my feelings, my breath caught in my throat and I caught Martin watching me. He came over and shook my hand, clasped my thumb, and shook my hand again. A speckled, tan butterfly fluttered across the back of the bull and came to an unsteady rest on his head between the heavy horns. Silence settled in a humid blanket over the three of us. A breeze played on my neck and I realized my shirt was sodden. The spell was broken by the baby-like cry of a trumpeter hornbill. "*Restez ici*" (Stay here), said Martin as he wandered off to fetch the others. As I crouched in front of the magnificent animal, the most indescribable feelings chased one another through my chest. Never before have I experienced the confusion of feelings—of joy, satisfaction, relief, sadness, triumph, thankfulness—to the same extent.

The rest of the team came jogging through the bush. Shouts, handshakes, huge smiles, hugs, backslaps, Antoinne lifting me off my feet and shaking me, photos and more photos, skinning, carrying, decorating the truck with branches, singing back to camp— *Mushi mushi wa bangena! Mushi mushi wa bangena! Whyah Whyah!*

Banging on the truck in time to the songs, we literally rocked into camp. The whole staff and their families running toward the truck, waving branches, yelling and ululating, Nicole hugging André, more photos, oohs and aahs, caping, ice cold beer, and a long, slow Dunhill . . . it just does not get any better than that.

I spent the last six days of the hunt in a state of euphoria. I felt as if I was walking six inches off the ground. A 32-inch bongo bull (in the top twenty in Rowland Ward) lay in the salt. Hunted hard. Hunted ethically. Killed cleanly. The bullet had mushroomed on penetrating the bush in front of the bongo and the entrance hole was quite large, although the round had not been deflected. The shot was exactly as I had previously discussed it with André, some ten inches down from the top of the shoulder, breaking the spine. Thank heavens for the .416 as we found the bullet under the skin on the opposite side of the bongo and I am not sure whether my .375 would have done the trick. At any rate, a wonderful blue duiker, a 15-inch warthog, and a magnificent, deep red northwestern buffalo followed before I left André at Mboki with his last client of the season.

The world record bongo, a lion kill measuring 351/8 inches, was picked up by Mrs. Beth Levitz, André's American agent, along the Kerre River in the middle of his concession. Martin also says that he knows of other bongo bigger than mine. Based on this, as well as my own experience, I predict that the new world record bongo could well come from this concession. By the way, all of André's clients who had giant eland at the top of their wish list took their animals, five in all, from 47 inches to more than 50 inches. I have already booked to go back in 1995 for eland.

It was by far the most beautiful area I have ever hunted. By far the best I have ever hunted. By far the most magnificent trophy I have ever taken. What can I say? I can only hope that the fairy tale continues and I live to hunt happily ever after.

BOZABO AKUYAWE

The tracks were crisp, clear, knife-edged, and the dung glistened olive green instead of the usual dull charcoal. I could feel no warmth in the large bull-size pellet that lay in the palm of my hand. I broke the oval ball. It was moist inside. They were not far. Their path was clearly marked by dark slashes through the newly grown, pale green, dew-laden grass.

They had come to drink at Baho salt lick in the night. They had come to relax on the wide, open expanse of the saline where no predator could approach unexpectedly. They had come to savour the mineral-rich, gray mud to complement their daily leafy diet. And then, as invariably happens, they were pushed aside by a bawling, blundering, snuffling, snorting herd of buffalo gate-crashers.

Without contesting the right of possession, they gently turned away, and on long, graceful, tanned legs, drifted into the gleaming green of the grasses, shrubs, and palms bordering Baho and ghosted into the gray tree line. It took quite a while to work this out from the tracks, as buffalo sign was everywhere, in many cases obliterating the underlying tracks. Finally, we arrived at the spot where they had stopped indecisively, milled around, nibbled a gardenia here, broke an *isoberlinia* branch there, and then, having made up their minds, were led by a large cow up the slope toward the hills of Zamoto, from whence they had come the previous evening.

Three hours later we caught up with the herd, which was traversing the slope of a hill, feeding as they went in a deceptively fast but graceful saunter. We circumscribed a crescent downwind of the herd and came to rest against the trunks of four young acacia terminalia describing a roughly shaped "w."

How lucky! My first week in the CAR. My first set of fresh giant eland (*Taurotragus derbianus*) tracks and here we were. We had them cold. The herd was going to walk right past us at a distance of some eighty metres. Piece of cake. Single out a good bull and then . . . and then chaos as a feather-light breeze gentled the few remaining gray hairs on the nape of my neck and the herd was transformed into a thundering replica of the charge of the "heavy" brigade. Huge animals materialized out of the green. A massive tan apparition made a right-angle turn in front of me, and I gawked at the huge hocks trotting away from me topped by an awesome set of corkscrew horns. "Cow," muttered André out of the corner of his mouth as my startled eyes found his. Amazingly agile, even dainty in flight, despite the obvious bulk.

More than four hours later we spooked the herd again. They headed downwind in a determined fashion for the Sudanese border. Reluctantly we turned for camp, now some eighteen kilometres away according to the GPS. That night, as I treated my aching feet—we reached camp in a thunderstorm some thirteen hours after spotting the first tracks—I had more questions than a child in a chocolate factory.

A few days later, at the main camp, we found a battered copy of Rowland Ward's *Record of Big Game*. It had this to say:

Discovery of this species was made by the 13th Earl of Derby. From the mid-nineteenth century it was rarely observed, being of a retiring disposition. Its wanderings are determined, at least in the dry season, largely by the presence of the tree *isoberlinia doka*, the young shoots and leaves of which form its favourite food. Its usual habitat is lightly wooded country and it continues to move even in the heat of the day, taking fright at the least alarm, when it may then travel a long distance. A gregarious animal, it is normally found in herds of about fifteen to twenty-five.

This species resembles the common eland, but is more impressive, being massive in body and head. The horns are enormous, are carried by both sexes, and in the bulls the projecting ridge of the spiral stands out strikingly. The ears are much larger than in the common eland, being broad and similar to those of the greater kudu; and the throat dewlap starts at the point of the chin. The general body colour is chestnut, rufous or fawn with a number of vertical white stripes. A stripe along the back and bands above the knees are black. The adult bull has a bushy chocolate-coloured tuft of hair on the forehead, and in winter, a dark mane on the neck, which has a wide oblique black band, becoming narrower toward the chest, with a narrow white band behind it; there is also an incomplete white chevron between the eyes.

Height at the shoulder about 66 inches (167.5 centimetres); weight 1,500 to 2,000 pounds (682 to 909 kilograms).

I had, however, come to hunt bongo, the most testing of the *tragelaphus* family of spiral-horned spirits, and had set aside five days to acclimatize, hunt savanna game, and generally sort myself out. Rain was beginning to fall regularly and heavily and the streams surrounding our camp were becoming increasingly difficult to ford and so, reluctantly, we packed up and moved closer to the aptly named rain forests, home to *Tragelaphus euryceros euryceros* or western bongo.

Now I was back. Almost two years had elapsed and it was with some trepidation that I sat in the main safari camp on the Bouye River reading Fred Duckworth's account in *Safari* about one of his client's attempts to shoot a Lord Derby eland. Four 21-day safaris! Have mercy! Involuntarily I wondered whether my forty-six-year-old body would be up to it. Maybe I would be lucky. Bump into a big bull on day one. See one from the truck on the way back to camp like the seventy-year-old American hunter who preceded me. I had met him at the airfield as we swapped charter aircraft for Land Cruiser.

I couldn't help a sneaky feeling of envy. Why did this kind of thing never happen to me? Nevertheless, I was really happy for him. Seventy-two and still hunting. Maybe there was hope for me yet. I was impressed by his spirit and outlook on life. It was there to be lived. To the full. Not so?

I was equally but unfavourably impressed by one of his traveling companions—a scrofulous, rodent-like creature from "Down Under, mate." Beady little eyes and tiny white teeth surrounded by an explosive growth of red fuzz. He reminded me most vividly of what I imagine some of the earlier and involuntary inhabitants of that large island must have looked like. He proceeded to give me the unasked-for benefit of his vast African and eland hunting experience, all miraculously garnered during the course of two whole safaris—the total extent of his African experience. He must have taken my silence for fascinated interest and even followed me into the brush at the edge of the landing strip where I went to rid myself of him and some equally noxious burden.

He shot his eland on the last afternoon of his twenty-one-day hunt and, man, was he proud of his achievement. "Never give up, mate; that's the secret. The hunting's all in here," he said, tapping his head. Well, he was right about that. Eland hunting is a bit like elephant hunting. It is often a case of mind over matter. What he failed to mention was that in the course of his hunt, he killed an eland cow by blazing away wildly into the herd against the specific instructions of his professional hunter. He also wounded and didn't find another big eland bull as well as a buffalo bull before he and his pro eventually claimed the trophy he was so proud of. It was not clear which holes in the carcass came from what weapon and the pro was not saying anything. He certainly lent new meaning to the phrase "empty barrels make the most noise."

Well, one thing was certain, I was about as ready as I was ever going to be. By the time I left Johannesburg, I was running about forty kilometres and cycling more than forty-eight kilometres a week, as well as doing my daily Canadian Air Force exercises. I felt fit and strong. I had learned a lot from my previous trip. I had brought two pairs of running shoes and a pair of light hiking boots. I always left a pair of running shoes and socks in the rucksack carried by Bert, our baggage man. Whenever my feet got wet after wading through a stream or swamp, I would quickly swap footwear and thereby avoid the crippling blisters I developed last time from walking hard on water-softened feet. I brought dark camouflage clothing, as much of the area had been or was about to be burnt—as is most of Central Africa in December and January of each year.

I know it sounds strange to be hunting in January, but that is the middle of winter in the CAR and it is the driest and coldest it is ever going to get. By that I mean you sleep under a blanket at night but midday temperatures seldom drop below 36 degrees Celsius. It is also the best time to hunt eland. With the 10- to 12-foot elephant grass having been burned, tracking is easier, an eland refuge is eliminated, and you can move around more quietly. There is a body of opinion that believes giant eland were originally forest animals, and at certain angles, their heads bear an uncanny resemblance to bongo. And like the bongo, their hearing and sense of smell is acute but their eyesight is less good.

On one stalk, a cow looked directly at me as I stood behind a scraggly piece of shrub some sixty-five metres away. She did not even break stride in passing. But noise is a major problem. Time and again when spooked, the eland were drawn like magnets into thickets of unburned grass or the potato crisp factories (those areas where the dry, brittle, crinkle-cut acacia terminalia leaves festooned the ground). When this happened, we would have to wait for them to leave or go around. To go through—even assuming the trackers could air-track the eland—was an exercise in futility as the five of us sounded like a battalion of infantry in hobnailed boots.

We burned these patches of bush wherever we found them. I never got used to this. For one, I was nervous that a fickle wind might alter the direction of the fire and pin us against some obstruction, or even worse, surround us. Secondly, despite protestations to the contrary, I was sure that the fires frightened the game and made them move away. Only the black kites who came in their scores to feast on the fleeing insects, rodents, and snakes were drawn to the fires we made. They often raged for days over thousands of hectares, leaving thick, black, greasy coils of smoke winding into the already murky, mildewed air.

Walking through these areas, even after the fresh, pale green shoots of tender new grass started appearing, was a dry, dusty, dirty affair. Wispy tendrils of blackened vegetation trailed down from the skeletal trees. Ash stirred by our footsteps rose like miniature landmine explosions and settled in, on, and over everything. But we could and did move quietly and quickly through these regions, often gaining time on the herd ahead.

We started off famously. A fresh, solitary bull track at 6 A.M. on the first morning. Was this the Bandit? The Moboso region north of the Mbomou River where we were hunting was home to this elusive, large, and solitary bull, which had eluded André over the past three years. But no, the tracks soon joined those of a herd and the game was on. Like elephant hunting, you kill a giant eland with your feet. They walk faster than you but they meander backward and forward. The trick is to use outstanding and instinctive trackers—those who think like an eland, who unravel tracks quickly, who can cut corners to make up time and who walk really fast. Otherwise, the best you can hope for is to catch them if they take a midday siesta. Of course, to try to winkle out a bull from the herd while they are still, listening and smelling in the fickle noon air is, in my opinion, like trying to outdrag a Ferrari in a Ford pickup truck. It's theoretically possible but you know the opposition would have to make a number of momentous mistakes for you to succeed.

At best, you must be still and they must be moving. At worst, you must both be moving. And that's what happened the first day. We caught the herd as it crossed a bare, laterite-strewn breach in the savanna. Using a tree-covered termite mound as a shield, we raced toward the herd. Peeking over the edge of the mound, we were in time to see the guardian's broad, tan buttocks disappear amongst the intertwined trunks of the terminalia trees, preceded by a gaggle of youngsters. Try as we might, we could not evade the cow as she wandered from side to side in the rearguard. Eventually, we got too bold (or desperate, you might say), and gave the game away. We were rewarded by the sound of thundering hooves fading into silence.

Then followed what was to become a well-rehearsed ballet. They ran, stopped, and watched their back trail. We tracked and walked hard to catch them, trying to guess once the tracks spread out (indicating that they had slowed to a walk) when they would stop. We then jogged in a crescent downwind and off the tracks to get ahead of, or at worst, come in from the side of the traveling herd. Guess wrong, go too far, and you lose the herd. Guess wrong, not go far enough, and you may have to repeat the maneuver or come in on the herd from the side, in which case, who sees who first is at best a 50/50 proposition with an alert herd. At any rate, you know the game is over, for the day at least, when the herd starts moving steadily and quietly downwind in a tightly bunched group. And that's what happened the first day.

But we went back, again and again. Each day the walk and stalk got longer. Each day I felt a little stronger, a little more confident that my body and feet, in particular, were going to last. Each day I was drinking a little less water, although I have to admit that, for the first time ever, my rifle was carried by one of the trackers. Yes, I reluctantly realized that my brain was writing cheques that my body could no longer cash, and if I wanted to be able to walk the four to nine hours a day, every day, which was what eland hunting required, I had to change.

At any rate, on the fourth day we confused ourselves and the herd, and quite by accident, they walked into us. There were sixteen animals in the herd. The bull was mature, the horns 46 to 47 inches in length and comfortably beat Rowland Ward's minimum trophy standard of 44⅞ inches. André dismissed it. "You can do better than that," he said, standing up and watching the nonplused herd fade away.

Nine days later, I wondered. Famous last words? Nine days in which we had not cut an eland track fresher than two days old. We changed hunting camps. We changed hunting areas. We changed hunting tactics. On one eminently forgettable twenty-one-hour day, we drove to Nguyo and back on a new path pioneered through the bush a few weeks earlier. The drive of some 170 kilometres took nearly fifteen hours as we dug ourselves out of streams and cut trees to widen the track for the truck. We passed through idyllic eland territory without a sign of them. We walked the swamps and plains around Nguyo—nothing. We saw pigs on the way to Nguyo and snakes on the way back. Six warthogs, a thin brown snake, two green tree snakes, and a forest cobra in hot pursuit of a shrew. But no sign of eland.

Dark, desolate thoughts abounded. Superstition reared its ugly head. Thoughts of maybes and might-have-beens wrestled with recriminations. Minor mistakes assumed unwarranted proportions. You started to lose your confidence, your belief that you are part of a competent, capable, professional and proficient team, each able to play his well-ordered part in this ancient ritual of ours.

At times like these, eland hunting can do strange things to your mind. Supposedly stable and mature men ride the roller coaster of despair and delight with differing destinations. It becomes a case of mentally hooking up and hanging on. But always, at the back of your mind, you are aware of the metronome gathering pace as the days tick by, 10, 11, 12, 13, and. ...

Day fourteen dawned. We were sitting on the edge of a salt lick some fifty-five kilometres from our latest camp as the gray gave way to early morning light. We started down to check the empty, unwelcoming pan for tracks. *Nada*—we straggled back to the truck, the early morning optimism having burned off with the sun. We stood around hanging over the back of the truck, sipping water, spitting, hitching up bits of equipment, looking anywhere but at one another.

"Now that we're here, we may as well check François's lick," said André, referring to the salt pan where our second tracker had spotted sign of a lone bull on the previous hunt. For no particular reason that I can recall, as we waited the few minutes that it took for the team to sort themselves out, André and I practiced, for the first and only time, me taking a rest over André's shoulder. Nicky had shown us how. If André bent slightly forward from the waist and placed his left hand on his left knee and right arm akimbo on his right hip, it provided a steady platform for me as I rested the rifle on his left shoulder and my right arm across his right shoulder and arm. We tried this a few times, as André is quite a bit shorter than my 6 feet 3 inches (in the old parlance). Eventually I found a stance that was about as comfortable as it was going to get and we were off to see the Wild West Show.

About an hour later, Martin, our head tracker, stopped so suddenly I nearly walked into him. "*Ici*," he said. Here and here and here, the fresh eland tracks spread out to our right. It took about an hour to unravel the tracks as the herd had milled around the spot during the early morning, feeding, breaking branches, and doing what eland do at rest.

We hunted well that day. We tracked well. We walked well. We discussed our tactics and while things didn't always go exactly to plan—we somehow managed a complete 360 degrees around the stationary herd during one of our crescent-like sneaks without giving the game away—we made no serious mistakes. Yes, we spooked them twice but not seriously. Not so that they changed gear into the famous, bunched eland, downwind jog trot. The second time, they ran briskly through a narrow section of forest, across a stream, and up a savanna-strewn hillside.

We were motoring on the tracks at a fast six kilometres an hour when François hissed us to a halt. "Often when they run through a forest they stop on the other side to see who is behind them," he said. André and Martin nodded in agreement. We moved downwind off the tracks. We had not traveled three hundred metres when André froze. We sank slowly into the golden brown, unburned grass. The guardian cow eland was looking straight at us. A crosswind must have blocked the breeze at the back of my neck, as the herd continued to spread across the hillside like melting rum raisin ice cream. And then the satellite dishes on the cow swiveled to my right and she started trotting. Down dip I could see two black heads waving in counterpoint to the golden grass as François and Bert strove to see the action up ahead. Murderous thoughts blasted through my brain but no time for that now.

As the herd of some thirty animals trailed briskly over the brow of the hill, we used their own confusion to mask the timpani of our trotting across the crinkle-cut terminalia leaves. The herd was skirting the fringes of the forest, seemingly unsure of why they were leaving the tender young *isoberlinia* shoots growing from the slim, elegant trees on the hill's crest. André motioned me one way, Martin the other. "I've seen the bull," hissed André, "You must stay with me!" I did—like the proverbial burr to the blanket. "There's the bull," pointed André. "Got it," I replied.

The bull was unmistakable. He stood out head and shoulders above the rest. I could see the black ruff of his neck, his horns hidden in the overhead leaf cover, the bulky definition of his huge shoulder muscles—my aiming point.

I was totally focused. This was what I had practiced and prepared for, mentally and physically. I was completely calm as my mind and body started an oft-repeated ritual. Forefinger and thumb moved the safety to avoid a click. Time was suspended. André bent slightly forward, his right hand moving to his right hip. I slid the rifle barrel over his left shoulder as my finger slithered alongside the trigger guard. And then . . . disaster struck! André unexpectedly straightened and pulled his binoculars to his eyes. The stock thudded into my cheek bone; the rifle jarred from my grasp! As I grabbed for the gun, a shot rang out and shredded leaves high in the kapok trees above the eland. The look of horror and disbelief on André's face mirrored my own. Martin asked whether I hit the bull, which had been only some eighty metres away. "An accident," I heard André mumble as he set off after the vanishing herd at a jog. We caught them and we lost them as they angled away, gathering momentum.

As reality returned, disbelief set in. After fourteen days, to blow it like that! We discussed what happened, both of us a little numb. We could have repeated the exercise a hundred times without a similar result. Recriminations were unnecessary and unwarranted. It had been an accident. André decided to check the bull one last time, unaware I was so close to firing. Still, it would have been the cherry on the top to have been able to celebrate alongside G. T. Ferreira, my friend and hunting partner, as he danced around the fire with the staff on his last night in camp.

"Bozabo akuyawe" (the eland is no more), they sang and danced to the rhythmic drumming. G. T. fired a round into the night air as part of the ceremony to celebrate his victory over the eland. I shared his euphoria and his success. He had worked hard for his beautiful 47-inch Lord Derby bull. He had worked hard—twelve days in all—and I relished his joy, even if second-hand. *Môre is nog 'n day* (Tomorrow is another day) I said to myself as I took my weary body off to bed at 11 P.M.

Next morning we were up at the normal time of 4 A.M. G. T. came over, shook my hand in farewell and "go get him" were his last words as we parted—he to the landing strip, me to try to pick up the pieces of yesterday.

Strangely enough, I felt calm and confident that today was the day. I knew now that finding fresh tracks in the morning would be half the battle won. I knew we could track them wherever they went. I knew we could walk them up before dark. I knew that we could outwit them and single out a bull. I felt I had paid my dues. I felt that today was my day.

And so it was. We picked up the tracks at 6:45 A.M.—fresh, fresh, fresh. We found them as they lay resting. François's razor sharp vision caught the flick of a long ear and saved us from stumbling into them and making an unforced error. It took me more than two minutes through 10X binoculars to spot what he had seen with the naked eye.

We circled ahead to the left. They moved to the right. We outflanked them to the right but couldn't find "our" bull. Three younger bulls, yes, even a 45-incher, but not our bull. One of the young bulls trotted off after observing me for some time as I lay like a lizard in my gray and black camouflage on the top of a termite mound gazing down the tube of my 1.5–6X Zeiss, the cross hairs unwaveringly fixed on the point of his shoulder. I knew he could not see, smell, or hear me, but some other sense took him and the rest of the herd away.

At 11:30 A.M. we stopped alongside a petite *marigeau* (little stream). In the cool shade of leafy palms growing alongside the tiny stream, the team drank water and ate a brunch of manioc (the local version of *stywe pap*–stiff porridge) and pumpkin fritters with little "raisins" of guinea fowl meat scattered throughout. André was impatient and hurried the men. *"Beaucoup de mush"* (Too many flies) he pleaded, swatting to no avail at the halo of sweat bees around his head. *"Igwe"* (Let's go), he said in Zande or is it Sango? They used these two local languages plus French interchangeably. "I could use a break," I said. We had been going nonstop for close to six hours, and in the end, this gave us the eland.

The eland were waiting on the other side of the forest for us. As the minutes ticked by, they relaxed and started to feed. It was François again whose keen eyes spotted them as we edged out of the gloom. A cow to the right. "There he is!" exclaimed André. "He's not as black in the ruff as some get, but he's really long," he whispered. One look convinced me. I slithered to the right. The bull also turned to the right and was now quartering away from me at a 45-degree angle. Seconds counted. The shot shattered the silence. The bull hunched and walked slowly away. The herd, confused, closed around him. He ignored them and turned slowly, ever so slowly to the left. We followed quietly but quickly. Martin took the lead. A second and third shot followed one on top of the other. Neither was really necessary. The first round had lodged in the bull's heart and he died gracefully and quickly.

I shall remember forever the last few, faltering steps the bull took toward us. I watched the huge, beautiful beast literally die on his feet. The episode lasted seconds in reality, an eternity in my mind. Perhaps I should have felt differently. I often have. But in this case my first feelings were ones of huge relief. Then, of course, the others came flooding in but relief was ever-present.

By the most conservative estimate possible, we had walked more than three hundred kilometres for this bull. I had not shot particularly well on the way. In fact, it had been a real hit and miss affair, if you will pardon the pun. I hit and killed everything that was stationary when I took the shot and I missed everything that was moving, including a yellow-backed duiker (which I really wanted), a blue duiker, two waterbuck, and, wait for it, a whole red, northwestern buffalo bull. Perhaps the lack of "actual hunting" (I had been forced to cancel three hunts during the preceding year due to business commitments) had been the reason. At any rate, when it mattered, Bertha, my battered old .375 Brno, did the trick.

Hunting the Oubangui Safari concession in the east of the CAR is an unforgettable experience. The area covers some 8,450 square kilometres, almost half the size of the Kruger National Park, and has only one village in it, very few tracks, and no fences. It is as close as one can get to the hunting experiences of the previous century. If you want the ultimate in fair chase, walk and stalk safaris—this is it.

Even though I have achieved the CAR double, namely bongo and Lord Derby eland, I hope to return as often as I am able. Quite simply, there is no other hunting experience in Africa today, to my knowledge, to rival it.

Hunt Mozambique

The evening light was changing to gray as I slid out of the Land Cruiser and leopard-crawled through the fine dust of the flood plain. As I came to rest to the left of a tall termite mound, I flipped out the legs of the bipod attached to my old, customized .375 Brno and focused on the picture through my 1.5–6X scope. The cross hairs came to rest behind the shoulder of a mature impala ram some two hundred paces away. The rest of the herd had already disappeared into the tree line and the impala's tense stance told me he was soon to follow. Without further ado, I adjusted my sights slightly, squeezed the trigger, and after the recoil, had the satisfaction of seeing the white belly of the buck lying where it had previously stood.

From the back of the truck, Magara nodded and smiled briefly as he held up his thumb. "Well done," said Joe, as I climbed into the front of the vehicle with him. "That's your first Mozambican animal."

It was the evening of the first day of my eighteen-day hunt along the shores of Cabora Bassa in northern Mozambique. It was the culmination of months of planning and the beginning of an adventure.

Heart of an African Hunter

What brought me here? In a word: elephant. Just the name conjures up controversy these days. "How can you hunt them?" people ask. After three unsuccessful attempts in as many years in Zimbabwe, I have asked myself the same question—many times.

The search for the elephant that was fixed in my mind's eye had, over the last four years, become something more than a hobby, more than just an idle pursuit. True, it fell short of an obsession but only just. Time spent on the previous hunts had not been wasted, however, not at all. I experienced some memorable hunts, shot some magnificent trophies, and made many friends. I had also used the time to discuss the elephant question with many professional hunters, safari outfitters, experienced sportsmen, and conservationists.

The results of my research pointed toward Mozambique and Safari da Caca, owned by Roger Whittal, Barry Duckworth, and Joe Wright, who are readily acknowledged by all as the foremost elephant outfitters in the region. In January, I put my money where my mouth was, paid the king's ransom that constituted my deposit, and booked the last three weeks of the hunting season in Mozambique, 8 to 29 September, 1990.

As is well known now, the Mozambican authorities, despite having granted Safari da Caca an elephant quota for 1990, canceled the elephant hunting in midseason. On reading the brief report in our local newspaper, I thought my Mozambique hunt was over. I had, however, not reckoned on the resourcefulness of Roger Whittal. At great expense he bought an elephant permit for me in Chewore, and after a total of some thirty-eight days of unsuccessful elephant hunting, I found the elephant of my dreams on the third day of my hunt in the Zambezi Valley of Zimbabwe. Two days later I was sitting on the shores of Cabora Bassa, Mozambique, ready, willing, and able to continue the rest of my hunt for lion and leopard. It had taken a day to drive from Chewore to Harare, Zimbabwe, and a further day to fly from Harare to Mkumbura on the border and then to drive to Cabora Bassa.

En route from Magoe (a little village roughly in the center of the concession area) to Cabora Bassa, there were many signs of past struggles. I saw burned out trucks on the side of the road and tracks that occasionally veered off and then paralleled the old roads for various distances because of land mines that had not been uplifted. We passed the "train," a huge rock outcrop, which looked for all the world like an old Wild West steam locomotive pulling a line of coaches. The locals call it *Garamaragafui* and it has some special significance in their culture. What, I do not know. On leaving Magoe, after being introduced to the local conservation officer who issued me with my hunting permit, drawn up by hand on a grubby piece of paper torn from what looked like an old school exercise book, we wended our way through the tiny outpost of Kasandira to the dam shore.

I had already been awake for some time the following morning, listening to the sawing grunt of a leopard and had been following its progress from the nearby water hole by the alarm barks of the baboons when, at 4:30 A.M., Twelve, our camp steward, tapped on my tent. After our successful elephant hunt in Chewore, Joe Wright, my professional hunter, Magara, another professional hunter who acted as my tracker, and I were all confident that we stood a good chance of finding a quality lion and leopard within a week or so, given the large number of cats in the area. Famous last words. We had reckoned without the intense heat that dogged our footsteps for the next week.

We ran into a brick wall. Day followed day and we developed almost a routine. Up early, a cup of coffee and a slice of toast, and then onto the flood plains. Shoot three or four impala as they hesitate in the tree line and then visit the baits that we had previously hung. Drive to near a bait, climb out, walk up carefully, look at the bait through binoculars, no luck. Look for tracks, turn back and start the process again at the next bait. Between baits, walk riverbeds, check the shoreline, check game paths. Nothing. On we battled through the soul-sapping heat; the tsetse flies that persisted in performing lobotomies on my bald pate; the infuriatingly dogged mutant ninja mopane flies that explored every orifice in my head. Worst of all, I developed a sinking feeling that we were going to return to civilization without having even seen a cat. Joe and Magara became as depressed as I was.

As the days ticked by, we resorted to humour to bolster our flagging spirits. We were going to set the world record for the number of baits hung without a take by a tom. We were going to shoot the world record pygmy leopard. We were going to can the smell of three-day-old dead impala and sell it to students instead of stink bombs, and so on.

And then, on day nine, our luck changed. A cold, stormy wind blew in from the northeast and the temperature plummeted. Almost immediately, we started to pick up tracks. A couple of our baits were taken by small leopards, and in fact, we actually saw one bound across the flood plain into the tree line. Our spirits began to pick up. And then we saw the mother of all leopard tracks.

Both Magara and Joe said they recognized the track. Three previous hunters had tried to shoot the big tom. On two occasions after he had eaten from the bait, he brought a female with him the following night. On each occasion, the hunters mistook the female for the tom. On the third occasion, he had jumped out of the bait tree before the hunter could take the shot. We decided that it was Jaws or nothing. The next three days were, if you will excuse the pun, a real cat-and-mouse affair. We tried to predict his beat and put baits up ahead of him. One night he walked to within two hundred metres of our bait before inexplicably veering off into a riverbed. The next night he got even closer. He walked to within one hundred metres of the bait, following our drag before turning around. The next night he hit a bait we hung in some gommos. The hunt was on in earnest.

For the first time in nearly three weeks, we took the afternoon off and went fishing. On the long trudge from the camp to the shore, lo and behold, two huge sets of lion tracks. Following the tracks through the dense, head high grass, with one rifle and a couple of fishing rods between us, was a character building experience. We saw vultures and then more vultures nesting in the trees at the water's edge. Then we came across a killing ground. Not one but twelve impala carcasses, killed over the previous three days, littered the ground. We could see where the cats had rested. We felt we were on a roll.

As if to confirm this, I caught the first of four tiger fish with probably no more than half-a-dozen casts. Being a non-fisherman who had not caught a fish for at least twenty years, it was a real thrill to see the iridescent fish leap out of the water shaking furiously. A shimmering rainbow of droplets formed around its jagged head as it tried to throw the hook. It was with a spring in our step that we walked back to camp. Leaving instructions for Magara to gather in the impala kills and hang fresh bait for the lions, we walked off into the gommos for our appointment with Jaws.

As the evening colours started to change, I heard baboons start to exchange excited warning barks. Later, the anxious, whirring *cheep* of a guinea fowl confirmed that our tom was on his way. We had a perfect setup. The wind was firm in our faces. The sun was setting behind our backs, silhouetting the branch at a 45-degree angle some sixty paces away on which we hoped the leopard would rest. Joe carefully hung the bait on the far side of the branch. This meant that the leopard would have to turn away from us to feed, making for a tricky shot, but with less likelihood of him seeing us.

Heart of an African Hunter

As the sun set and before the moon rose, I went through agony. What if he came now? What if he ate and left before I could see? I felt more than saw Joe as he eased himself into a sitting position on my left. He was looking intently through his binoculars. After what seemed like an age, he put his mouth close to my ear and whispered, "Don't move;" don't make a sound; he's there!" This big tom had a Ph.D.; he probably ate with a knife and a fork and had a secretary to make appointments. He sat in the crook of a branch for nearly twenty minutes, partially obscured by the foliage, just looking, looking, and looking. Eventually, satisfied that all was well, he glided up the branch, turned around and started to feed. The sound was awesome as he thrust his head into the chest cavity of the impala and started to chew off the lower rib bones.

I wanted to shoot but Joe made me wait. "Let him start feeding properly," his voice ghosted into my ear. The moon was now up and with the added help of the light-gathering powers of my telescopic sight, I could see the cat at a three-quarter angle facing away from me. He pulled the hindquarters of the impala up onto the branch and it slithered off. As he reached to pull the impala toward himself a second time, I aimed at the off-side front leg and squeezed the trigger. The thunderous crash of my .375 was greeted by a roar from the leopard. He launched himself out of the tree like a RPG7 rocket. I could hear him grunting, snuffling, rumbling, roaring, smashing through the undergrowth, a big crash as he hit something more substantial, a final furious grunt, and then silence.

The silence was total and I could hear my own breathing and that of Joe's as well. My eyes must have been the size of saucers as I turned a questioning look toward Joe. He reached over, grabbed me by the upper arm and squeezed hard. "Well done, you have your leopard!" he said. And I had. When Magara eventually arrived with the vehicle, we carefully worked our way up to the bait tree. We found his first tracks some ten metres from the tree and then blood and more blood and then the most beautiful leopard I have ever seen, stretched out, at peace, as if fast asleep.

He had a huge track. He was an old, old tom. His incisors were blunt. In fact, he had lost his bottom right-hand incisor as well as two of his bottom front teeth. His nose had been broken in some terrific fight and the bone had not grown properly closed. He was starting to lose condition and the skin around his neck was hanging in folds. He measured some seven feet in length, weighed a ton, and is the last leopard I will ever hunt.

No huge celebration that night, as we had lions to look for the following day. As luck would have it, Magara had seen two big, black-maned lions en route to setting up the bait. One made a mock charge and it was only after a tactical retreat that he was able to go about his business. We freshened the bait the next day and 3:30 P.M. saw us sitting in Joe's portable blind. The zinging of tsetse flies gave way to the whining of mosquitoes to be followed by the grunting chorus of hippos. Our blind was backed onto the water some twenty metres away. We were surrounded by head high *Panicum riepens* grass and it was not long before the soggy, squishy, mud-sucking sounds of hippos emerging from the water could be clearly heard. And then we made a fatal mistake.

Assuming that the lions had already fed and were too full to come back to the bait, at 9 P.M. we called Magara on the radio to come and fetch us. Our disastrous decision became clear the following morning. Our bait was eaten. The next night we sat until dawn. No lions came to visit and the proceedings were only enlivened by the sound of a hippo crunching grass some six feet from my head. The lions never returned. We looked high and low for them. We walked the waterfront. We walked the riverbed on the eastern side of the flood plain. We drove and walked up into the bordering hills. Not a track. Not a moan at night.

Our other baits were rotten by this stage and we had to start afresh with only three days of my hunt left. We moved to the western side of the flood plain, determined not to give up until the last minute of the last day of my hunt. Joe was even prepared to let me hunt one day longer, the final day of the hunting season in Mozambique. Gone were our thoughts of returning to Chewore to look for the 47-inch buffalo we had passed up during the course of my elephant hunt. Gone were the thoughts of flying down to Chiredzi to look for a big kudu and a southern bushbuck to complement the monster 17-inch Chobe bushbuck I shot some years previously. *Shumba! Shumba!* That was all that we had on our minds.

Battering a path along a granite outcrop forming the natural border to the western side of the flood plain, Magara miraculously spotted the head of a lioness peeping out of a mass of dry, yellow grass. Our flagging spirits were once again revived. We followed her to see if she had company, but as she disappeared up into the granite kopje, we could see that she was alone. Undaunted, we hung our last bait. That night two big cats devoured our entire impala ram, leaving only the head dangling from a scrubby mopane tree. The next night, while we sat in the blind, the lions grunted and roared. They moved backward and forward across our front in a semicircle, moaning, groaning, and roaring from dusk to dawn. At times it sounded as if they were in the blind with us. Just before dawn, they were so loud that I could feel the sound in my chest, and then they retreated into the kopjes. They missed our drag by about thirty metres, and as they had stood upwind of our impala, never came to the bait.

We wandered around aimlessly the next day and even went fishing, although my heart wasn't in it. As if to emphasize the hopelessness of shooting a lion on my last day, not even Joe could catch a fish. Well, what else do you do on a Saturday night in Mozambique but sit in a lion blind? The old phrase, "all dressed up and no place to go," rattled around in my head. We had hardly settled down in the blind when the distant moaning of a lion told us that the big cats were early on the move. They came straight to the meat. No messing around this time, chasing impala helter-skelter through the grass. They did not even stop for a sundowner at the water's edge. There were three of them. All maneless. One of the cats walked straight in, reached up to the bait and started feeding.

The tearing, ripping, crunching noises he made put Jaws the leopard to shame. I could feel the adrenaline start to pump through my system as one of the cats started to walk straight toward our blind. She sat down on her haunches like a dog, facing us some fifteen paces away and looking intently at the blind. Maybe she picked up a movement or heard a sound as I readied myself for the shot. Joe said afterward that he had been on the verge of asking me to shoot her. Fortunately, her curiosity satisfied, she turned and padded back to join her companions.

I switched my focus to the feeding lion that, reared up on his back legs facing directly away from me, was tearing at the carcass. I heard Joe's voice faintly.

"They all look the same to me; you will have to decide which one you want."

From somewhere came the thought that the biggest lion would probably take precedence and feed first. I eased the safety back with thumb and forefinger to avoid a *snick*, raised the cross hairs between the lion's shoulder blades and squeezed the trigger. The lion collapsed like a wet sack at the foot of the tree. I put in an insurance shot but it was not necessary. We spent the next hour, while waiting for Magara to fetch us, chasing away the other two lions that repeatedly returned to the bait and wandered around in the bush near our blind. And so ended our Mozambique adventure.

Flying to Johannesburg the following day, so many different scenes from the past few days flashed through my weary head like 35mm slides on a carousel. I knew I wanted to go back again. I knew I wanted to hunt Mozambique one more time.

Why, you might ask? Where else can you hunt 5.5 million acres in unspoiled Africa today? The territory we hunted stretched from east of Mukumbura on the Zimbabwe border to west of Tete and included both north and south banks of Cabora Bassa, a truly massive dam. The area measured some 100 miles by 100 miles!

Apart from three small villages, Magoe, Daque, and Kasandira, the region is largely devoid of people. The successive political struggles, the Zimbabwe civil war, and other political unrest has denuded the population and, I believe, contributed to the resurgence of wildlife in the region. The other contributing factor may be the resettlement of people in the Mavuradona Wilderness Area across the border in Zimbabwe. They pushed game and particularly big game across the border into areas vacated as a result of past strife.

The unrest has also compressed the people in the area who, for the most part, seem reluctant to leave the immediate vicinity of the remaining villages. Hurriedly vacated villages and old military encampments can still be identified. The cooking utensils and other personal items that remain are stark testimony to the haste in which the inhabitants departed. This, coupled with the huge discrepancy in the age groups of the locals (there were children and adults but extremely few teenagers or young adults), was a constant reminder of the harsh consequences of Mozambique's recent history.

And recent it was. A few days before our arrival, the Matsangas shot and killed a man on the road between Magoe and Daque. During the course of our stay, they also kidnapped four women and a man from this little village and right under the noses of the local garrison.

As luck would have it, one of the professional hunters working for Safari da Caca, who was showing an American booking agent around the area, managed to rescue one of the kidnapped women. According to her, there was a group of seven Matsangas who were leading them away from Daque into the foothills. Fortunately for her, the sudden and unexpected arrival of Dirk's vehicle surprised her guard, and as he tried to melt back into the bush, she seized the opportunity to dash for Dirk's vehicle. We also came across an old man whose nose and lips had been cut off by the Matsangas.

I can only take my hat off to Joe, Roger, Dirk, Mike, and the others for the downright guts and courage they have shown in opening these areas. For repairing the roads, for traveling the untraveled tracks, for cutting new roads, for giving the locals employment, food, and clothing, for offering transport to the older people and children between villages, and for giving the locals some degree of comfort and security. According to Joe, since they have been there, the locals have slowly started to extend their areas of cultivation, not without some inconvenience to the safari company, as the local method of bush clearing seems to involve setting the bush alight regardless of where or how far the fire burns.

These local people are the poorest I have seen in Africa. They are dependent on the few crops they can grow, the little fish they can glean from the dam, and the odd animal they can trap. There are no telephones in the area and the sole first aid facilities at Magoe were of the most primitive kind. I saw one tiny thatched school in the whole region and the only means of transport, other than an odd bicycle and scotch cart, was one little 50cc motorbike.

In regard to camping facilities, the water's edge had retreated some two kilometres from its level the year before, and this made water something of a problem. The edges of the dam were encrusted with a dense mat of water hyacinth and thickets of *Panicum riepens,* which often made access to the water difficult. As such, our main camp was located because of its accessibility to water at a nearby water hole and not because of the aesthetic value of the surroundings. What with having to bring everything, and I mean everything, from Harare, camp facilities were limited to the bare necessities. Ken, our cook, and Twelve, our camp steward, did everything they could to make us as comfortable as possible, but they could not make up for the safari tents, the worst designed and constructed tents I have ever used. They could also not make up for the plague of mice that infested the area and that nightly performed the latest disco dance in, on, and around me. Before tiredness took its toll and I learned to sleep through the mice mambos, the nightly *nachtmuziek* was a real pain.

On other occasions, due to the vast size of the concession area, we made use of a fly camp, all the paraphernalia being transported on an accompanying Unimog. Overall, the facilities were comfortable but Spartan, and as the hunt progressed, the time spent in the camp was minimal. Up at 4:45 A.M. and back at 7 P.M., a beer, a shower, a bite, and bed.

All of this, however, pales into insignificance when compared with the experience of hunting this huge, unfettered area. An experience which, for me, was the closest I believe I will ever come to knowing what it must have been like for Selous, Harry Manners, and the like. And despite the drawbacks, such as they were, if I am spared and remain whole in mind and body, politics permitting, I will be back.

ELEPHANT HUNT

As the little tail dragger, flown by Mike Thornycroft, started its descent over the burnt and blackened escarpment of the Zambezi Valley toward Chewore, I could feel the butterflies starting to stir. Scattered thoughts of my previous three elephant hunts wandered randomly through my mind. Day after day of picking up tracks, walking on them for hours, sometimes never catching up to the elephant, sometimes finding the elephant had crossed the border of the concession area, sometimes finding the animal but knowing it was not what I was looking for. Well, what was I looking for? Over the years my thoughts had crystallized and I knew that I was looking for an old elephant bull. One no longer breeding. On his sixth and last set of molars. An elephant who was on his own, whose tusks were long, elegant, and matched one another. An elephant whose tusks I could hold above my shoulders. Weight was not that important to me. I could never imagine selling the tusks anyway as I only wanted this elephant.

I had previously hunted the National Forestry Commission areas around Sijarira and the Deka Safari areas around Hwange. I looked at dozens of elephant and it was clear to me that the short, thick, heavy ivory of the elephant in these areas was not for me. After a great deal of research and numerous discussions with professional hunters, safari outfitters, experienced amateur hunters, and conservationists, I booked a twenty-one-day elephant hunt in Mozambique with Safari da Caca, an associate company of Hunter's Safaris, run by Roger Whittal and Barry Duckworth of Zimbabwe. They had an enviable reputation for extracting extremely large elephant, and my professional hunter, Joe Wright, assured me that if I was fit and prepared to walk, I stood an above average chance of earning the elephant I was looking for. As Joe said, you kill an elephant with your feet and this was born out by my friend, Philip Pascall, who hunted Mozambique the previous year with Joe and came away with a superb 75-pounder.

In January, I swallowed hard, breathed deeply a few times, and then signed the cheque as deposit for my hunt. Words like "king's ransom," "insanity," and "crass stupidity" rang though my brain. But I did it. I decided there was no way to hunt big elephant on the cheap. Imagine then my despair when, in August, I read a small article in our evening newspaper announcing that elephant hunting had been canceled in Mozambique. My initial feeling was disbelief. Surely the reporters made a mistake. No one could summarily cancel previously approved hunting in midseason. Telephone, telex, and telefax lines between my office, Maputo, and Harare were constantly under pressure the next few days. My worst fears were confirmed. The hunt was off. How can I describe what I felt? My wife said I handled it pretty well. She was not nearly as worried about me as she was the last time South Africa lost a rugby test.

And here I was, all dressed up and no place to go. I had spent four years getting ready for this hunt. Over the previous nine months I lost seven kilograms in weight and was down to what I weighed in my first year at university. I ran, cycled, and played squash virtually every second day. I fired hundreds of rounds in practice on the shooting range, including more than sixty rounds with my customized .460 Weatherby Magnum built for me on a Brno action by "Silver" Bill Ritchie and fitted to a specially made and weighted stock that left the rifle weighing some twelve pounds in total. Despite its weight, the .460 kicked like a castrated camel. Unless I held it tucked tightly

Elephant Hunt

into my shoulder, the 1.5–4X variable compact scope gave me a nasty tap on the forehead and I was reduced to bandaging it to prevent an involuntary lobotomy.

But I was ready. I was the fittest I had been in years. I was shooting well and was confident that, if the good Lord would only give me the luck, skill, and determination to find the elephant I was looking for, I could do the job. And then a phone call from Roger Whittal saved my hunt. At great expense he managed to buy an elephant permit in Chewore. Would I like to take it and then continue the rest of my hunt in Mozambique? Are the Kennedys gun-shy? Chewore was No. 2 on my list, after Mozambique, as one of the best elephant areas in southern Africa.

As Mike greased the charter plane onto the dirt strip in a perfect three-point landing, I already knew that my predecessor had just taken a superb 80-pounder. I confess that, on congratulating Arthur Chamberlain on his beautiful elephant, I had mixed feelings. Had he taken "my" elephant? Would I find one nearly as good? My doubts started to evaporate on seeing the enthusiasm of Joe Wright and his tracker, Magara, also a professional hunter, who told me that, if the three of us could join our spirits and work together, "Gospel" would see that we found the elephant we were looking for.

After sighting in my rifles, we headed off for the Mkanga Valley for a brief five-hour stroll to get the feel of Chewore, to stretch my legs, and, I guess, for Joe and Magara to get a feel for how far I could actually walk. The next twenty-one days, if necessary, would be spent on our feet from dawn to dusk looking for "my" elephant, to the exclusion of all else.

The pips of my alarm at 4:30 A.M. the next morning in our little fly camp in the Mahonde Valley sounded surprisingly loud in the still morning air. Within half an hour we were on the road as dawn started to break. We started to cut elephant tracks almost immediately, none of which, however, were of interest to Joe or Magara. Down to Mkanga we drove and up into the foothills. Joe had seen the tracks and dung of an old elephant bull on his previous hunt and we were going to spend the first day in the hills glassing for him and seeing if we could cut fresh tracks.

The previous day, Joe pointed out undigested vegetable matter in his dung and his large, cracked, and broken tracks, showing quite clearly how smooth, scuffed, and worn the heels of his feet had become. Elephants use molar teeth to chew their food. In total they produce six sets, one set replacing the other as it becomes worn down. As the sixth and final set deteriorates, the animal's food is not chewed properly and passes through the elephant's system in a relatively undigested form, hence the clearly identifiable vegetable matter in the dung. Eventually, of course, the elephant loses condition and dies of starvation due to its inability to extract sufficient nutrients from the food. Research shows that this occurs about his fifty-fifth year. However, as an elephant's tusks continue growing throughout his entire life, the chances of an old elephant having better tusks than a young one are good. Certainly this is a better basis for determining whether to follow an elephant track than the mere size of a track itself.

High into the hills we climbed. Fit as I was, toward midday I began to battle. I was using soft-soled tennis shoes, which continually slipped on the grass-covered rocks. The grass, being head high in many places, made it difficult to watch my footing and I slipped and fell on a number of occasions, finally taking a chunk out of my scope mounts, before we slowed the pace of the walk.

Outside of Tanzania, I have never hunted among such rapacious tsetse flies or such persistent mopane flies and I was reminded how hostile the African bush can be. Every bush had thorns of one kind or another. Even the grass scratched and drew blood from our bare legs, not to mention the tsetse flies whose every other bite felt like Mike Tyson jabbing a red hot syringe into my soft, unsuspecting flesh. No clothes, no insect repellent, no nothing seemed to deter these demon flies, but I think I would still choose them above the maddening persistence of the mopane fly, whose sole goal in life was to explore every orifice that I possessed and some I had not thought existed.

Elephant Hunt

The discovery of a big elephant track thrust tiredness aside and the next hour confirmed once again for me that there is nothing to touch elephant hunting. The tingle of anticipation when you pick up a big bull track, the growing excitement as you discover signs that you are catching up. Fresh dung here, a newly tusked tree there, and then a glimpse of dusty, gray hide! Is this the one? An anxious search for tusks. No. He was a beautiful 50-pound bull. Short, thick ivory with almost no taper from lip to tip, but not what I was looking for.

Probably to practice our final stalk, as we had never hunted together, Joe took me in on the bull. I was surprised at how assertive he was and aggressive in his approach to the bull. Once we got the wind right, we walked directly at the bull from slightly behind and to one side. We walked at a steady pace but were careful not to make any noise, stopping as soon as the bull stopped eating or dropped his trunk to test the wind. After getting to within forty paces of the bull, certainly quite close enough to make the shot, we did not dither around and turned and left the bull oblivious to our presence.

The long hike to the crest of one of Chewore's many hills saw me sweating blood and gasping for breath. I was starting to consume water at an alarming rate and needed a rest, despite the fact that it was only 2 P.M. Looking down into the next valley as we ate our sandwiches, we could see three different herds of elephant cows and calves and one enormous old buffalo bull. In fact, in our approach to the hill, we could quite literally have pulled the tail hairs of the last of four buffalo, or *dagga* boys, as we call them, grazing along the banks of a little stream. I had to fight the tremendous urge to take the biggest of the four, which, depending on whom you listened to, Joe or Magara, varied between 45 and 47 inches. A truly magnificent bull and one of many I saw during my stay at Chewore.

Coming down off the hill (although I'll swear it was a mountain), we passed close to all three of the elephant herds, at distances varying from thirty to one hundred metres. Only one herd became alarmed on noticing us and moved off briskly, tails held out stiffly, their ears flapping against the sides of their bodies. Joe explained that once they start running with their tails stretched out behind their bodies like that, they were unlikely to stop for quite a while, and if you wanted to trail such a herd, you better bring your lunch.

We reached our fly camp after dark and it was all I could do to drink a cold beer, shower, and have a mouthful to eat before my camp stretcher claimed my tired forty-two-year-old body. It seemed as if I had not even laid my head on the pillow before the alarm rang again.

Today's plan was to tackle a new series of hills and valleys, and Joe warned me that it was going to be a forty-kilometre walk and even tougher than the previous day. Very soon we were into the foothills and from there on it was a steady upward climb, made easier for me this time by a change in footwear. Even so, I had to stop three times on the two-hour climb. Coming over a false crest into the wind, we caught an enormous kudu bull totally unaware. The temptation to take the magnificent bull, which Joe estimated at 57 to 58 inches, was almost overpowering. We even started to make a half-hearted stalk when, to my relief, the decision was taken out of my hands as the bull spotted us and glided out of sight.

Following the general direction the bull had taken, we came over a neck in the hills and looked down into a deep, green valley. In the distance, looking for all the world like a charm on a bracelet, stood an enormous, lone elephant bull. Even at this distance and with my naked eye, I knew he was huge. My 10X binoculars soon confirmed my initial impression. He was a superb bull. I could see his straight, elegant tusks descending into the grass at his feet. I knew, instinctively, that this was the elephant I had spent more than forty days hunting. "That's him, Joe," I said with a degree of finality in my voice that brooked no contradiction. "He looks pretty good," said Joe more cautiously. "He's got long, black ivory and that often means he's a good old bull. Let's have a closer look before we decide."

"That's him; I know that's him," I repeated as we started a swift descent of the hill. We discussed our tactics en route and maneuvered downwind of the elephant, realizing that the wind in the valley would be blowing from a slightly different direction from

Elephant Hunt

the wind on top of the hill. Again we bumped into three *dagga* boys on the valley floor as they boiled out of the thick grass on a riverbank to stand and glare at us some forty paces away. We stood dead still, afraid they might run in the wrong direction and spook the elephant that was now only some four hundred metres away. With a brief snort and a flick of the horns, they trotted off across the wind, noses in the air, indignant at our intrusion.

Breathing a sigh of relief, we started to close quickly on the elephant directly from his rear. I had a very good view of the long tusks. I could see that the right-hand tusk was longer and a little thinner than the left, but could also see that they almost matched one another. "There's over four feet of tusk sticking out from the lip," Joe said. *That means the tusks will go about 6½ feet,* I thought. Exactly what I was looking for. "He'll go about 58 to 62 pounds," continued Joe. "Let's take him," I said, and with a nod from Joe, we started the final approach. Careful not to make a noise, but not timidly, we moved directly in on the elephant. I had always wanted to use a side brain shot and was pleased when Joe agreed with me. As such, we were closing in on the bull's flank, slightly above him. About forty paces from the vast gray beast, I sat down and rested my rifle on my knees to take aim. Suddenly the bull took three or four paces forward, obscuring his head from view behind a bush. Quite calmly, Joe motioned to me to move a few paces to my right.

The angle became more acute but not a problem. I remembered Bell's tip. Imagine there is a broomstick thrust through the earholes of the elephant and then try to break the broomstick in the middle regardless of the angle of the head. I could sense, however, that the elephant, although not aware of our presence, was becoming restless. "Take him now just behind the ear," whispered Joe. I felt surprisingly calm. I eased off the safety with two fingers to avoid a *click,* glided the sights up smoothly behind the earhole and squeezed the trigger. A split second later I heard Magara, off to my right, fire his .450 Ackerly and saw that his shot was not necessary. The .460 round killed the elephant with surgical precision. He was knocked off his feet and almost rolled 360 degrees before coming to rest with his back facing me. It was only upon walking up to the magnificent animal that I started to tremble slightly, and although my insurance shot went where it was intended, I would not have liked to attempt a third. I had to turn away as a confused flood of emotions swarmed though my system. The grip on my shoulder and the firm hand-shakes and looks from Joe and Magara made me realize that these two hardened pros shared some of my emotion.

Shaking off the feelings that threatened to get the better of me, I checked the tusks to ensure that they had not been broken by the fall. My next move was to look at the bull's tail as I had long wanted an elephant hair bracelet made from my own elephant. Imagine the laughter when we found that the elephant's tail was as bald as my head! It took until dark that evening before we were off the mountain with the tusks and I shall long remember the peace-ful and quiet feeling of satisfaction as we stood on the brow of the hill looking down into the valley as the light changed. Joe took some pictures and we girded our loins for the final descent to the vehicle. Fourth time lucky! It all seemed worth it in the end. He was a magnificent animal. The matched tusks measured 6 feet 6 inches and 6 feet 4 inches, and weighed 50 pounds and 58 pounds respectively. Both tusks contained excessively large and long nerves, which accounted for the difference in Joe's initial judgment. Not that I cared. I found my elephant.

THE BOSS AND OTHER TALES

Sitting in my hotel bedroom in London, John sounded far away. He was. He was talking to me from Johannesburg, two days after he had been badly gored by a buffalo in Zimbabwe. "When the buffalo was on top of me, pushing me along the ground with his boss, it wasn't too bad," he said. "It was like being at the bottom of a loose scrum. Make that a springbok/all black loose scrum," he chuckled. I was relieved and amazed that my old friend could be so cheerful.

According to John, the client had wounded the buffalo. On the follow-up, like the good and experienced professional he is, he allowed the client to take another shot as they caught up to the buffalo that was lying down and facing away from them. "You know what it's like," he said. "You don't want to shoot the client's animal unless you absolutely have to." The client's second shot was no better than the first and John and his coprofessional hunter, Kontela (who doubles as a tracker), both fired at the bull as it boiled off into the tall, tallow-colored grass that grew thick and long after the good, recent rains. Entering a particularly dense patch, Kontela spotted the buffalo at close range. Having the better view and angle, John motioned him to take the shot. "It was like the starter's pistol for the one hundred metre Olympic sprint final!" At a distance of three metres, the buffalo exploded out of the screening grass allowing John time only for a snap shot from the hip with his .450 Watts. "The bullet punched a hole in the buffalo just below the boss and above the right eye, but I might as well have been using a pea shooter for all the good it did. In a nanosecond he was all over me like a rash. When he's on you, you just go where he puts you. You're not going to poke him in the eye. You're not going to punch him on the nose. You're too busy going where he puts you. And then suddenly you're sailing through the air. There's no effort. There's no struggle. There's no heaving—one and two and three! You're just suddenly eight, nine feet in the air. And you know when you come down there are no cold Cokes waiting for you. But he is.

"And he's going to pound you and pound you and pound you some more—not once, not twice. He doesn't even start counting 'til he's reached ten. Then he's going to pound you some more until you're dead or he is. He knows exactly what he's doing. He is killing you. He really wants to. If anything, he's overeager. Stamp, hook, butt, pound. Everything all at once, all together, all the time. And he's really enthusiastic.

"When the horn ripped into my groin and the buffalo threw me over its back, I knew the ball game had changed. *Oh, oh,* I thought, *big trouble.* I started to lose track of which way was up. At the same time, the client and Kontela were blazing away at the buffalo but to no apparent effect. He hooked me again, this time under my left arm and threw me a second time. Instantly he was on me again. Kontela ran up, stood over the buffalo and fired down at it through and between the shoulder blades while it pushed me along the ground. The buff carried on regardless. Kontela then ran around to the side and shot the buffalo through the ear. It collapsed half on me and half off.

"I could see the blood soaking down the top of my thigh in a broad band. Kontela was frantically ripping his T-shirt into shreds. Undoing my belt. Pulling my pants down. It was his involuntary 'Jesus Christ!' as he saw the wound in my groin that got my attention. Until then it was like the time I split my calf open when trying to cut the throat of that wilde-beest. You remember the one we shot on the Limpopo? You knew something bad happened but the reality of the ugli-ness had not hit home."

While I listened with mounting horror to John, memories of our first buffalo hunt together nearly twenty years ago came flooding back. Four of us booked a hunt at Londolozi with John Varty. It had been a momentous decision. Wives and bank man-agers were consulted. Budgets were massaged and reviewed. The cost created soul searching of biblical proportions. Today the R1,600 price tag seems a joke. But in those days it was an immense amount of money for each of us.

Then began a process that I am convinced nearly every first-time buffalo hunter goes through. Oh my! We read every book and magazine we could lay our hands on that dealt with buffalo hunting. We talked to everyone and anyone who had ever seen a buffalo, let alone hunted one. We scared one another half to death with all the gory Capstick-type stories. And we trained. My, how we trained. We ran. We went to the gym. We practiced on the shooting range. We visited the zoo. Whenever we met, our dis-cussions consisted almost exclusively of the three Bs—buffalo, bul-lets, and ballistics. Our wives, of course, added a fourth B for boring—pronounced as if it were a four syllable word.

When we arrived in the lowveld, we were so excited we were like a bunch of wound up clockwork mice—rushing hither and thither, banging into the furniture and creating nothing but confusion. Eventually we settled down, and that evening agreed to split into two teams and play matches for who would have the first shot. Derek, John Varty, and I were in one team and Curt, Map Ives, and the other John in the second. We hunted for some five days before our luck changed and Derek shot his first buffalo. I remember it as if it were yesterday. By then familiarity had bred a degree of contempt. I was getting used to this buffalo hunting business. That morning, for the first time, I had not awoken with butterflies in my stomach. We were big game hunters, not so? I had been studiously trying to acquire John Varty's nonchalance as we tracked past elephant, rhino, and on one occasion, two snoozing lions. I felt I wasn't doing too bad a job, and as my tan gradually caught up with his, I made a mental note to buy a couple of copper bangles to wear on my wrist, just like those worn by the other professional hunter, Map Ives.

Within seconds, however, after Derek downed his buff and the realization set in that it was now my turn, I noticed an immediate and distinct change in myself. Try as I might, my pose and poise evaporated like spit sizzling on a hot plate. My heart beat faster. Adrenaline flooded through my body. I could see. I could smell. I could hear. I felt more alive than I had ever felt before.

The last moments of my first buffalo hunt are etched forever on the hard drive of my memory. The "late finals" (to use a flying term and as I have always thought of it) saw us hunkered down in a glade of still, green mopane trees. I sat with my .458 Brno, topped with a 1.5–6X Bushnell compact, resting on my knees, waiting for one of four buffalo bulls to walk into a natural avenue created by the tree trunks. The buffalo were grazing toward the avenue from my right. I could make out a hoof, the flick of an ear, the swish of a tail. My heart was thundering in my chest. I was breathing so hard that if I made the same noise over a telephone, the police would have arrested me for making obscene phone calls. I was sweating bullets.

The first buff hit the break in the trees. Not that one! Then the second buff. Not that one! Then the third. That one! Before the word "one" left Varty's mouth, the .458 fired itself. I did not hear the shot nor feel the recoil. Suddenly the mopane scrub was alive with a mass of bodies like Putco buses boiling backward and forward. Hooves thundered; dust rose. Big, bloody great big bodies battered through the bush. A wild staring eye here, a wet nose there.

The Boss and Other Tales

Fresh buffalo patties slapped into the ground like mortar fire. I had the bizarre need to shout "incoming" and started giggling to myself as we ran into the maelstrom. Suddenly, hard on the brakes and left hand down! There in front of us stand the four bulls, facing us head-on like Apocalypse Now. "Shoot!" screams Varty. "Which one?" I bellow. Before I can say, "I'm a first-time buffalo hunter," Varty has his .416 locked into his shoulder and lets drive. The bulls charge past us to the right. We tear after them—through bushes, over stones, under branches, leaves lashing across faces, grasses whipping bare arms and legs. In midgallop, the legs of one bull fold and he ploughs into the ground, never to rise again. I remember a lot of shouting. "Stop! Careful! Shoot it again!"

Slowly we retreat from our state of mayhem. The noise dies down. Dust settles. Derek and I grin inanely at one another, covered in dirt and sweat and panting like tired dogs. The buffalo has only one bullet hole—on its left shoulder. The solid broke the left shoulder, cut one of the arteries above the heart and lodged under the skin on the right shoulder. There is no evidence of any frontal shot. What happened to the other buffalo is not for me to tell. My first buffalo was the smallest of all the fifty-one I have shot to date. It had a soft boss and the spread measured a mere 32 inches. Knowing what I know today, I would never have taken the shot nor would I have charged after the buffalo like we did. Knowing what I know today, no self-respecting professional hunter worth his salt would have let me take the shot, and although John Varty may now be an expert conservationist, game lodge owner of international repute, and world-famous TV star, at that stage, a professional hunter he was not. In the interim, I'm sure we have both learned a lot about our chosen endeavors. I know I have.

Having said that, it was and always will be my first buffalo and so it has a special place in my heart. The small horns, with the boss filled in with fiberglass by my taxidermist, hang next to my fireplace on my ranch. A framed copy of the photograph of Derek, myself, and the buff resides behind my office desk as a permanent reminder of a wonderful hunt. It had been on foot in a huge, unfenced area of the lowveld and shared with some wonderful men who are my friends to this day.

One of them was John. Yes, the same John with whom this chapter started. John Oosthuizen is now one of the best professional hunters in Africa. Buffalo hunting is his specialty. A couple of years ago, he won the top award of the Professional Hunters Association of South Africa for a 48-inch buffalo he took with another good friend of mine, Bob Israel, from New York. Curt went back to the town where he was born in Texas and is currently a judge. He barely hunts at all. Derek is the chief executive of a major advertising agency and still hunts, but only as an occasional pastime. As for me, well, what can I say? My wife says that I suffer from the worst case of arrested development she has ever seen. Approaching fifty, I am still obsessed with guns, hunting, and fast cars. And it is true that my passion for hunting buffalo has never left me.

There are two kinds of hunts that I enjoy above all else. One is the sneaky type of hunt, which, in my case, is largely confined to spiral-horned antelope. The other is the kind where you pick up tracks, walk on those tracks, and try to outwit the lucky packet you find at the end of them in those "late final" moments mentioned earlier. These are the hunts for elephant, eland, and buffalo.

Africa has three distinct types of buffalo: *Syncerus caffer caffer*, the big, black Cape buffalo bruiser; *Syncerus caffer aequinoctialis* being the red northwestern buffalo, which you find north of the equator from Senegal in the west to Somalia in the east; and then the cheeky, nasty little forest buffalo, *Syncerus nanus caffer*, found in the rain forests in and around the Congo and sometimes called Ituri buffalo or dwarf forest buffalo. I have only hunted the two bigger species but have promised myself that, all things being equal, I will go back to the rain forests and hunt the little beasts in the rain.

I have only had one bad experience with buffalo, possibly because I have never lost my respect for them, nor if the truth be known, that tingle of fear when I am really near to them. You know the feeling, when you are so close you can see the bloodshot, red veins in the eyes of an old bull with your naked eye. When a cow thirty metres away lifts her head and stares over yours with that thousand-yard stare. And you know you don't want that focus to shift to you. When all your senses are working at ten tenths and your whole body is so concentrated and alert that it tingles. Certainly that is the foundation on which my respect is built.

That old adage, "get as close to the buffalo as you can and then get half again as close before taking the first shot," has guided my buffalo hunting all these years. It is probably worth repeating that, in ninety-nine out of one hundred cases, the *pawpaw* only hits the fan after you take the first shot. And so it is that I have hardly ever taken a shot at a buffalo more than forty yards away; nor on one that was standing anything other than exactly side on and which gave me a clear shoulder/heart shot; nor with anything other than a .400 calibre. In fact, all my buffalo have been shot first with a .458, then a .460, and the last few with a .416. And I have been more than happy to accidentally spook the buffalo in trying to get close and watch them run away or turn down an awkward shot and try again. There are lots of buffalo, after all, but only one you. I should also say, although this may be a controversial topic, that I have hardly ever shot a buffalo in a herd, nor with anything other than a solid bullet. Most of my buffalo hunting has to date been a fruitless search for that elusive plus-47-inch *dagga* boy. Why 47 inches? Well, that was the original Rowland Ward trophy standard spread before the late Steve Smith, the then editor and publisher, reduced the limit to 45 inches.

In the twenty years that I have pursued these animals, across six African countries and over innumerable hunts, I think I have laid eyes on a grand total of two such bulls. One bull stood gazing at me across the Timbavati River (which was flooding at the time) with that classic "you owe me money" look. I went back to the area for the next three years in an attempt to find him again, but to no avail. I can still see in my mind's eye that proud and massive figure glistening black in the torrential downpour, oblivious to the teeming rain and crashing thunder. I know the pitfalls of anthropomorphic thinking, but I sensed then, in one of the few times that this has ever happened to me, that a connection was established between hunter and hunted. Despite my numerous inquiries, I have never been able to establish whether he lived out his one score and five or died at the hands or teeth of some two- or four-legged hunter, as the case may be.

I could have pulled the tail of the other 47-incher as he ambled absentmindedly down the banks of a trickling stream high in the Chewore Hills of the Zambezi Valley in the company of three old, tattered, and battered mates. We were on the tracks of a large bull elephant and Joe Wright made it clear from the start that we were not going to be sidetracked from our quest for a trophy elephant by other "unimportant, uninteresting, and irrelevant miscellaneous animals." You can tell that Joe is a dedicated, and I mean *dedicated,* jumbo hunter. His tracker, Magara, had a slightly different view and kept on telling me, "biggest *nyati* I ever see—*madoda."* I have never been good at piggie in the middle, and after thirty-nine fruitless days of elephant hunting, spread over the previous three years, I was not prepared to take the shot and run the risk of seeing another 80-pounder (like the one the hunter preceding me had shot) run over the hill in front of me. And so, to Joe's acclaim, we silently pulled back into the riverine bush and let the four old *dagga* boys continue their breakfast unmolested. I still think about that buffalo.

In fact, the biggest buffalo I ever took was the first time I tried something different than the side on, shoulder/heart shot. I was hunting with Campbell Smith in the lowveld of South Africa at the time. It was during the course of that hunt that Campbell taught me the trick of moving downwind, off the tracks and then running parallel to the buffalo so as to get ahead of them and allow them to come to you. It sounds a bit easier than it is in practice, but when it works, you achieve the classic situation where the hunter is still and the game is moving.

The Boss and Other Tales

We tried the tactic a couple of times on that trip and it was a nerve-racking experience for me. On the first occasion, we were so close that all that separated us from a large and curious cow was a small shrub some four feet in diameter. To crown it all, the rest of the forty-strong herd was spreading out to the front and left of us. I am still not sure what kept me sitting there, but I think that paralysis of the lower limbs had something to do with it. To this day I think Campbell believes I am a lot cooler and tougher than I look, because when he whispered that we should pull back, I merely remained sitting there, gazing steadfastly at the approaching herd. To this day, I have never told him that I did hear his whispered words but was quite incapable of moving. Fear had nailed my feet to the ground.

This was a little different, however. The small group of some ten animals, all bulls from what we could see, were moving toward us with the largest bull aiming to pass to our left. At a distance of some twenty paces, he put his head down, changed direction toward us and started grazing. "Shoot him just over the boss in the middle of the neck," whispered Campbell. I looked questioningly at him and he repeated the instruction adding, "It's a devastating shot." The bull was now some fifteen paces away and I could see the hairs on his neck clearly through my scope, even though it was screwed down to 1.5X. Despite the fact that this was my sixth buffalo, I knew I was not at home sunbathing next to the pool, even though I had a much greater hold over myself than before. I consciously and gently squeezed the trigger and the huge bull collapsed in a heap in front of me. It did not twitch, groan, or tremble. It was down. Dead. Deceased. It had passed on to the happy grazing grounds in the sky without a murmur. I was astonished. It was the first buffalo I dropped in its tracks and is still one of only two cases where I achieved the same feat—the second being in a much more complex and confrontational situation where I shot the bull between the eyes at a distance of some twenty paces. But that's another story. On closer examination, the reason for the 43-inch bull's dramatic collapse was clear. The bullet had traveled through the spinal column, through the middle of the heart, and had lodged in the back leg of the animal. Campbell was right; it was and is a devastating shot.

But not all buffalo hunting is "death or glory" stuff. I can remember many days that, had they been spent in an office, might have been counted as boring. On the other hand, many days on the tracks were beautiful. Stunning, crisp mornings. Breathtaking scenery. And then the odd and interesting things you see when you spend many days on your feet in the bush. A column of army ants. A martial eagle swooping on a green pigeon. A cuddly, cute hyena puppy peeking curiously from its den and . . . humour.

I have the incident on video. We were hunting out of a tranquil grove of sausage trees in the Okavango. Two of our group were novice buffalo hunters. One brought his dad along, and the other was a friend who doubled as the cameraman—and he was good. His running commentary, in a very well-bred English accent, was erudite and interesting as he filmed dawn breaking over the swamp. He filmed the first fresh buffalo tracks. He filmed the first fresh buffalo patty. One poor tracker had to insert a finger to test the warmth. He filmed some curious reedbuck and then red lechwe bounding through the shallows in their plunging, rocking-horse style with spray surrounding their heads like halos.

By midafternoon, the novelty had worn off. Picture the scene: Cameraman and friend (bearing a light calibre plains game rifle) have dropped back and are some 150 metres from the action. The action is centered on a small island shielded by trees and in deep shade. Obviously there is something of interest on the island as the pro, Patrick, and his father (bearing the cameraman's H&H Royal double rifle—a fact he was shortly to regret for more than one reason) have been standing knee-deep in water and gazing intently into the shadows for an inordinately long time. So long, in fact, that the cameraman has lost interest. Eventually a shot is fired. The cameraman leaps into action and starts filming. A buffalo boils out of the shadows toward the hunters. Another shot. Patrick's father belly flops into the swamp, complete with double rifle. The hulking buffalo bull humps through the shallow water, spray and clods of mud exploding in his wake. Thinking the buffalo was wounded by the hunters, the cameraman's mate opens up with the popgun. *Bam! bam! bam!*

At the third shot, the buff stops. His huge head swivels. Who is making all this noise? Who is shooting at me? He focuses on the cameraman and his helper. He starts his charge from a long way out. The cameraman loses his plumby and proper English accent. The picture on the video alters even more dramatically. Sky, grass, and sky again. A fourth *bam!* Over the picture you can hear a voice trailing into the distance. "What the h— do you think you're doing? Run! Run! The d— thing is coming for us!"

What happened was that Patrick had been struggling to see a buffalo standing in the deep, dark shade on the island. He eventually took the buffalo with a perfect frontal heart shot. This buffalo turned and ran out the opposite side of the island, where we later retrieved it. Nobody, however, saw the second buffalo. As it brushed past Patrick in fright and in an attempt to flee, the pro instinctively fired at it, hitting it through the lungs. The person with the pea shooter assumed wrongly that the buffalo was the one shot by Patrick, but correctly, that it was wounded. Equally correctly, he believed that, although his weapon was inadequate for the job, the more lead he could put into the wounded bull the sooner it would be put out of its misery. All but one of his shots were ineffective but the last one broke the bull's right shoulder, stopping the charge and putting him down where nature took over and he died.

The cameraman sheepishly returned, dusted off the camera and dried his rifle. He made amends the next day by downing a good bull with one well-placed shot from his big banger, although it will be some time before we allow him to forget his rapid retreat or the choice language he used.

In all the years I have hunted buffalo, I have had only one really bad moment and this is how it happened. During the drought in the early '80s, I was lucky enough to be asked to help reduce the number of buffalo on a friend's game ranch. The ranch was game fenced and buffalo, being bulk feeders and consuming up to sixty pounds of grass a day, were placing themselves and all the other animals at risk. My friend put off culling the buffalo until the last possible moment and I had already participated previously in culling impala on the ranch in the hope that the drought would break before it became necessary to transfer our attention to the buffalo.

On this particular day, we awoke before dawn, breakfasted, and moved out with our individual hunting teams to different parts of the 9,000 hectare (20,000 acre) property. This might not sound that big to some, but in my experience, if you can thoroughly hunt 2,000 hectares in a day, you are doing well and are in fit hunting condition. At any rate, the area was more than big enough for us. During the course of the day, I shot four buffalo out of the same small group of bulls. In each case, I adopted Campbell Smith's technique. In other words, once the buffalo stop running, settle down, and their tracks start to meander as they begin to feed, I move off the tracks, downwind and parallel to their course, and let them graze toward me.

It was now about 5 P.M. The sun was sinking. I was hot, sweaty, and tired. My thoughts were already turning involuntarily to that first ice cold bottle of beer back at camp. My mouth was dry. I could see the cold beads of moisture forming on the surface of the glass bottle. What was left of the bulls were moving to the right across my front as I lay like a lizard on the hot sand, my rifle at the ready. I couldn't help it. It was the size of the bull that made up my mind. He was a beauty. Solid, broad boss, classic deep curves, and a good spread of more than forty inches. I had seen a couple of inches of clear daylight between an imaginary line drawn from the tips of his ears and the inside curve of his horns. That is always a good sign that a bull is of trophy standard.

The bull was moving past me. I hurriedly made up my mind. I let the shot go. He wheeled sharply to the left, stumbled over some rocks and went down about twenty paces from where

I lay, facing directly away from me. To compound the error of my snap shot, I then proceeded to make a whole series of stupid mistakes that nearly cost me my life. I did not pay attention to the fact that the bull ran only a very short distance and not the 100 to 200 metres that most heart-shot bulls run. I did not sit down and have my customary cigarette or apple or wait for the mournful death bellow of the bull.

Instead, spurred on by my tracker's admiring comments of "*Makulu sterk!*" I strolled up to the bull from the rear. Kneeling quickly, I slid a second solid into what I thought was the back of his brain. Only later did I discover that I had been so casual and close to the bull that I barely creased his boss. Then, to compound my crass stupidity, without reloading, I walked around to the front of the bull to examine the fantastic trophy that he was. Sitting on my heels about three feet from the nose of the bull, I don't know who got the bigger fright when he opened his eyes. As the bull bounced to his feet like a rubber ball, my rifle and I parted company. To this day, I have no clear recollection of how I climbed the mopane tree. It was only later, much later, that I discovered I had taken the skin off the inside of my elbows and knees. When I half came to my senses, I was in the tree with the bull resting his boss against the trunk some four feet beneath my running shoes. I was shaking uncontrollably like a country outhouse on a very windy hill. It took me some minutes to realize that, under my arm, in a fancy handmade shoulder holster, I carried a .44 calibre Ruger Redhawk. In those days, although I had already trimmed down the amount of equipment I carried in the field, I still carried either a Colt .45 in the small of my back or the .44 in the shoulder holster when hunting big game.

Pulling it out of the holster with trembling fingers and taking exaggerated care not to drop it, I waved it at the back of the buffalo. It took me several more minutes before I could align the sights properly. After the first shot, I thought I missed the bull completely. It took a moment to realize that the little black spot on the back of his neck was, indeed, the bullet hole. I was aghast that this most potent of handguns, which I confidently expected would halt a charging lion or leopard in its tracks, shoot through the engine block of a car and bowl over the biggest burglar, did not interfere with the rhythmical rocking that the buffalo was imparting to the tree in which I was precariously perched. After the fifth shot, I threw the revolver at the bull.

About 9 P.M. the bull slumped to the ground, and still later, let out his last mournful moan. I felt certain the bull was dead but was still in a quandary as to what to do. The night was full of the sounds of jackal and hyena and the last thing I wanted to meet on my way back to camp was one of those four-legged garbage disposal vehicles. I was also worried that the trail of dead buffalo I left behind me would attract lion from the neighbouring park. The moon eventually gave me the confidence to climb out of the tree and I reached camp after midnight. The only humour that I have ever seen in the situation, although I cannot say the same for my friend, was when my tracker returned after three days. When I asked him why it took so long to return, he replied that it took him a full two days to stop running and one day to hitch a lift back.

I have obviously never forgotten that experience, and to be absolutely certain, a shoulder mount of that 42-inch buffalo hangs in my study where I can see it every time I lift my head from my desk. Since then, one of my friends has been killed by a buffalo, an employee and another friend put in hospital, and a third stopped a charge from an unwounded and unmolested buffalo at ten paces. I have never lost my love of hunting these big animals, but I have also never lost my caution or my care when doing so. When I do, that is the time when I hope I have the sense to stop.

HOW NOT TO HUNT A LION AND STILL GET ONE

Is modern cat hunting an overrated pastime? In a funny sort of way, it reminds me of the army. "Hurry up and wait." And wait you do. You wait and stare at bits of rotting meat and wait some more. And then—if you're lucky—suddenly the cat is there and *boom* it's over, or *boom* it's . . . "Oh, Dear!" Or maybe that should be "OH, DEAR!!!" Hours of boredom followed by seconds of excitement.

I know that's simplistic. A bit like describing fox hunting as the ungainly chasing the unseemly. I know it's also a generalization. And generalizing about cats is difficult, if not impossible. In fact, the only thing most people will agree on when it comes to cat hunting is that, whatever you think they will do, they invariably do something different. And this probably explains why there are so many cat hunting "experts." Every hunter, amateur or professional, seems to have his own idea of how to hunt the big felines. All I can say is I have seen many methods work and equally many fail.

I have had the privilege of hunting cats with two of the modern experts: Lou Hallamore, coauthor of *Chui*, in Zimbabwe, and with Nicholas Blunt in Tanzania. Nick's dad, Commander David Enderby Blunt, wrote the book *Elephant*. Between the two of them—Nick and Lou, that is—they have hunted cats for more than fifty years. And that's not all. I have also hunted cats with John Oosthuizen, André Roux, Keith Vincent, Jannie Meyer, Frank Dyason, Joe Wright, and Campbell Smith. Good professional hunters all. And I have learned valuable lessons from all of them.

Today, almost all cat hunting in Africa consists of shooting lions and leopards off bait. I would hazard a guess that less than 10 percent, and it may be as little as 5 percent, of cats are shot differently and then most of these exceptions will be chance encounters or walking toward the sound of roaring lions. Lions taken by tracking on foot are few and far between. Habitat shrinkage, the lack of experienced trackers, and the lack of willing hunters (professionals and amateurs alike), are all contributing factors.

What kind of bait to put out to attract a cat? Some hunters prefer one particular kind of animal—impala, warthog, or baboon, for example. Frankly, I don't think this is important. More important is the fact that there must be enough meat to last more than one meal; the meat should be as inaccessible to vultures as possible; and must last as long as possible before deteriorating to the extent that not even a hungry leopard will eat it. For these reasons, I believe hippo makes a good bait. The skin is too tough for vultures to penetrate; it can be hung in such a way that vultures can't sit on it and eat the flesh; the legs provide a substantial meal, and as old Hatibo, one of my skinners, once said, "The *simba* that has tasted hippo dies on the meat."

Next is the question: Where to hang the bait? One thing you may want to ask yourself in this regard is whether cats cover their territory at random or according to some sort of pattern or beat. If you believe the latter, then of course, there is no point in hanging the bait near fresh tracks as the cat is gone and won't be back for some time. At the end of the day, the best areas are probably along paths frequented by cats, close to water, where the cat has a secure and comfortable route to the meat and where he can lie in cool cover to keep a watchful eye over his possession.

How you hang the bait is also important. For lions, you want to hang the bait using chains or very strong rope to prevent the lions from taking it away. The bait must also be high enough to prevent hyenas from demolishing it. For leopard you want to hang the bait much higher, and in all cases you must take into account the prevailing wind, the direction of the setting sun, the site of the blind, vultures, and the effect of silhouettes.

And don't forget the blind. Do you build it on the ground or in a tree? Clearly the latter is much safer, but because it requires more time and effort, the surrounding commotion is something of a trade-off, even if the materials needed are assembled away from the site. For this reason, and the scarcity of suitable trees close to the bait (trees can be unnecessarily difficult like that sometimes), most blinds are built on the ground and allow the hunter to sit or lie comfortably while he waits for the cat to arrive.

I stress comfortably because the greater the comfort, the less likely the hunter is to fidget and make cat-alarming noises. This is one of the reasons why I prefer blinds where the hunter can lie instead of sit. They are more comfortable (sometimes too comfortable) and I don't think I am the only one to have nodded off in a blind. But for me, I shoot most accurately off my bipod while lying down. My bipod (which attaches to the reinforced pin for my rifle sling) fits me perfectly, much better than the rests contrived by blind builders.

Having said that, I have also shot cats sitting and standing. Of the two, the sitting blind probably makes more sense, particularly as it lends itself more easily to a mobile blind. Many pros carry a series of rolled up reed mats and sticks, which can be quickly, quietly, and easily used to form the framework of a blind (sometimes this includes a roof to avoid reflections on moonlit nights), which can be equally quickly camouflaged with resident bushes, shrubs, and grasses.

The really "high tech" pros not only have semidetached blinds in their vehicles, but also a variety of listening and lighting devices—where night shooting is allowed. The most advanced technology I have seen was so sensitive that it allowed the pro to listen to ants crawling up the tree trunk via a remote-controlled listening device the size of a thumbtack, and then light up the scene with a red-filtered, rheostat-controlled light. I suppose the client used a laser sight fitted to a carbon fiber-stocked, titanium-barreled .460-338 with electronic trigger. God help us!

Having said all this, maybe a recent hunt in Tanzania will illustrate some of the things that should and should not be done. On this trip we hung the back half of a sable in a stick-like tree, devoid of leaves, on a bare patch of ground, fifty metres from a car track. At the time, I had other animals on my mind and I wasn't terribly enthusiastic about cat hunting. But it was expected of me to at least go through the motions. A day and a half later, we were in the vicinity and went to check the bait. This "checking" can of itself be converted to a separate art form. I have known pros who park a kilometre from the bait, sneak in as if they were stalking a Rowland Ward kudu, check the ground for tracks, the tree for scratch marks, and the meat for animal hairs, all in an attempt to work out what is eating the bait and how big it is. Discussion is in whispers. No one smokes and certainly no one piddles.

We just drove up. Reluctantly I got out and walked to the upwind side of the meat. To approach from the other side is the best diet tool ever devised. If you could bottle the odor or include it in an aerosol, one spray a day would put the most determined fatty off his food.

Not very promising, I thought. *No tracks, no vultures in the trees.* As we pottered around in different directions, a startled, abrupt grunt erupted from the grass to my front. One, then two, then three lionesses appeared and skulked away at a tangent. We slipped into action mode in half a dozen nanoseconds. The pro, myself, the tracker, and game guard in line astern. A threatening rumble rising in pitch and volume from the front. I saw her cocked, teddy-bear-shaped ears first as she peered around the side of the antheap. I saw the black tip of her tail flicking the dead, golden grass behind her. A whispered consultation. We back off. The game guard and tracker insist there is a fourth lion. A *kubwa sana* (very big one) and they mime a big mane.

We hastily build a makeshift blind against the side of an antheap almost due west of the bait 114 paces away. We cut a shooting lane to the bait. We drop the bait to the ground although still tied to the tree with stout rope and we duck into the blind at exactly 5 P.M. Two hours of daylight left. Almost immediately, two vultures descend. Dressed as undertakers, they hop toward the meat in their ungainly yet somehow menacing way. A large lioness erupts from the grass to the right of the bait and the gate-crashing birds beat a hasty retreat to the top of a nearby acacia tree. The lioness stalks around the bait and stares straight at me as I lie still as stone, rifle at the ready through my shooting port.

The pale yellow eyes bore a hole through the back of my skull. I feel naked, almost embarrassed at having been so easily exposed and a tad apprehensive as she takes a few steps toward me to confirm her suspicion. With a flick of her tail, which seems both dismissive and contemptuous, she returns to the bait and starts eating. The other two lionesses gingerly approach. She growls the low, rumbling warning we heard earlier, but eventually allows them to approach and join in. Almost casually, without lifting her head from the carcass, she clubs the youngest lioness on the back of the head when it gets too close. The youngster skitters away in fright.

Shooting time winds down. The bush stills, and as quiet descends, I am reminded again how noisy it normally is. It doesn't stop the umpteenth tsetse, however, from trying to crawl into my inner ear for a taste-test. Its normal buzz changes to a hysterical pitch caused no doubt by the claustrophobic confines of my eustachian tubes. I lose control and instinctively slap myself hard against the side of the head.

The stroppy lioness looks up at me over the back of the bait and walks toward me. She stops about thirty trigger-finger-tightening paces away, lies down in a sphinx-like pose and stares and stares and stares. The truck is about three hundred metres away hidden in a bush, and as twilight descends swiftly into darkness, discretion gains the better part of valour and we slink away from the blind, tails tucked between our legs, heads bowed, beaten by Her Majesty.

But only for the time being. Next morning, before dawn, we are walking down the car track. We had no time yesterday to cut and sweep a quiet approach to the blind. A few hundred metres from the bait, the polite, tentative twitters of an early morning guinea fowl are deafeningly drowned out by the thunderous roar of what can only be a very large male lion. I can feel the sound in my chest as it tails off into discreet *uh, uh, uh, uh,* chuffs. Immediately I am sure of one thing—I am not at home in my favourite armchair watching the evening news on TV. All senses, and some I didn't know I possessed, are alive and quivering. Right now I can hear a fly wing flap at one hundred metres.

We tiptoe off to the left into the shoulder high grass in a semicircle to come into the blind from behind. Each twig, each stalk of dry grass sounds like a claymore mine exploding as it snaps underfoot. Eyes popping, hyperventilating through open mouths, we sneak into the blind. Nothing. No. Yes! We see the head of the lioness peeping out around the side of a leadwood tree trunk. Eventually she saunters up to the bait, looks at us and disappears in the direction of what we subsequently discover is a well-populated hippo pool. And that is that.

We hold a war council. We call in the consultants. Nicky Blunt happens to be in camp at the time and the Professor, as I call him, has forgotten more about cat hunting than I have been taught. We also draw Hatibo, our skinner, into the debate. I would guess his age at close to sixty. The old man introduced himself to me as Hatibo—gunbearer, skinner, cook, and lover! But in looking through his well-thumbed photographs, it is clear that he has been on more lion hunts than I have eaten hot breakfasts. Decisions are made. We need a hippo to freshen the bait and we are going to build a *machan* (a blind) in a tree. It's a professional, all-action, team effort. Some people cut poles, others grass, still others manufacture a ladder. We summon the help of an antique local fisherman in his leaky bark canoe to help in the recovery operation. I clobber a hippo in the head and drop him stone dead in the shallows.

Back we rush. Jarring over the pitted black turf of the dry *mbugas*. Rush, rush, rush. By 4 P.M. we lie like lizards on the logs of our *machan*, swaying gently to and fro in the treetops. We are smothered in hopelessness. We know it has all been in vain. When we got there, the vultures were everywhere. They had demolished the bait. If the lions were around they would never allow this to happen—or so conventional wisdom dictates. As if to confirm our pessimism, a herd of impala accompanied by a lone topi graze peacefully beneath our *machan*.

Every now and then they give us false hope by gazing fixedly in the direction of the bait. They only really get concerned when the evening airs tantalizingly waft our odor down and around them. Like a buck caught in the headlights of a car, they stop, twitch on stiff legs, and dart off in different directions before returning to their starting point. I seriously consider shooting the topi. He is a good one and I want him.

Somehow I climb down from our precarious perch in the pitch dark without breaking my neck or damaging my rifle. Now what? We eventually convince ourselves that Hatibo is right. They won't be able to resist the hippo meat. Next day we build a top quality stand-up blind at the foot of the tree that houses the *machan*, some 135 metres from the bait, cut another shooting lane and hang another hippo leg. We leave. We have persuaded ourselves they are early morning feeders.

As we exit the Land Cruiser the next morning in the dark (the almost full moon has set), we hear the lion. And boy, do we hear him. He is a *duma* lion and proud of it. He is so loud I can't hear myself think. We push on as fast as possible, the first inklings of dawn appearing pink before our path. We find the tape that marks the entrance to our carefully prepared and swept 300-metre path to our blind. We are quiet, oh so quiet. We cruise down the path like cat burglars. All is still. I hear the blundering blur of a bumble bee or some such large insect and then a rumbling sound I cannot place.

My being is focused on the wall of the blind. Behind its protective embrace I rest my .375 Brno loaded with Federals topped with 300-grain Nosler Partition bullets kindly found for me by Robert of Swaydns in Alberton and lent to me by Frans Knox. I quietly remove the bung from my shooting port, which has been carefully fashioned by Hatibo and tied to a stick so it will not accidentally fall and hit the ground with a thump. Even more carefully, I ease Bertha through the shooting port, put my drab, olive green jacket in the "v" of a pole cut for a rest and ease the forepiece onto the jacket. I'm as ready as I can be. Clean rifle, clean Zeiss 1.5–6X Diavari low light scope, clean body, and cool head. Right, let's go. This is what all the practice and preparation has been about. And I'm calm, imperfectly calm, my breathing almost steady, hands reasonably dry, still, and tremor free.

A first quick scan. Nothing. A slow careful sweep. Nothing. Out come the 10X25 pocket Leicas. Nothing. The three of us in the blind look one another in the eye and slowly shake our heads. We hunker down beneath the protection of the dry grass shield and put our heads close together. "What do we do now?" I whisper. "Wait" is the unanimous decision. Jeog, our trucker, stays sitting. The pro and I stand. I can hear my knee joints creak. Getting a touch old for this, I think.

"On the right—he's on the right!"

"Where?"

"Walking toward us. The lionesses are behind him!"

I can't see. I'm looking too far right. In fact the three lions are walking almost directly toward me as I spot them appearing out of the gray dawn, their coats perfectly matching the background of dry, dead, yellow grass and dull, gray, slender tree trunks. I note the halo of pale mane around the enormous head of the enormous male. I find time to wonder where the long, black mane hair came from that Jeog found on the bait as I watch him slouch toward me, flicking out those huge padded front paws.

I sense the massive power in the almost sloppy, slovenly plods of the lion as he narrows the gap between us. He takes no note of his surroundings. His eyes seem focused toward my left. He is still some 130 metres away and approaching the point where the lion tracks invariably head down to the hippo pond.

He starts veering to my right. *He's going back! He's going back!* my brain yells silently to me. He is still partially obscured by the gray secondary growth of stick-like saplings. He straightens out and again moves directly toward me. I have the cross hairs resting on the middle of his chest just beneath his chin. As he clears the scrub, I let drive. The lion swaps ends, spins, rends the air with terrible, unearthly roars, falls, stands. As he comes erect, I pound him again on the point of his right shoulder. The roaring reverberates around the small clearing. He disappears from view behind a thin screen of grass. I can't believe it. He is struggling to stand, pushing himself up with his huge shoulders. My third and final shot rolls him over. He lies with his back to me as I watch him, all my senses on full alert. His great chest rises and falls. His breath escapes in heaving chuffs like an old locomotive in the shunting yards. And then there is silence.

"I didn't know you were going to shoot."

"That shot took me by surprise."

"Where did you hit him?"

"What a big bugger!"

"I was listening to your breathing."

"Amazing."

"Did you hear those roars?"

"I couldn't believe it when he kept on getting up–like Punch 'n Judy."

"What's that rumbling on the left?"

"Be careful! It's the lioness!"

Blathering away like a bunch of arrow-marked babblers, we nearly blunder into the big lioness as she lies crouched over one of the hippo legs some fifty paces to our left. The rumbling sound I'd heard earlier had been her. So much for Nicky's guarantee that no cat had ever got away with a bait he tied up with his rope instead of the chains we wanted to use.

She must have pulled the leg down in the night and dragged it over to our first blind. We were in full view as we sneaked into our stand-up blind, but she was content to let us off with a rumbled warning. It hadn't been an insect after all.

To completely confound us, she stayed put throughout the entire recovery operation, only moving to tug at her hippo leg and to greet the two younger lionesses who returned, saw us, and beat a hasty retreat.

And yes, he was every bit as big as he first seemed. He had a full blond mane tinged with black under his chin. The five of us battled to load him onto the Land Cruiser. In the end, we had to cut a pole to push under his haunches to raise him onto the truck bed. His skull easily beat the Rowland Ward minimum trophy standards while his body, from tip to tail, measured a tad under ten feet.

Only the first Nosler Partition remained in the body and it performed poorly—only the stem of the bullet remained under the skin at the end of the ribcage, although it penetrated nearly four feet diagonally through the chest cavity. The worst performance I experienced on my entire trip from what I still consider to be a premium bullet. Both the first two shots killed him, the third and last round being possibly a little too far back. Thankfully it wasn't the other way around.

When I look back over the five days that covered the hunt, how we blundered our way from mistake to mistake, it seems that this was the classic way not to hunt lion and yet still get one. Consider this. We hung the remains of the sable carcass (after we caped it and took the fillets) to a pole; using ordinary rope; in the middle of nowhere. No wiping down the tree with dung, no dragging the intestines around the area. We chased the cats off the bait. They spotted us when we hid in the blind. They pulled the bait free. Saw us as we walked into the blind, and so on and so on. Quite pathetic, really. But look at the scoreboard.

And, by the way, earlier in the safari we accidentally bumped into two lions on a freshly killed, monster warthog boar. The Professor orchestrated everything, from the choice of the tree, to hanging the bait, to positioning and building the blind, and the course of the carefully swept path to the blind. We waited and watched as the lions returned to the fringe of the clearing where the bait hung. They eyed the bait while lying in thick cover some fifty metres away, turned, and slunk off never to be seen again.

It only goes to show—whatever you think they will do, they invariably do something different. And maybe, at the end of the day, that's the challenge.

pretty hackneyed pose, but I was so pleased to beat this old, wise, and battered
m that I just did not want to let go after off-loading him from the truck. Pride
so accounts for the silly grin.

A better photograph of same tom. There was no scale or tape measure but a piece o string, cut to the leopard's length, later revealed that the cat measured 7 feet, 2 inches.

A maneless male lion typical of this region. This lion's skull beat the minimum Rowlar Ward trophy standard of 25 inches—Mozambique.

The tiger fish I caught on Cabora Bassa the afternoon before I shot the leopard—Mozambique.

Bullet-ridden town gaol—Magoe, Mozambique.

Joe Wright, me, and elephant—Chewore, Zimbabwe.

Me and elephant—Chewore, Zimbabwe.

big elephant bull that
wandered out of the Kruger
National Park onto a game
ranch where I was hunting in
the South African lowveld.

An even bigger elephant bull—
Mhlaralumi, South African lowveld.

Me and some very nice tusks—Chewore, Zimbabwe.

Intermediate colour variation in northwestern buffalo—CAR. Although not clear from the photograph, the underneath of the neck, chest, and belly were a dusky tan.

Old dagga *boy—South African lowveld.*

...sed a custom-made .460 Weatherby on a Brno action by Bill Ritchie for this Cape buffalo—
...ambezi Valley, Zimbabwe.

...y old friend Derek Carstens and me with his Cape buffalo—Zambezi Valley,
...imbabwe. I used an H&H .475 Royal and Derek a .375 H&H Royal.

If memory serves, this was my sixth buffalo, which I shot with Campbell Smith, then a part-time professional hunter, now one of the more experienced South African pros.

Old dagga *boy—South African lowveld.*

lack version of northwestern buffalo—CAR.

ly red northwestern buffalo—CAR.

Bob Israel, a good American friend of mine, carries this photo in his wallet at all time. The bull has a spread of 48 inches and won another good friend, John Oosthuizen, the Professional Hunter of the Year award in South Africa. The bull was taken in the South African lowveld.

Me, Phiri-phiri (tracker), and Cape buffalo—South African lowveld. This is one of only two buffalo I have shot that dropped in its tracks. A frontal shot over the boss as it grazed toward me did the trick.

After bunking off and going river rafting below Victoria Falls, my old friend, Derek Carstens, probably didn't deserve this lion, but it did make up for nearly drowning after our raft overturned. All in all, the end to a perfect African day.

Me and lion—Rungwa River, Tanzania.

A once in a lifetime trophy.

Mpumulanga Parks Board officials with the rhino horns.

Wound on right foreleg of the rhino suffered during repeated clashes with younger bulls. He also had numerous stab wounds on his rear and one under his right foreleg.

The rhino let out a long, gentle, hissing sigh and died.

ight to left: Pottie Potgieter, Richard Flack, Louis Marais, and Mpumulanga Parks
oard staff.

Tyghe Carstens, one of my favourite godsons, and his very first springbok—Agtersneeuberg Nature Reserve, Karoo, Eastern Cape.

Me and my son with fallow deer. This was Richard's first game animal, guided by r friend and partner, Louis Marais.

guided Richard to this
presentative mountain
edbuck ram high in the
)oiberge (the Red Mountains),
1roo, Eastern Cape, on the last
)ur of the last day of our hunt.

ghe Carstens and his rock
rax (dassie) taken as part
his training prior to his
ringbok hunt.

Typical defassa waterbuck. A good 200-metre shot off shooting sticks dropped this 29 inch bull where he stood—my first Tanzanian trophy—Rungwa River, Tanzania.

Kirk dik-dik—Masailand.

record book Harvey duiker—Mweka Wildlife College, Mount Meru, Tanzania. ...e college has now raised the minimum daily rate to three days at $600 US ...llars per day, and, nice as it is, this is a bit steep if all you want is a bushbuck, ...iker, or suni.

...me scout, me, Nicky Blunt, tracker, and gerenuk—Masailand.

Jane, my wife, and me with East African impala—Naibermut, Maasailand. Jane's clothe did not make the trip from Johannesburg, so every other day her wardrobe consisted c my spare shirt, longs, and underwear.

I nearly lost this fringe-eared oryx after a poor first shot. A suspicion that it was th same bull I had seen two days before paid off, and, on driving to the area, I foun the bull and the second shot did the trick.

ving out with Jane from the landing strip on Gary Hoop's farm in Masailand at the end
the safari.

auty and the beasts.

Jane, me, and Grant gazelle—Masailand. The second victim of Nicky *psychological stalk.*

Nicky Blunt with my Chanler mountain reedbuck, taken on the Masaila *escarpment, Tanzania.*

WORLD-RECORD RHINO

I suspect that in every serious trophy hunter there lurks a collector, in some shape or form, waiting to escape. While I know a couple of hunters who seem happy to concentrate on one animal, to the exclusion of almost everything else, I am not one of them. Yes, there are animals I have hunted time and time again and the enjoyment, wonder, excitement, and sadness have never worn off: kudu, bushbuck, mountain reedbuck, buffalo.

In fact, the sheer thrill of hunting, every facet from practice to preparation, from calibres to cameras, from traveling to trophies, I love with a passion. Although, over the years, I must have shot hundreds of impala, for example, I still enjoy hunting them today almost every bit as much as when I hunted them in the early days along the Limpopo. But I don't want to become the world expert on the animal.

Much as I admire the kudu stalkers, the bushpig baiters, the springbok cullers amongst my friends and associates; much as I admire their specialist knowledge and skill, I have always wanted to hunt in as many different African areas for as many different African species as possible. And that is the collector in me, although all the hunting books and magazines I have read have been at least partly to blame, certainly a contributory factor. Reading about hunting comes under the same heading as window shopping does for my wife.

As I have hunted in different countries for the different species endemic to that region, so the numbers and types have increased. So, I sometimes find myself in a situation, almost by accident, where I've collected three different species of hartebeest—lelwel, Cape, and Lichtenstein. I then tend to make a deliberate effort to include say a Coke in one of my next trips. Or, once having put together a series of four types of reedbuck—common, mountain, Chanler, and bohor (some deliberately, some by accident, some by good fortune)—it seems natural to do the homework to find out what other kinds of reedbuck are available and where and how to complete the collection.

Some collections developed quite quickly from the time I made a conscious decision to commence the quest. It only took a few years, for example, to find good specimens of common, typical defassa, and sing-sing waterbuck. Crawshay, Angolan, and Ugandan defassa are missing—all subspecies of typical defassa (*Kobus defassa defassa*). On the other hand, it has taken me half a lifetime to complete the Tiny Ten. Some collections I might never complete and maybe that's a good thing. I have been consciously and assiduously seeking to complete a collection of the nine major species of spiral horns since 1983. These hunts have included my best and worst hunting moments, and after a recent trip to Ethiopia, I am battling to come to grips with the fact that I may never see a free, adult, male mountain nyala, let alone have the opportunity to shoot one.

I said earlier that an incomplete collection is not necessarily a bad thing. It certainly gives me something to look forward to. It becomes the focus of a future trip even if it does make people look at you strangely when you wax lyrical and enthusiastic about planning a hunt to Namibia for Damara dik-dik and black-faced impala. Of course, if you are passionate about your hunting, not to mention those of us who can become just a tad obsessive, the missing species can drive you to . . . what? To drink? Not such a problem if moderation is kept in mind, but what if the obsession leads to unethical hunting? What if the self-imposed pressure leads to staking out water holes, shooting from vehicles, hunting with dogs, or worse still, canned hunts?

Then, trophy hunting degenerates from the best kind of hunting to the worst. Then, trophy hunting—the search for old, big, lone bulls or rams out of the breeding cycle—can become a competitive chequebook collection of animals taken regardless of conservation constraints, regardless of ethics, without respect for the animal but to satisfy ego, or worse still, to win some award or competition.

So it is that rhino have always been a problem for me. I have for some time now wanted to hunt one, to experience the sensation of tracking, stalking, and shooting one of the prehistoric three-ton behemoths. I have for some time also wanted to complete my collection of the Big Five. The problem has been that I have just not been able to find an acceptable hunt. Every time I have investigated the hunt offered, it has turned out to be a relatively small, young rhino in a relatively small enclosed area. Many of the rhino were bought from the Natal Parks Board specifically for this purpose. Somehow I could not reconcile myself to this.

And so the years rolled by without a rhino. Louis Marais, my partner in Karoo Safaris (a South African safari outfitter) and I checked out numerous rhino hunts on offer in Natal, the Northern Cape and the Northern Province in particular. No go. In the meantime, prices went up and up, driven there primarily by overseas hunters. Medium-sized rhinos (24- to 25-inch front horns) started hitting huge prices of R85,000 and more. Rowland Ward-class bulls of more than 28 inches started at about R125,000. A king's ransom!

I resigned myself to a rhinoless future, to reading about rhinos and rhino hunts as opposed to getting out there and doing it. One of the recent books to include a chapter on rhino is *The Big Five* by Anthony Dyer and illustrates that our southern white variety (*Ceratotherium simum simum*) is no dozy bus-bodied blimp. (Incidentally, there are two varieties of square-mouthed rhino—northern and southern. The former variety differs from ours insofar as skull formation, teeth, and skin are concerned, and used to be found from western Kenya to Chad.) Dyer writes:

> I was so lucky in my one really close encounter with rhino. There had been many confrontations or charges but I had always been able to get up a tree or to some safe place before the rhino caught me. I was trying to induce a family of giant forest hog to leave a bamboo thicket so that the people on the other side could see them. The bamboo had been fed on by elephant to the extent that it consisted of an almost impenetrable stand of clumps of bamboo about seven feet tall. I wandered, absent-mindedly, along a very narrow trail in the hope that the forest hog would move along in front of me. There was a sudden snort, and a rhino horn swept up inside my right trouser leg. It ripped out of the trousers at belt level, continued upward to smash my rifle stock, and on up under my right armpit, lifting me quite high in the air. I fell on the rhino's back, and quickly tumbled to the ground.
>
> In an instant the rhino spun around and had another determined go at inserting his horn into my wriggling, shouting figure. Then he circled around and charged upon me again to finish off the business. Again I was airborne, together with a certain amount of broken bamboo. My return to earth was heavy and my open, bawling, mouth engulfed a stem of bamboo.

World-Record Rhino

The rhino then disappeared. I stood up, coughed up the stem of bamboo, and set out to find my rifle and binoculars. The rifle had traveled some distance, and ended up muzzle downward with a foot of barrel embedded in the soft soil. My binocular strap was broken but the glasses themselves were intact. A black bruise quickly appeared from ankle to armpit, and the trousers were ruined. I had undoubtedly been saved by the thickness of the bamboo that did not give the rhino a fair chance to aim his horn as he would have liked.

I have never met Anthony Dyer—only heard and read about him. He became an apprentice professional hunter in 1947 at the age of twenty-one. He hunted with famous safari companies in Tanzania like Ker and Downey and Safariland for many years before becoming president of the East African Professional Hunters Association in 1965. He clearly knows what he is writing about. This is what he says about the white rhino:

> The more one knows about rhino, the more one must think about them with compassion. All that they do is logical to them. It is within their own normal pattern of behaviour. Their rushing around, their bellicosity, their little mewing calls, are proper behaviour for a rhino. Mules have achieved a reputation for kicking anything from generals to hand-grenades; so rhino have a reputation for charging anything in front of them. Within reason this reputation is justified, but let us look at why they behave like this. Men move through rhino country mostly in the daytime when a rhino is asleep, alone, and unwarned. Suddenly tick birds chatter a shrill warning. A foul whiff of human scent comes to his nostrils. The noisy progress of a trespasser offends his ear. This sudden shock is most apt to induce an immediate charge, sometimes from over a hundred yards away. Having scattered the enemy in a whirlwind of confusion,

the bitterly upset rhino will hurry off seeking peace. Sweet peace, nothing else.

If a rhino has any advance warning of danger, he will behave differently. If he has had a chance to become alert and plan his action, he will invariably choose the option of flight. An experienced Bushman, when passing by where a rhino may be sleeping, will deliberately make enough noise to alert the great brute, so that it will move off.

The hearing and scenting of a rhino are so highly developed that they amply make up for his poor eyesight. The ears turn like funnels and can catch the slightest sound. They seem to have an ability to sense the direction of a sound. This is shown by the way they will charge straight at it, as though they had pinpointed the offender with complete conviction.

This refined sense of hearing has evolved naturally as a result of life in thick cover where distant vision is no asset, and where there is seldom any steady drift of air to carry scent. The eyes are on the sides of the head and seem to be at a disadvantage when looking straight ahead. A rhino will tend to turn his head from side to side, straining one eye at a time.

It is difficult for a man on foot to remain aloof to wild rhino and a wild rhino is any rhino that is not actually in a cage. It is true that rhino in the national parks become quite indifferent to the presence of cars, but if you get out of the car you are in for a surprise or two. Sensible men treat these great beasts with respect. They will, if they can, avoid a sleeping rhino.

Directly in front of me, some twenty-six paces away, I could make out one and a half of the funnel-like ears of a sleeping rhino. Nothing else was visible through the thick vegetation. A squirrely, midday wind wafted the blistering hot January heat against my left cheek. Cicadas buzzed and burred. My shirt changed colour to dark green. I sweated through even the peak of my baseball cap. Perspiration ran in rivulets down my sunburned face and splashed silently onto my 1.5–6X, 30mm Zeiss Diavari scope sitting solidly on top of my Ritchie custom-made Rigby .416 Brno action, Walther barrel, Timney trigger, and hand-carved stock with a comfortable palm-fitting swell in the pistol grip. A real heavy "hook up and hang on" type of stock. I like it. A lot.

"I've only got the brain shot," I whispered to Louis as he peered over my left shoulder as I crouched behind a shrub sprouting from the bowl of the Heilboom to my left. "Don't shoot!" Louis whispered urgently. "We must see his horn first. We must make sure he's the right one."

Well, what was the right one? The right one was the one the Mpumulanga Parks Board put out to tender at their Loskop Dam Reserve. The Reserve was established in 1948, and over the years, has grown to 20,000 hectares (or 44,000 acres). It is home to more than forty white rhino, the originals of which had been imported from Natal many years previously. One of their oldest bulls—about thirty-five to forty years old (it is difficult to age rhino accurately)—was coming under steady but increasing pressure from two to three aggressive younger bulls. He had lost three consecutive fights and the last one left him with a deep stab wound in the armpit of his right front leg, raw patches on his rump and right front foot, and stab wounds on his ample rear end—a sure sign that he was losing.

Although he was regaining condition and strength and was still vigorous, the Parks Board decided that now was the best time to cull the bull before he was killed or died of his wounds. They put him out to tender. The terms were clear. The Parks Board provided a guide; you did the rest. Find it, shoot it, skin it, and hand over the carcass at an appointed place as the meat was to be sold cheaply to the neighbouring communities. The funds went directly to the Reserve, which had only started culling excess game in the previous three years. Oh yes, and the bull was a monster. The tender terms indicated that the front horn measured nearly 37 inches. It might, it just might be the Safari Club International new world record. It wouldn't beat the Rowland Ward world record as this measuring system takes only the length of the longest horn into account and that length, believe it or not, was 62¼ inches—shot in South Africa in 1898 by that famous early African hunter, Gordon-Cumming. Nevertheless, no bigger rhino than the one on tender had been hunted and registered by Rowland Ward for more than sixty years.

What to do? I heard about the tender on a Monday. The tender closed the next day and the results were to be announced the following Thursday. The bull had to be hunted within the following month. It seemed ideal. A free ranging rhino. A huge and beautiful area in which to hunt it. The proceeds being ploughed directly back into conservation. A clear case of sustainable utilization in practice, and to crown it all, the possibility of a new SCI world record, as this measuring system takes the lengths and circumferences of both horns into account—a much fairer and more representative system of measuring, in my opinion.

Only problem was that many hunters would think the same. Some rich American or German with hard currency was sure to win. I couldn't help it; the thought nagged at me. I wanted the rhino to remain in South Africa. I believed it was a once-in-a-lifetime opportunity. I discussed the matter at length with Louis. I suggested a price. He kept quiet. I suggested a higher one. Still he kept quiet. I swallowed. In a squeaky voice, more query than suggestion, I mentioned a higher figure. *"Dis 'n goeie prys"* (That's a good price), Louis replied in a gruff voice. Louis put in the bid. I won.

After the initial excitement subsided, reality surfaced. Assuming we were successful, how would we recover it? Who had ever skinned a rhino? How much did it weigh? How many people and vehicles would we need? Eventually Louis took control of the logistics. He would arrive the day before, clear the paperwork, run off the heats, and make the initial reconnaissance. Pottie would join him from the lowveld with a Land Cruiser, loading gear, and labour.

They phoned that evening. Louis sounded nonchalant. Piece of cake. Everything was organized. Oh, and by the way, they'd found the rhino late that afternoon. And then the excitement bubbled through. The bull was a bruiser. Built like a battleship. As he explained, *"As daai ding sy horing in jou . . . indruk gaan jy soos 'n toffee apple lyk!"* (If that thing sticks its horn in your backside you will look like a toffee apple!)

My son, Richard, and I arrived from Johannesburg the next morning along with the foreman of Trans African Taxidermists, the people who have mounted all my trophies. Louis was waiting impatiently. "Come, we must go now. The bull has moved to another valley," he urged. Unpack. Repack. Equipment check. We're off. No time for nerves.

A few hours later we are moving in line astern up a slight rise along a red, dusty dirt track. Over the saddle, between the two low, round, tree-bedecked hills to our front, I can see the sun sparkling and twinkling off the brilliant blue surface of a large, inland lake.

Shortly afterward Louis spots the rhino to our right. How, I don't know. I see nothing. We don't muck about. If Louis has seen it, that's good enough for me. We detour to get the wind right and move in on the bull's right flank. We are worried about the fickle midday breeze. But we need the bull to stand. Louis's first attempt to throw a stone to the off side of the rhino is poor. The second attempt is worse. Louis is an ex-rugby player; cricket is foreign territory. The rhino remains unmoved. Then an ear flicks and swivels toward the sound. Sweat burns my eyes. I wipe a forefinger across my forehead. Water runs down my finger in a stream into my palm. *Hold the throw,* I think but don't say out loud.

I reposition myself, left elbow on left knee, right rear on right heel. My rifle barrel clears the intervening thick clumps of green grass—just.

Louis's third toss taps the tree trunk behind the bull. Through my scope (screwed down to 1.5X), the huge bulk of the bull levitates effortlessly like a phoenix from the camouflaging cover. I focus on his right foreleg but am aware of the Eiffel Tower rising from the front of his forehead. I'm not distracted. As the rhino reaches his full height, the shot flows down the barrel. The giant battleship-gray block is instantly transformed into a huffing, puffing, whistling, snorting, runaway locomotive. I listen to the Trans Karoo train smash, crash, and bash through and over the tree-filled terrain downhill to my right. Suddenly silence.

I wait a moment longer, rise and move to my left. My second round lies ready in the chamber of my rifle. As I come over the brow of the hill, the rhino has reversed ends and is boiling silently back on his tracks to my right. If I had followed immediately in his footsteps, we'd now be about to shake hands—before taking part in the well-known Dyer waltz mentioned earlier, that is. In the nanoseconds that follow, *Uh, oh!* is all I remember consciously thinking. Out of the corner of my eye I see Louis screw his .416 into his shoulder.

Then everything seems to slow down. I am totally focused on the rhino. I am completely calm. I lean into my .416 and rest my left shoulder against a tree. The cross hairs of my scope are clamped onto his shoulder. The sight picture is my whole world. As the rhino clears the surrounding scrub twenty paces away, I can see the whole of him. I shoot him a second time on the point of the right shoulder and turn him to his right and back down the hill again. The rifle reloads itself and the third shot takes the three-quartering rhino a foot behind the left shoulder about one-third up. He thunders into a thicket and is shielded from sight.

World-Record Rhino

Trees, branches, grass, shrubs fly in different directions from the thicket. I am not aware of any sound. I kneel and reload. As I rise and move forward, I make out a gray aircraft carrier among the olive green cover. The bull is down, and as I carefully close in from the rear, his last breath escapes in a long, gentle, hissing sigh.

The whole affair from first shot to last has probably taken no longer than two minutes. As the adrenaline rush starts to fade, I feel the first fluttering tremors in my hands, knees, and stomach. My son rests his hands on my shoulders and they drop back to position normal. "I thought I was in for a short, sharp run up a tree back there," he says, looking directly into my eyes. I grin uncertainly, slowly coming to grips with what has happened, with the enormous size of the bull, his battered old body, massive horns, and my emotions.

As we stand beside the amazing animal, we are all silent. In awe. Louis eventually breaks the silence. *"Daai .416 van jou slaan geweldig hard. Sy hele liggaam het geruk met die skoot. Ek het geweet dis verby met die eerste skoot."* (That .416 of yours hits extremely hard. Its whole body jerked with the shot. I knew it was over with the first shot.)

Gradually the rest of the team filters through the trees toward the little clearing made by the bull. Handshakes. Grins—some sheepish from the late arrivals. Photos. Everyone wants a photo with the bull.

The recovery operation lasts until after dark and would have taken much longer but for the kind help of Jannie Coetzee, warden, David Bradfield, ranger, Billie Swanepoel, head of field and public support, and their staff and equipment. We need a small TLB (tractor, loader, backhoe) to load the skin onto a truck and guess it weighs at least 500 kilograms. Jannie offers to store the amazing horns in the Parks Board safe for the night. Jokingly he points out that, as they've been implanted with a microchip, there is no chance they'll get mixed up.

We recover the 400-grain Federal solid—my first shot (which had bisected the bottom half of the heart)—from under the skin behind the left shoulder. Almost in a state to be used again. The other two bullets are lost somewhere in the massive structure of the beast.

That night, over inch-thick rump steaks and a bottle of bull's blood, we rehash the hunt in fine detail. Each of us adds a different perspective to the day's events. Pottie, who captured the events on video, even admits that, after the first shot, he may have filmed a lengthy section of grass. As I drop off to sleep that night, my last thoughts are of the rhino. The horns measured 36½ by 29¾ inches and 12 by 25¼ inches, amounting in total to 103 inches, a green score more than 7 inches bigger than the current world record. What a wonderful way to start the new hunting year!

Despite my wife's vociferous protests, I think, just this once, I may defy her wishes and do a full mount. I honestly think it is the only way to do this magnificent beast justice. What do you think?

TRAINING FOR TOMORROW

People sometimes ask me why it is I so enjoy teaching youngsters to hunt and how I go about it.

Well, for starters, I've always enjoyed teaching. In fact, in my penultimate year in high school, I wanted to become a history teacher. Would have too, but for the fear that I would not earn enough to live in the manner to which I wished to become accustomed.

I gave tutorials at University, and as a young articled clerk in a law firm, I lectured company law to students studying to pass the Chartered Institute of Secretaries exams, to supplement my meager salary. A monthly income of R250 to be precise. I started by standing in for my boss who promised to pay me what he earned. It was only much later that I found out that the stingy son of a gun kept back a substantial portion of the hourly rate for himself.

As for the youngsters, well, for whatever reason, I've always got on well with kids. My wife says its because I've never grown up myself. Everything I really like revolves around fast cars, rifles, and hunting. According to her, I suffer from a terminal case of arrested development.

I'm sure this is all true but I do think, in fairness, there are a couple of other reasons. First, I come from a large, extended family. We are all close to one another, and in the family, children always receive pride of place. None of that Victorian rubbish of children being seen but not heard. The kids were and are never spoken down to but rather treated as members of the family whose views, opinions, achievements, and failures are listened to, discussed and debated, if anything with more enthusiasm than those of the adult members. I grew up like that and tend to treat children the way I was brought up.

At any rate, as I said, I really like kids, and to my intense pleasure, they seem to like me. Along with dogs and horses I might add, and for some unknown reason, these facts please me. And you know the old maxim—you're good at things you like and you like the things you're good at.

Finally, it is hugely rewarding to see a slice of life, no matter how small the sliver, made new for you through the eyes of a child. It is also rewarding to give a little something back to the sport that has given you so much and to know that if you can persuade only one youngster that wildlife represents a viable alternative to teenage sex, drugs, and rock 'n roll, that it will all be worthwhile.

In fact, I believe it was precisely this that led the first father to send me his unruly teenage son. But for the fact that he was a valued client, I would probably have refused. He was an obnoxious little . . . . Almost the archetypal product of a broken home—rich father, attractive second wife, hectic social life, kids packed off to an expensive, private boarding school and PRESTO! Add water, stir for five minutes, and instant anarchy and rebellion.

I fetched the youngster. He had a serious case of jaw drag. His sullen bottom lip was stapled to his chin. He wouldn't look at me, and on the way to the range, answered my questions in monosyllables. By the time I arrived, I figured out that, if I worked really hard, I could do without his father's business. I ignored the little twerp. He ignored me. But he couldn't ignore the sleek, gleaming rifles I unpacked from my gun case.

I set up the bench, assembled my spotting scope and bench rest, unpacked the ammunition and taped the target to the stand. It was when I screwed the silencer to my .22 Brno that curiosity got the better of him. "What's that!" burst from his lips, catching him and me by surprise. So I told him. And that is how we started.

After three months of range work, I guided him down a gulley on a game ranch in Warmbaths, Transvaal. When we crawled up the opposite bank, the impala ram was facing directly toward us at about seventy-five paces. He shot the ram neatly in the middle of the neck with my wife's 7x57mm Brno topped by a fixed 4X scope. His beaming face and shining eyes looking up at me while I painted the buck's blood on his forehead were all the thanks I needed.

Over the years, my "training course" for youngsters has evolved and I have taken out a number of young men, ranging from eight to eighteen. One of these experiences stands out, however. I picked up the young man, ten years old, at the end of his solo journey from Chicago. Six hours later, we drew up outside the farmhouse at Bankfontein in the Karoo—just the two of us. "Two thousand and thirty seven," I replied in answer to my godson's question as to how many other questions he had asked on the way down. We started with my twenty-seven-year-old .22 Brno. Before he got to shoot on our range, he had to name each part of the rifle and scope and show that he could clean it properly.

A day of practice. On the bench, sitting, standing, kneeling, lying, and then all over again. Over a hundred rounds. It never ceases to amaze me how quickly these young men learn. It's like talking to blotting paper. Not a drop of information escapes. How keen and enthusiastic they are.

A day of *mossies* (sparrows) and doves with one of the farmhand's sons. Another day of practice. After lunch we graduate to my wife's 7x57mm Brno. At the first shot, his head spins to look at me. "Yoh!" he gasps. The look of shock in his bright, brown eyes reminds me of a stunned mullet. After that, things get a bit ragged as his brain warns his shoulder, "Look out, here it comes again!"

We regroup and return to the .22. Before dark, we try the 7x57mm again from the bench. Better, much better. We take the target home and discuss the neat three-shot cloverleaf nestling an inch above the bull while I barbecue some bite-size Karoo lamb chops on the *braai* on my front *stoep* (veranda). Tyghe is dog-tired and battles valiantly to stay awake while I finish my glass of red wine. "Tell me about my dad and you and the bushbuck at Londolozi," he asks around a yawn that swallows half his head. We hear the mountain reedbuck whistle in alarm from the fields of Sudan grass we have planted along the river as they pick up our scent. He drags himself off to bed as the day ends. The time is 9 P.M.

The next day, my neighbour's young son, Bernard, and he head off for a day of *dassie* (rock hyrax) hunting. Big adventure, strict rules. Only one .22 between the two of them. I map out their route. I promise to check on them at random. The magazine may only be inserted in the rifle and the rifle loaded when they are ready to shoot. If I find to the contrary at any stage, that is the end of the hunt. Period! They both believe me.

That evening is taken up with an action replay of the day's events. And stories. As much about the how and why of hunting as the what of hunting. Of course he wants to hear about the buffalo that chased me up a tree and the lioness that took my tan away, but more importantly, he inhales the aroma of hunting. Why do I hunt? Why does he want to hunt? And what he needs to do to make his dreams a reality.

Training for Tomorrow

The next day is *the day*. Three A.M.—a timid knocking on my bedroom door. "Is it time yet?" I hear a small voice ask. Four-thirty A.M. brings an action replay. Eventually we get up.

To cut a long story short, Tyghe's dad is a very experienced, highly ethical hunter and this has rubbed off on his son. We are going to hunt springbok (the young man's choice), on foot, just the two of us, on the open plains.

Late that afternoon, after a 500-metre leopard crawl, he cleanly kills a springbok ram at 120 paces with one shot. As trained, he stays down, immediately reloads and concentrates on the downed buck. The rest of the herd mills around. We don't move a muscle. We wait. Yes, the buck is dead. When we stand up, the herd stays transfixed. "Where did they come from?" they seem to ask one another. They eventually move off—reluctantly it seems. Next to the trophy buck, eyes shining, Tyghe jumps up and hugs me. "Thanks, Pete!" We are both very, very happy.

I leave him "on guard" with his buck—in case a jackal or crow comes along to despoil his trophy, you understand. I make the long walk back to the truck. I could have left my jacket over the buck, but this was, and will always be, his first buck. There are times and things to share and others to savor alone. This was one of the latter.

When I return, the wonder has not worn off. It shines from every windswept pore. I take photos—lots (one more for my gran)—and paint his forehead with blood. He holds the legs while I show him how to remove the insides. The "city" in him makes him pull a face but he manfully pays close attention and even gets some blood on his hands.

We take the representative ram back to the butchery and we watch Alfie meticulously skin the buck with a razor-sharp, soft steel kitchen knife and his fists. Only after the carcass is washed and hung up inside do we leave. Tomorrow is *B* day—biltong (jerky) making day.

I am sure there are other and better ways to teach young people how to hunt, but show and tell and do seems adequate, and if nothing else, each and every youngster except one has thoroughly enjoyed himself. Most of them write and call and visit. Tramp around the trophies in my study, watch my videos, page through my photograph albums, and ask questions—lots of them. Some even borrow and read the books on hunting and early African exploration from my collection. These are the ones who are going to become serious and ethical hunters—or at least so I believe.

Of the many, many lessons I have learned from teaching these youngsters, the most important lesson was not to teach my own son. I realized that, in my eagerness and enthusiasm to share my passion, I was putting him under pressure. I was impatient for him to learn and learn quickly. I wanted him to graduate so that we could hunt together in the places I enjoy and for the game I love.

In the nick of time, my partner recognized what was happening and took my son under his wing. A good friend took Richard for his first gamebirds, and Louis took him for his first buck.

Last year, the two of us hunted together in Natal for ten days. I don't know who enjoyed it more—him or me. And if all this has sounded like a recommendation to send your son or daughter to a third person to learn to hunt, you're right, it is.

PREPARATION
+
OPPORTUNITY
=
LUCK

There is more, much, much more to hunting than buying a weapon and shooting an animal. But then I suppose that begs the question: What is hunting to you? Hunting seems to mean so many different things to different people in different places and at different times.

It is hard to compare the hunting activities of an Alaskan Inuit, Amazonian Indian, or Kalahari Bushman to that of a Scottish laird, Karoo game rancher, or Austrian "high sitter." But all will argue that they hunt.

For some, hunting is a means of survival. Food, clothing, utensils, rope, thread, basic ornaments are the goal. For others, the search is merely meat. For still others it's a hobby, a passion, an obsession. Then again, it can be a test—a test of courage as in the case of the Masai or a test of endurance or of yourself. And this is by no means an exhaustive list. The more I think about it, the more difficult it is to be dogmatic. For example, I know many fishermen who will argue, and argue convincingly, that they hunt. And what of falconry and so on and so on?

For me, hunting has evolved over some thirty-nine years. I remember the days of my boyhood—of airguns and *mossies* (sparrows) on a farm outside Bredarsdorp, Cape Province. A *bosduif* (bush dove) was the sought-after trophy. And then culling in the Karoo with the adults. What a thrill just to be included. All we wanted to do was shoot as much as possible, as often as possible. We couldn't even spell conservation. The mysteries of different places and different species followed over time. A long time—many places and animals—from duiker to kudu. And then the fascination with those animals that could stand on you or chew you—the Big Five and the good fortune of being able to follow the adrenaline addiction, the reliving of *Boys' Own Annual* dreams—an advanced case of arrested development my wife calls it.

Then began the current phase, which overlaps all other phases and is, in fact, a function of all of them put together: trophy hunting. The search for old male animals, out of the breeding cycle, ever more exotic, in ever larger and more remote and isolated areas. It has been a period of intensity; some might say insanity. Intense training, intense preparation—mental and physical. Periods of mental despair and physical exhaustion and injury. And as compensation, as recompense, moments that defy description. Memories that will last a lifetime etched into the very fabric of my brain.

As a necessary balance, wildlife photography grabbed ahold; the search for the smaller species, and best of all, the teaching of youngsters. For whatever reason, a number of fathers have entrusted their young sons to me. I thank each one of them because teaching, training, and sharing their first buck with these fine young men has been one of the most rewarding experiences of my life. It has made hunting new again to see it afresh through the eyes of the youngsters.

But back to trophy hunting. Because some of the more exotic animals—bongo, mountain nyala, Lord Derby (or giant) eland, and sitatunga (the top African trophy animals and in order of difficulty, in my opinion) are found in remote areas, preparation becomes vital. Preparation, more often than not, is the difference between glorious success and miserable, depressing disappointment. Luck, after all, occurs when preparation meets opportunity, to quote André Roux.

Training for Tomorrow

In order to prepare properly, you need to know what to expect. You need to know as much about the animals you seek and the areas where they are found as possible. Unfortunately, like most of life, in trophy hunting there is no free lunch. The best areas are often held by the best outfitters and professional hunters. Supply and demand dictates that they are also the most expensive. Through bitter personal experience I have come to learn that only an idle, rich man with lots of spare time on his hands can afford to book cheap trophy hunts. Equally unfortunately, the more remote the area, and the more unusual the species, the fewer people there are to ask for advice. And asking is the obvious starting point.

My checklist of questions starts with the animal and moves on through the area, costs, outfitter, professional hunter, trackers, skinners, trophy care, travel arrangements, best times of year to hunt, weather, clothing and equipment, medical matters and general advice, and recommendations. But who to ask? *The Hunting Report* published by Don Causey files reports of hunts by species and area. Subscribers receive prompt and efficient access to these, and follow-up inquiries to the originators of the reports more often than not are met with friendly and helpful advice. True trophy hunters want those following in their footsteps to be successful. Beware, however, of first-timers who file glowing reports! You know the kind—the pro is the best in Africa, the hunting area the most wonderful in the world, and so forth. Oftentimes they know not of what they speak.

The early books by hunters, explorers, and missionaries are a fountain of knowledge and one of my favourite and most important sources of information, but more about that later. Taxidermists are an excellent source of information on trophy quality. Safari outfitters and professional hunters should be consulted but are clearly not unbiased, and don't forget regular contributors to hunting magazines or experienced members of your hunting association.

It is the latter part of 1996, and I am planning and preparing for a mountain nyala hunt in Ethiopia some fourteen months from now. And there hardly seems enough time. I know little or nothing about Ethiopia or mountain nyala and am begging, borrowing, and buying all the books on the animal and the country that I can lay my hands on.

Hunting has been closed in the country for four years prior to 1996, and the dated reports available from *The Hunting Report* may not have been relevant. Modern books are few and far between. Even the book I found by a naturalist researching mountain nyala did not have a picture of a live animal.

It has been fascinating, however, learning about the people and regions of this country on the horn of Africa. Without wishing to sound like a Chappies bubble gum wrapper, did you know that, in terms of Ethiopian legend and history, they claim that the Jewish Arc of the Covenant is kept in the Ethiopian Orthodox Church, Maryam Tsion in Axum?

Queen Makeda ruled the northern part of Ethiopia and parts of Yemen in the tenth and eleventh century B.C. That region was known as Sabea, and during her thirty-one-year reign, she also became known as the Queen of Sabea or Queen of Sheba. This region traded extensively and there are records of the trips her seventy-three ships and many camel caravans made. During the course of one of these forays, she visited King Solomon. It must have been some visit, as on arriving home, she gave birth to Ibn-al-Malik whose name, in time, became converted to Menelik (the same name as the Emperor of Ethiopia who gave the Italian army such a *snotskoot* [bloody nose] at the Battle of Adwa in 1896). As the story goes, the Queen's son paid a visit to his natural father, and on his return to Ethiopia, was accompanied by a son of each of the ruling Jewish families. One of these sons was a priest by the name of Azariah, and it was he who brought with him the Arc of the Covenant. Graham Hancock, in his fascinating book, *The Sign and the Seal*, gives you the benefit of his nine years of research in support of this fascinating aspect of Ethiopian legend and history.

And preparation can be a chicken and egg exercise. Preparing for a hunt can often unearth interesting facts and these facts can often spark interest in a hunt, which leads to more preparation and so on and so on. For example, I came to bongo hunting in the Central African Republic because of Sir Henry Morton Stanley, yes, the "Dr. Livingstone, I presume" Stanley (born Rowlands, however, in a tiny coal mining village in Wales). Fascinating man. The blacks nicknamed him *Bula Mutari* or Breaker of Rocks. A better nom-de-plume might have been "Ball-breaker." His were certainly made of titanium. After the Livingstone encounter, he led a British-sponsored relief column up the Congo River via the Ituri rain forests to rescue Emin Pasha (actually an Austrian named Eduard Schnitzer—but that's another story), governor of the British outpost Equatoria, then about to be invaded by the Mahdi (a Muslim insurrection leader), and his fanatical Fuzzy-wuzzy warriors.

His trip, particularly those parts through the equatorial rain forests, fired my imagination. Then I discovered that bongo, one of the nine spiral-horned animal species that have monopolized my hunting life, inhabited these rain forests and that was it. My curiosity got the better of me. The closest I could get to the Ituri in Zaire was that tiny corner of the Central African Republic (CAR) where it joins the Sudan and Zaire, and off I had to go.

It took me three years to find the right area, outfitter, and professional hunter, not to mention the money to pay for it all. And it was Sutherland, the great elephant hunter, whose books taught me about the local Zande people in that eastern corner of the CAR where I hunted. After all, he should know, they poisoned and well-nigh killed him. In fact, although he survived, he was never the same again. Marcus Daly hunted through the region. And Anderson had his camp near Ouagou in the northern part of the two million hectares we hunted. You can see the ruins of it to this day.

They all taught me something about the people, the places, and *Tragelaphus euryceros euryceros*. For example, did you know that it is preferable to hunt bongo in the rain? The forests are too noisy when dry. And the colour of your clothing should be green, dark green. Soft shoes, not boots. Gardening clippers are useful to snip the creepers that snag your feet, arms, rifle. Tape on the foresight of your rifle will prevent it hooking on the undergrowth.

Low light scopes are a must—it's dark in those forests. An extra pair of shoes and socks will prevent your constantly wet feet from rotting. Heavy calibres—minimum .375. Yes, to shoot a glorified bushbuck, but through very, very thick vegetation. I used a .416.

The preparation has always made the whole experience so much more than buying a gun and *skiet 'n bok* (shoot a buck). Sometimes I think that the preparation and anticipation it brings are as much fun as the hunt itself. It certainly lasts longer and the enjoyment can be drawn out. No sooner does an actual hunt start than it's over—in a flash. Preparation allows you to live in the footsteps of the Sutherlands of the past and the Robin Hurts of the present, to join an elite group of driven men who have hunted ethically on foot, been successful, and lived to tell the tale. I also understand why the two groups of pygmies we surprised while sneaking through the rain forests ran away screaming when they saw our Zande trackers—the Zande still hunt and eat them. It prepared me mentally for the claustrophobic effects of the forest. At least I did not break down and start yelling like one of my successors when twenty feet from a big bongo bull. I also did not spook the bongo like a predecessor by snicking my safety immediately prior to pulling the trigger. And, after losing seven kilograms during the course of the three-week hunt, my body was strong enough after months of training to last the pace and hunt every day, all day, if only just.

Oh! and I almost forgot. The only language the natives speak, other than various local dialects, is French. And yes, the language tapes did help me make it through customs and immigration, although nothing prepared me for my hotel room in the capital, Bangui. It was perfectly clean, but some previous inhabitant had lit a fire in the room, leaving a large, burnt hole in the carpet and severely singed and tattered curtains.

A QUESTION OF ETHICS

Some months after a bongo hunt in the CAR, I was browsing through *Safari,* the official publication of Safari Club International. What I read made my blood boil. The article told of an American hunter who took six trophy animals including bongo and sitatunga, north of Moloundu. The article reported: "Bongo are hunted with trackers and dogs, by following tracks found after rain. Dogs do not track; they are only used to surround bongo when found and keep it from running away. He said that all eight hunters got bongo, plus two more were taken by PHs."

The thought of cornering any animal with dogs, let alone a bongo, offended my very being as a hunter. "Only used to surround bongo"—give me a break! Why not trap them in a pit? Why not shoot them in a zoo? I was enraged at the thought that anyone could debase our sport by such a practice. I was furious at these hunters for providing ammunition to the antihunting brigade. I was also sickened at the thought that this practice might proliferate and cheapen this, the finest of all African trophies.

So I was, feeling somewhat less than charitable when immediately thereafter, I read of a warthog "hunt" in *Magnum.* This "hunt" consisted of driving around a farm on the back of a *bakkie* (truck) hoping to cross paths with a pig. When this failed, the intrepid hunters hid in a pump house at a water hole where they successfully ambushed a warthog on its way to water. I fired off a letter to Ron Anger, editor of Magnum, the top South African hunting and firearms magazine. "Whatever this may be, it is not *hunting*," I thundered. "How about writing on the subject?" he suggested. *Piece of cake,* I thought. *Here's a chance to strike a blow for ethical hunting.*

As I started to plan the article, I quickly realized that it was not as simple as I thought. Well, of course, one has to exclude shooting birds over dogs from any criticism of hunting with dogs. And then, of course, Americans have been hunting deer, bear, and mountain lion with dogs for decades. And what about jaguar hunting in South America, and so on?

But why exclude wingshooting with dogs? Sure, dogs retrieve wounded birds that might otherwise suffer a lingering death. Sure, they recover dead birds that might otherwise be lost. But, most importantly, they are used to find and hold birds to enable the shooter to come within range before the birds are flushed. Now my wingshooting friends have often told me that it is impossible to shoot certain kinds of birds without dogs, gray wing partridge in particular. And yet I know of an American who, one afternoon, accompanied my friend and partner, Louis Marais, into the higher reaches of the Bankberg of the Karoo, where they shot seventeen of these elusive game birds. The nearest dogs were on the neighbouring farms.

About a month ago, I was hunting wild turkey in Texas with an American friend, Mike. He is an ardent hunter and conservationist. When you see the five black rhino on his Texas ranch, you know he puts his money where his mouth is when it comes to conservation. "So how do you view hunting with dogs?" I asked. "Well," he drawled in his soft, Texan accent, "I suppose it probably began with our subsistence farmers in years gone by who farmed in the thickly wooded parts of our country.

A Question of Ethics

They used dogs, first for protection and second to help supply their families with food. The overgrown forests made it difficult to stalk deer. On top of that, their weapons were fairly primitive by today's standards. This led them to breed and train dogs to chase and bay animals that would be shot for food or eliminated as predators. In time, this became accepted as an ethical form of hunting."

As we continued our discussion over dinner, one of his friends asked, "Well, don't you bait for leopard and lion in Africa? Isn't that an artificial form of enticing and holding the animal so that it can be shot?" I had to concede that he had a point. I would hazard a guess that more than 80 percent of cats hunted in Africa are shot either over bait or natural kills. There seems to be a clear analogy in that the animals are not tracked on foot.

Mike went on to add that the sport lay in breeding and training as well as hunting with dogs. The actual kill, although not irrelevant, was merely the natural conclusion or adjunct to the sport. Thinking back on the four occasions that I hunted in Texas, I realized that he was speaking the truth. On the first occasion, I categorically refused to hunt with dogs and the landowner refused to let me hunt without them. It was only after huddled conversation between my American host and the landowner in which words like "crazy African" were repeatedly uttered that I was allowed to proceed on foot with a rather bemused American guide trailing behind. The successful conclusion of my hunt did nothing to convince the landowner, who put it down to beginner's luck. My next hunt passed uneventfully, as I could not persuade my hosts to refrain from using dogs, and so I spent the duration of the hunt lying on my back among the roots of a large tree where I read a book until the hunt was over.

What was clear, however, was that the dogs were the central feature of the hunt, not the shooters. The sport lay in breeding and training the dogs, and the ability to control them using whistles over vast distances through dense forests while handlers and dogs were separated. The handlers used the dogs almost as an extension of their own senses and moved them backward and forward, to the right and left, through the woods. Once the dogs sighted or picked up the scent of the quarry, the handlers and shooters still had to catch up with the dogs, that in turn had to chase and hold the quarry at bay. This was easier said than done, and in talking to the handlers I was told that the animal being chased quite often succeeds in getting away. As for the shooters (and I deliberately call them that as opposed to hunters), there was little skill involved for the most part. In fact, most handlers were more concerned that the shooters not shoot one of their dogs than they were about bagging the quarry.

Now it seems to me that all ethics, let alone hunting ethics, are difficult to cast in stone. They are shaped by the norms, the morals of our society, and equally clearly, these differ from region to region, from country to country, and from age to age. Some ethics are clear cut, apply throughout the world, and are enshrined in custom and legislation. For example, "Thou shalt not steal" is a common sentiment in hundreds of societies. However, there are probably more differences than similarities from country to country and from age to age, and one only has to think of male and female issues to realize that there are huge discrepancies with regard to matters such as sex, abortion, and the like.

And maybe that is the determining factor when it comes to hunting with dogs. In Africa we do not use dogs to hunt game other than birds, and we consider it unethical and immoral to do so. In America they use dogs to hunt deer, bear, and mountain lion, and it is considered ethical and moral to do so, despite the fact that, in the case of deer and bear, more of these animals are hunted without dogs than with them.

Nevertheless, it is the application of dog-hunting techniques to sport hunting in Africa that I feel is wrong. In my opinion, it is unnecessary, unsporting, and certainly debases the value of the trophy taken. If it were in my power, I would outlaw the practice. At the very least, I think that ethical hunters should lobby for a separate trophy categorization, whether it be under Rowland Ward, SCI, Boone and Crocket, Pope and Young, or whatever trophy-measuring system is adopted by the hunters concerned. In other words, in each of these systems, there should be a separate category for animals shot over dogs.

For the sake of completeness, I would add that I do not believe it is unethical to secure wounded animals by tracking and baying them with dogs. The onus is on a hunter to use whatever means are at his disposal to secure and put an end to the misery of a wounded animal in the shortest time possible.

After speaking to a variety of hunters in different countries, I come to the conclusion that hunting ethics are like beauty—in the eye of the beholder. In Africa we believe that sport hunting using dogs to track, corner, or bay animals is unethical. While we accept that an exception is made when shooting birds over dogs, we should not allow the customs and ethics of other countries to pervert and bastardize the hunting morality that Africa has developed over scores of years. In essence, while I accept the old adage "When in Rome, do as the Romans do," I would urge that in the interest of our sport, we do not import "Roman" morality into Africa.

TANZANIAN TROPHY TRIALS AND TRAVELS

When I close my eyes I can still see the nodding heads of the Grant gazelles as, line astern, they bob off at a tangent through the pale yellow grass, disappearing into the shimmering heat across the Masai plains of Mbuga wa Makame. I was sad to leave, not only because I had not found the lesser kudu I was looking for, not only because the safari company had messed up my bookings and allowed me only five instead of fourteen days at their Masailand (Tanzania) camp, but because I had experienced one of those rare moments in life where excited expectation meets reality, and reality wins.

I had found the hunting fields of my boyhood dreams: *Out of Africa*, *Boys Own Annual*, *Rolux Magnum* advertisement, and Speke and Burton all rolled into one. From the moment I set eyes on the green canvas safari tents hunkering in the shade of huge, flat top acacias, rising from the undulating ocean of golden grass on the edge of the Masailand escarpment, I felt an almost tangible sensation in my chest. As trite as the words may sound now, they rang in my head, *This is what it's all about!*

I looked at my tiny wife as she turned to me, eyes shining half with apprehension, half with excitement, to ask, "Are we here?" "Here" was to be our home for the next five days—her first on a big-game safari.

I had already spent three weeks in Tanzania on what was meant to be a relaxing plains game hunt. The first two weeks were to have been devoted to lesser kudu in Masailand; a week to the southwest along the Rungwa River for Lichtenstein hartebeest and topi, and then down to Lake Rukwa for puku and bohor reedbuck before heading back to Masailand to give Jane a three-day taste of safari life. After that we were looking forward to continuing our holiday at Ngorongoro Crater for a few days.

Sounds idyllic, doesn't it? Too good to be true, right? Well it was—too good to be true, I mean. No good deed goes unpunished as they say, and the professional hunter who begged for the hunt booking let me down badly. He had not arrived but ten days before me in Tanzania to scout the hunting areas as promised. He had not learned Swahili as promised. He had not confirmed my itinerary with the safari company. His "had nots" went on and on.

Shunted off to Ipenyero camp on the banks of the Rungwa River, I found a French professional hunter, Alain Lefol, plus apprentice, plus client in my camp. They had not shot the lion they were looking for and were not leaving. Eventually they did leave, only to set up a fly camp a little distance away, where they remained and hunted in my concession before rolling their vehicle, injuring the apprentice, and leaving for Arusha. This kind of poor organization by the safari company characterized the entire trip.

Trying to put a brave face on things, the next morning we set off on our first hunt in this huge piece of Africa. Easier said than done. We had no map, no GPS (the pro left his behind); we could not communicate with our tracker or game scout, and did not know where to begin to look for game. There were only two car tracks in the area—one accessed the road to the north and the other looped toward the Rungwa River in the east. Oh, and shortly before leaving camp, we discovered that whatever gifts our "tracker" may have had, tracking was not one of them.

An unmitigated recipe for disaster? Not so. Well, almost. What saved the day was the presence in camp of an old East African hand, Nicky Blunt. Nicky was cutting a third car track in the area while waiting for the start of a three-week safari. As luck would have it, the clients failed to materialize, so I had his expert, if intermittent, help over the next four weeks—and what a godsend that was! To be explicit, without his help I would have returned home before the end of the first week.

As it was, my safari took on a totally different shape and form and I saw a cross section of Tanzania that would otherwise have escaped me. I ended up hunting from the Rungwa River down to Lake Rukwa—a distance of about 160 kilometres. Then up to Arusha and on to the northern shores of Lake Manyara, in the shadow of the Rift Valley wall, where Iain Douglas-Hamilton researched his famous book on elephant. After the blistering heat and reflected glare of the over-grazed calcrete flats of Kwa Ku Chinja near Manyara, the contrast of the glistening, green gloom of the rain forests on the slopes of Mount Meru near Arusha was a total surprise and revelation.

And then, unable to restrain myself any longer, I made two visits to the Masailand escarpment while waiting for my hunting camp to clear. These two trips, over what were possibly some of the worst "roads" in Africa, took a bone-jarring seven hours there and another seven hours back. Up at 4:30 A.M., we returned close to midnight. But the trips were worth it. The incredible luck of taking a Chanler mountain reedbuck, the only reedbuck species I was still looking for, and one that many hunters have sought in vain, more than made up for the fact that the trip in the ancient Nissan 4x4 (held together with wire, hope, and prayer) turned my liver to foie gras, my brain to bran mush, and my spinal discs to dough.

For the week I spent hunting in and around Arusha, my safari camp was the Dik Dik Hotel on the slopes of Mount Meru. Not your typical safari camp, and certainly not what I imagined when I left for Tanzania. Nevertheless, the hotel is run by an inventive and efficient Swiss couple, and they and their well-trained and friendly staff went out of their way to make my stay a happy one. The food was good, the Tanzanian Tusker beer welcome, and more importantly, they were prepared to serve meals at any time, day or night, and that certainly made our early departures and late arrivals endurable.

But I am getting ahead of myself. If you look at a contour map of the region between the Rungwa National Park, the Rungwa River, and Lake Rukwa, you will see that it consists of a series of parallel drainages following a northeast to southwest inclination. These undulating depressions, *mbugas* the locals call them, are interspersed with sandy-floored miombo forests on the ridges, not unlike the mopane forests of the South African lowveld, but with a greater variety of trees and vegetation. At this time of the year—mid-August to mid-September—the *mbugas* are burned and blackened, brittle tufts of spiky grass that are hell to drive over and worse to walk through. To crown it all, the fine, gray dust penetrates and permeates everywhere.

Midday temperatures range between 34 and 38 degrees Celsius and the tsetse flies are a torment. Worse than anything I experienced in Zimbabwe or Mozambique, they attack in waves. For the first time ever, I checked a water hole for tracks with a rifle in one hand and a jumbo spray can of Doom [insecticide] in the other.

And there was not a lot to check. The game was sparse and widely scattered and yet the variety was there and the quality good—if you hunted hard. So that's what we did. Out before dawn, back after dusk, only returning to camp if the delivery of a trophy required the trip.

Apart from these handicaps, the concession area was liberally sprinkled with fishermen, wood cutters, and honey gatherers—euphemistic terms for poachers. In fact, on our first walk we came across the carcass of a freshly killed, young, female elephant. She could not have been older than twenty, and if her tiny toothpicks weighed more than five kilograms a side it would have been a lot. Later we heard them fire a shot, and still later, the poachers twice set fire to the veld upwind of us to warn us off. Needless to say, reporting the incidents was like talking into the proverbial "black hole."

Speaking of poachers, on our trip to Lake Rukwa we bumped into a professional hunter whose concession included a substantial portion of the lake shore. He told us that the previous week the local police commissioner, accompanied by the local head of forestry in the region, shot twelve buffalo at night along the lake. He told of frequent shootings at night with powerful lights, and reported having been shot at with automatic weapons when trying to apprehend the poachers. To say he was dejected and demoralized would be an understatement. Despite the area being a nature reserve, we found thousands of head of cattle and their herders. When we spoke to one young herder (dressed in a fetching combination of lilac dress, black fedora, and spear), he complained about being chased and beaten by nature conservation game guards. So I asked, "Well, why do you bring your cattle here? You know it's not allowed."

"Because there's nowhere else to take them. If we go back to where we came from, the people are unhappy. If we come here, the game guards are unhappy, but there are fewer of the guards than the other people."

"Why are the people where you came from unhappy for you to return?"

"Because we have much more cattle now."

R.I.P. Poor Africa!

At any rate, I had a productive time along the Rungwa. I shot good quality lion, Lichtenstein hartebeest, topi, defassa waterbuck, and Sharpe grysbok—all beating the respective Rowland Ward minimum trophy standards. I also shot a very respectable sable, bushpig, and zebra, the latter being smaller than our Burchell and without the shadow stripe—a very pretty animal. Down at the lake, I shot a very average puku ram, at 259 yards according to my distance-measuring Leica Geovid binoculars, and a good bohor reedbuck, which really made my day as I had wanted one for ages.

I took both in the thick reeds along the shore. In neither case did my shooting fulfill the promise that my earlier attempts along the Rungwa hinted at. I missed the ram with my first shot, and although I dropped the grazing reedbuck with a shot through the neck at 159 yards from my .375, I actually missed my point of aim on the tip of the shoulder by about nine inches. Still, *amper mis as amper raak* (almost missed as opposed to almost hit).

Back at Ipenyero camp along the Rungwa River, I made abortive attempts to hunt Patterson eland, which seems indistinguishable from the Livingstone eland of Zimbabwe and Zambia. After a few futile days of fumbling around—Nicky had now left and it was a case of the blind leading the blind—I had quite enough. I won't bore you with all the gory details but the atrocious performance of the pro continued, in fact got worse, and the lack of a tracker, let alone one with whom we could communicate, turned this part of the trip into a game of roulette. As the Cessna 404 banked away from the sun setting over the kopje at the end of the runway en route to Arusha, I was glad to be leaving. I would not be going back.

The next day at Arusha, the now-familiar safari company mess was meandering along at its usual pace. The company representative eventually arrived at 9 A.M., thankfully sober this time. The area set aside for hunting Thompson gazelle and white bearded wildebeest had changed. They didn't have licenses for the new area. They had not made my bookings to hunt on the slopes of Mount Meru nor had they obtained the relevant permits for this hunt. Rather than spend the day sitting on my thumb, Nicky suggested we try for Chanler reedbuck along the Masailand escarpment. That afternoon found us sneaking along the hilltops of the escarpment, looking over a massive expanse of Masailand. I was entranced, bewitched, hooked. It was truly beautiful, this vast expanse of Africa. The blue mountains fading away to paler and paler blue reminded me so much of the mountains of the Karoo. And the hunting had that familiar feel. Easing up the hills, the wind on my left cheek, I carefully glassed the opposite hillside through the camouflage of a bush, looking for the telltale signs of a bedded buck. Every now and then, as we leap-frogged one another, Nicky and I made prearranged contact. By 6 P.M., however, my thoughts were already turning to the long and wearisome trudge back to Arusha. As I moved quietly up the back of the hill Nicky was glassing, I spotted him gazing intently into the valley. I whistled. He waved. Urgently. I quickened my pace. "Come quickly, I've spotted a ram!"

Peeking through a narrow avenue down the bushy hillside, I spotted the buck staring in our general direction. I slid into a sitting position, pulled out the extensions to my bipod, rested the feet on the tops of my boots and edged forward on my backside. Still there, but a difficult downhill shot. "One hundred and seventy-three yards," the Professor whispered into my ear as he read off the yardage from my binos. What a help. I had estimated this, the smallest of all reedbuck, to be about 250 yards away and was taking aim an inch or two over his back. Lowering my sights, I took up the pressure on my 2½- pound trigger. As I rocked back from the recoil, I could see the white of the buck's stomach through the grass.

"Why didn't you lie and shoot?" asked Nick. After replying that the grass was too high, I looked back at the buck. No buck! I scrambled to my feet, marking the spot where I had last seen it. As I dashed down the slope, the old refrain rang tauntingly through my brain: *The animal that runs and falls is all yours, the animals that fall and run—the "fun" has just begun!*

After a major anxiety attack lasting all of ten minutes, we found where the ram rolled down the steep slope. The Professor wouldn't hear about it, and fifty-seven-years old or not, carried the ram out of the valley halfway to our hunting car. The easy part he left to me, nine years his junior. We were all very happy and me particularly so.

Before leaving on safari, I had read William Astor Chanler's book, *Through Jungle and Desert*, published in 1896, and after whom the buck is named. I had never thought that I would ever find this unusual and smallest of the reedbuck. I knew from previous reading that many had tried and many had failed, and here, on my first afternoon, I had found a good representative specimen. What an unexpected bonus!

Redunca fulvorufula chanleri as described by Rowland Ward:

> Distribution is from northern Tanzania through Kenya and along the Rift Valley to southern Ethiopia, especially in the Awash Valley and the Torit district of southern Sudan. The horns are shorter than in the southern race; the colour is gray rather than rufous; and they live in smaller parties of three or four. They become very difficult to see as their grayish colour merges into the rocky background. Height at shoulder about 28 inches (71 cm); weight about 55 pounds (25 kg . . . minimum 6¹/₈ inches).

There are only fifty-eight entries in my 22nd edition of Rowland Ward, and the latest is 1987, taken in the Arusi

Mountains of Ethiopia. My ram of 5½ inches did not qualify but who really hunts just for the record book?

This little adventure was quickly followed by my worst day on the safari, hunting the Mweka Wildlife College area to the north of Lake Manyara. From the unhelpful, rude, and unpleasant college official at Kwa Ku Chinja who told us, "Maybe in one hour I find you a game guard;" to the useless game guard himself; to the Samburu and their cattle who turned the plains bordering the lake into a fly-infested, cow-dung-bedecked wasteland.

By late afternoon we threw in the towel, one mediocre Thompson gazelle to the good. There was little or no game. What there was turned out to be of poor quality and I could find no pleasure in the sorry state of the landscape. Kwa Ku Chinja is like bad wine—to be laid down and avoided.

But I will remember it always for my very first "psychological stalk."

"Look," Nick said, "it's no good trying to stalk as you would normally; there's not enough cover"—understatement of the year. "The animals are used to cattle herders. We must imitate them. Swing your arms, talk, walk in single file. When I tell you, drop down and shoot. The rest of us will carry on walking. The psychology comes when it's time to shoot. Do you stop before the bucks run or do they run off before you stop? Note which way most of the animals are standing. Don't try to walk past their fronts, they'll run. All their predators try to head them off. Rather walk to pass behind them; I normally try for around two hundred yards."

And that's what we did. The Tommie never even lifted his head from the bush he was nibbling.

The next morning before dawn, we arrived at another Mweka Wildlife College area on the slopes of Mount Meru. It was one of those magical, crisp, clear bush mornings. Silence, perfect silence, reigned as I looked up at the cloudless, star-punctured canopy over the clearing in the forest. First one, then another, bird started its tentative twitterings as the sun rose from behind Kilimanjaro. Breathtaking. The light drizzle the previous day cleared the atmosphere, and as I sat on the edge of the clearing with Dr. von Nagi's cottage at my back, I felt that God was in His Heaven and all was well with the world. The good doctor, by the way, had owned the concession to hunt on these slopes and built the cottage (perfectly sited), as well as many of the tracks through the forest.

Without a doubt, this day was the highlight of my trip. It was like hunting in a fairy tale world. The forest was home to suni and Harvey red duiker, both species as numerous as fleas on a dog's back. Every second belt of forest was alive to the pitter-patter of little feet, and I had a chance to really study the rabbit-size suni—this species being called *Neotragus moschatus moschatus* and slightly smaller and lighter in colour than *Neotragus moschatus livingstonianus*, which we normally associate with Zululand.

I love this kind of hunting. Sneak, stop, spy; sneak, stop, spy in the deep, dark shade of the heavy tree cover, broken every now and then by a fairy glen or water-lily-covered pond. The echoing grunt of a hippo guided our footsteps silently along the hillside. "Watch the stinging nettles," mimed Augustino, our guide and twenty-year veteran at Mount Meru.

A scuttling flurry off to the right. Rapid movement through the glossy foliage. One, two, three . . . five Masai bushbuck! The biggest of all the bushbuck species. Two hurtling back and forth. Three spectators. Which one? Without noticing us, the two combatants drew apart and drew breath. Bertha glides to my shoulder. I rest on Nicky's shoulder and at eighty paces I shoot the larger of the two. The bushbuck bombshell in panic. I watch the ram display all the characteristics of a heart shot—convulsive, hunched leap and desperately paced run—and track his flight. I hear him thrash through the underbush while the others ghost away almost silently. I hear him run into something solid, and then the thump as he falls. We find him about eighty paces away on the side of a gentle rise. Augustino is beside himself with joy and excitement. Confirms over and over that he told me he would get me a *kubwa sana* (big one) and he did. He nearly shakes my arm off, and, after the obligatory photos, takes his shirt off and carries the whole bushbuck some three kilometres to the truck, stopping only twice to rest. Awesome!

That afternoon, a Rowland-Ward-class Harvey duiker joins the bushbuck in the back of the truck. Unfortunately, as the safari company messed up my bookings and I have only one instead of two days at Mount Meru, and as you are limited to two animals per day, no suni. I try and console myself with the fact that I have an excellent southern African suni from Phinda near Hluhluwe in Natal. I am not successful.

I want to return. I want to hunt out of Dr. von Nagi's cottage. I want to try for buffalo and suni. I want to hunt with Augustino again. I want, I want . . . well, who knows? With a modicum of luck, stranger things have happened.

And then, at long last it's off to Naibermut camp in Masailand. We arrive a day late because the safari company is unwilling to pick Jane up from the airport and take her to the charter flight, despite the fact that she is paying full observer rates. So I do it. I lose two hunting days as a result, and to make matters worse, Tanzanian Airlines leaves her suitcase in Johannesburg. She has to make do with some of my spare clothes. She looks wonderful, this waif, of 5 feet 4 inches and 120 pounds, wearing clothes designed for my 6 foot 3 inch and 190-pound frame.

Again there are hunters in my camp when I arrive. One grumbles that he was only due to leave the following day; the other says he never wanted to come to Masailand in the first place. All he wants to do is go back to the Rungwa River to try for the leopard he hadn't managed to find. If only he had spoken to me!

Heart of an African Hunter

The really bad news is that Nicky has been delayed in Arusha by the safari company. Why? No one knows. In the end, he arrives three days late. In the meantime, it's a case of the blind leading the blind—again. Fortunately, the game guard speaks a little English. Unfortunately, he insists on using it to tell war stories. Apparently one of the previous hunters shot at and missed four lesser kudu and wounded a leopard, which had not been recovered. Wonderful. All we need—a crazy hunter blazing away at everything that moves and a leopard without a sense of humour wandering along the escarpment.

We have five days to find a lesser kudu. The safari company has kindly extended my hunt by two days, free of charge, but this has cost Jane and me our trip to Ngorongoro Crater and I am still waiting for the return of my deposit. I am by now irritated, frustrated, and deeply disappointed. The professional hunter, as my Texan friends would crudely point out, is about as much use as "tits on a boar hog." When I confront him with all the broken promises and blunders and ask him how he would feel if he were me, he hangs his head and mumbles, "The same I suppose."

I pull myself toward myself and put the past behind me. I am reminded of Moaner van Heerden's famous words, "Cowboys don't cry," and determine to make the best of things.

We are hunting big, big country. We try to scout the area to get a sense of what gives. One day we follow a car track for 200 kilometres in a rough north to south direction and we do not leave the concession area. We walk along the tree-lined escarpment; we climb the rocky outcrops and glass the bush-strewn valleys. We drive the plains and check the water holes. We see a few lesser kudu cows and calves and a few immature bulls. At least we know they are here.

In three days I shoot one mediocre Grant gazelle and a very large hyena. I have always wanted a hyena but have never been prepared to put in the effort to really go after one. I suppose I always believed that, one day, our paths would cross. The hyena was facing directly away from me, and I took the shot while lying behind Bertha with the bipod attached to my sling swivel, in extended mode. I am rock steady. There is not a bullet hole discernible anywhere on the hyena although I find the bullet nestling under the skin under its chin. The Nosler Partition mushroomed perfectly but the bullet lost all its lead. Amazingly, after the shot flattens the hyena, the dog somehow manages to find the strength to half stand and turn to the right before finally collapsing.

Nicky arrives at midnight on the Tuesday. Only three days left but my spirits lift. He has a plan. He knows where to look; he knows how to look. Immediately our "luck" seems to change, and in one unforgettable day, I take a good fringe-eared oryx and dik-dik and a very good gerenuk, which was second on my wish list. By carefully questioning the "tracker" in Swahili, he ascertains that the previous American hunter had missed a very good gerenuk at 2 P.M. not far from a well where the Masai water their cattle. At precisely the same time we are at precisely the same place. And so is the gerenuk.

After a tense stalk through a large thicket of whistling thorns (the ants hollow out and make holes in the fruit of the thorns, which then make a whistling sound when the wind blows through them), during which I can just make out the tiny, bobbing head of this unique animal, I eventually find the narrowest of gaps between the thornbushes. The gerenuk obligingly enters the gap and the .375 nails it to the ground. It is one of the strangest, yet most gracefully beautiful of all the antelopes. To watch it pause, and with delicate, ballerina-like grace, unhurriedly rise on its hind legs, its long, slender forelegs poised against the overhead branches while it stretches its elegant neck to sample the tender leaves, is poetry in motion.

Everything it does is done with style, ease, and grace. The gerenuk is the Dame Margot Fonteyn of Masailand.

Like a tracer bullet, seemingly slow as it leaves the barrel, yet gathering momentum ever faster as it approaches, the remaining time speeds past. And suddenly, we are standing at the side of the little airstrip on Garry Hoop's farm, the evening shadows lengthening as the little 206 swoops in to land. The disappointment lies heavy on the three of us, not because I didn't get a lesser kudu—that's hunting. After all, if you could rent-a-herd or dial-a-bull, it would be no challenge, no fun, no sport. No, this was not the first hunt where I hadn't gotten what I had come for. The disappointment was in the people, not the game.

Tanzania is a beautiful if bankrupt country trying to retreat from the brink of destruction brought on by the suicidal social experiments in the '80s and '90s of a Nero-like dictator. Its people are friendly and the Masai, in particular, as proud, colourful, and interesting as I had always imagined. But, as happened in our own country, those who could, have left. For the most part, the remainder are not going to win any prizes for reliability, efficiency, or productivity.

The country is worth visiting for its natural beauty alone. The variety of its wildlife and the way they vary from our wildlife in southern Africa make the trip a fascinating must for any hunter. But if you do decide to go, you may want to consider some of the following:

• Check out your safari outfitter carefully.

• Insist on references from experienced hunters who have recently hunted with them.

• Deal directly and in writing with the safari company, not through third parties.

• There are very few working telephones in Tanzania.

• A two-hour air charter can cost anywhere between $1,600 and $2,400.

• Do not pay all your costs before the hunt—try to retain at least 10 percent of the daily rate.

• Everything takes much, much longer to do.

• If you do not take it with you, it is highly unlikely that you will be able to beg, borrow, or buy it there.

• Take a GPS, a compass, and a good, large-scale map of the area you are to hunt.

• Insist on an experienced tracker, or better still, take one with you.

• Insist on a resumé of the professional hunter assigned to you and check his references.

• Take a Swahili phrase book.

• Take a snakebite kit—we killed both a forest cobra and puff adder in our Masailand camp and I saw the biggest mamba of my life crossing a track in front of me.

I believe that the safari industry in Tanzania is complacent. Possibly, it has been spoiled. Hunting has dried up in east Africa due to unrest, wars, and the ill-considered Kenyan ban. Further to the south, apartheid largely took South Africa out of the equation and Mozambique and Angola fell to the age-old African problem: African politicians all too prepared to destroy and devastate their countries rather than reach an accommodation with their political opponents. Tanzania got fat on the hunting spoils. It has had no real competition, certainly not in this neck of the woods. They seem to be used to driving wealthy foreigners around the veld. After all, if you mainly shoot everything from a blind or within a few metres of the vehicle, who needs a tracker?

One good thing flows from this, however—the camps are excellent. Beds, showers, toilets, good food, and well trained and friendly staff to cater to your every need. Maybe I am being unnecessarily cynical on the strength of one trip, but the kind of hunter who doesn't walk and stalk probably pays particular attention to camp comforts. He certainly is not going to sleep on the tracks in Tanzania!

The pickings have been good. The prices are the steepest in Africa. The living is easy. If you don't like it, there are plenty more to fill your place. From this it is a short "jump to the right" and the client becomes the original "sausage in the machine." The safari company knows what you want, it knows best and so has no need to consult the customer.

Very few businesses have survived with such a philosophy and I don't expect the Tanzanian safari industry to buck the trend. Unless they change, particularly as Ethiopia reopens, Uganda finds its feet, and South Africa re-enters the fray, they are in for an unwelcome (if not overdue) surprise.

An African in Alaska

It was Curt Goetz who saved the day. But for him, I am not sure that the great Alaskan bear hunt would have gone past day four. Because Curt is not one for doing without his creature comforts or falling prey to whimsical, enthusiastic bursts of exercise, I started to smile and ended up laughing out loud at myself as I imagined my fastidious friend's horrified reaction to my present condition. Here I was, an innocent from Africa, freezing to death in the Chugach Mountain Range of Alaska and in a state of advanced discomfort. My friend and hunting companion of some fifteen years, Derek Carstens, looked up inquiringly at me from his arctic sleeping bag and joined in my laughter as I shared my thoughts with him. Nothing that we had seen on film, read in books, or heard had even vaguely prepared us for this brown bear hunt in the late autumn of 1991 in the middle of the Alaskan wilderness.

For years Derek and I had harboured four hunting dreams—to hunt the Big Five in Africa; to stalk stag in Scotland; to hunt tiger in India from the back of an elephant; and to hunt brown bear in Alaska. We have done the first two, the third was out of the question, and after a year's research, many telephone calls and much correspondence, we met at the Captain Cook Hotel in Anchorage on Thursday, 24 September 1991. We were like two school kids that evening as we dined on Alaskan king crab, catching up on news and speculating on the hunt ahead.

We spent the next day and some $2,500 each on outdoor gear and hunting licenses. It came as quite a shock to pay substantial amounts for a license in advance, regardless of whether you shot the animal or not. For the most part, in Africa, you only pay a trophy fee should you kill, or heaven forbid, wound an animal.

Laden with outlandish clothing such as rubber hip boots, waterproof climbing boots, thermal underwear, 30 degrees-below arctic sleeping bags, gigantic aluminum-framed backpacks, rain gear, special socks, gloves, and head gear, we trooped back to the hotel suffering from jet lag and not a little apprehension as to what lay ahead. It all seemed very different from the shorts, short-sleeved shirts, and running shoes that constitute our normal hunting clobber. The stories we were told in the various stores we visited about the size of the bears in our hunting area (anything up to 10½ feet tall) and the hunting conditions themselves made us realize, for the first time, that the hunt was not going to be a walk in the proverbial park. How right we were!

The next morning we flew in a twin-engine plane to Cordova, a small fishing village in the south of Alaska. We then swapped to a single-engine amphibian that flew us between snow-covered mountain peaks and across some of the most beautiful scenery I have ever seen, en route to Deadwood Lake. We looked down on tranquil lakes fed by clear, pastel green streams, surrounded by emerald green spruce trees dusted with snow, on a crisp, overcast day. As we landed, the first tentative drops of rain began to fall and they continued to do so, ever harder, for the next eight days and nights. While we transferred our gear to the lake shore, a small Super Cub float plane splashed down to ferry us to Wolf Lake. With a warning from the pilot to Derek to load his rifle and chamber a round, we left him standing apprehensively on the lake shore as we barreled down the lake to our rendezvous at Wolf Lake. (The aircraft was so small I sat on the floor behind the pilot with my legs stretched out on either side of him. There was no room at all for any of my kit, which had to be ferried in separately). Ed Stevenson and his fellow guide, a red-haired, 6-foot, 5-inch giant of a man named Will Stephens, were waiting for us at Wolf Lake.

Things were not as they should have been. Ed, Will, and Deb (Ed's wife) had been delayed in leaving their previous hunting camp at Sheep River due to horse problems and had only arrived the previous night. The supplies still had to be ferried from Deadwood Lake to Wolf Lake, a tree platform built to store the provisions out of the reach of bears, and then backpacked to our base area some one and a half hour's walk away. Now a walk this long is normally a doddle, but in Alaska, it takes on a whole new meaning when you realize that this has to be done with a 60-pound pack on your back, in hip boots, along bear trails, and for the most part, using swollen rivers as pathways. With darkness fast approaching, wearing our unfamiliar gear, we stumbled off down a bear trail along the lake shore. If a bear trail conjures up visions of a wide, smooth, contoured elephant trail in the Zambezi Valley, you would be making a big mistake. These bears have a peculiar sense of humour and only seem happy if they are either going up or going down.

Moving off the bear trail, we entered a turbulent, fast-flowing stream (a "crick" as Ed and Will pronounced it). I can't remember if it was the third or fourth crick we entered because, at that stage, my entire being was focused solely on putting one foot in front of the other. At any rate, my boot hooked under a root and down I went. The shock of the icy water took my breath away, and if that wasn't bad enough, I quickly realized that I could not get up. The weight of my pack falling over my head and the fast-flowing river conspired to keep my head in the water. Fortunately, like a giant crane, Will came to my rescue and ignominiously plucked me out of the water with one huge hand. Cold, wet, and with knees feeling like worn out shock absorbers, Derek and I stumbled into camp as darkness fell. The last part of the trek had been character building as we negotiated a slippery, muddy, eight-inch-wide bear path along the side of a steep mountain slope overhanging the glacier-fed Gravina River. One slip would have sent us tumbling into the roaring main channel of the river.

The next four days reminded me of those old-fashioned trials by ordeal reserved for witches and other undesirable characters in the Dark Ages. Between trips to Wolf Lake that would have taxed a Green Beret or Selous Scout, in order to fetch stores, we made the odd scout for a couple of days at a time to nearby valleys. During this whole period, it rained or sleeted night and day with the temperature never reaching much above freezing point.

The differences between an Alaskan hunt and an African safari are in stark contrast—I mean *nothing* is similar! Derek and I completed what we thought had been a relatively hard but successful ten-day buffalo hunt through the Chewore Hills in the Zambezi Valley in July. I had been fit for this safari and since then had intensified my fitness program, which consisted of daily Canadian Air Force exercises supplemented by jogging or cycling on alternate evenings. Shortly before I left for Alaska, I was running 8.5 kilometres in about 45 minutes and cycling 20 kilometres in about the same time. I thought that I was in really good shape.

I failed to take into account a number of factors, however. For example, on returning to camp at the end of a long day on safari in Africa, there is always a welcoming fire; a cold beer will more often than not be thrust into your hands to be succeeded by a hot shower, a fresh change of clothing, and a delicious meal cooked by the camp chef. A glass of wine with the meal is not unknown, followed by a peaceful night's sleep between dry sheets and warm blankets. At the end of the day on our hunt in Alaska, there was no fire (the wood was too wet). We had to pitch our own tents and boil a meal of freeze-dried food (which closely resembles lukewarm polystyrene). There was nothing to drink other than water, tea, or coffee, as anything else would have been too heavy to carry, and the only way to dry out wet clothing was to climb into your sleeping bag with it on. We slept on the ground on thin, inflatable mattresses in our sleeping bags and our clean clothes were the previous day's dirty clothes. In fact, during the eighteen days of the hunt, we did not bath or shower as there were simply no facilities to do so.

This was quite a culture shock for Derek and me. Over the past fifteen years of big-game hunting in Namibia, Botswana, Zimbabwe, Mozambique, and South Africa, often in what we thought was fairly rugged terrain, we flattered ourselves that while we were certainly less than professionals, we had also become more than run-of-the-mill amateur hunters. Our egos were taking a serious bashing, and here we were on day four of the hunt, tired, cold, miserable, and with aches and pains in muscles that we had not known existed. Day four was the day on which, but for my bemused thoughts of Curtis George von Goetz III, I think we both would have been prepared to consider a radio call for the float plane back to Cordova en route to Anchorage, had the other one suggested it. Somehow, the laughter did it. That and the fact that, miraculously, my body stopped smelling like a toxic waste site, or at least I thought it had until I caught the horrified looks of guests in the lobby of the Captain Cook Hotel on my return to Anchorage some fifteen days later as they walked downwind of me.

I remember a Lufthansa air hostess, in particular, walking jauntily toward me. At a distance of some four feet, it looked as if she walked into a brick wall. Her nose crinkled and her face became contorted. She gave me a brief, horrified look from under her eyebrows before scuttling off to the right, all the while looking over her shoulder at me. I misunderstood the look, thinking it was possibly my appearance—unshaven, calf-length drover coat, rolled-down hip boots, and broad-brimmed African safari hat. It was only when the registration clerk greeted me with "You smell kinda high, Buddy!" that I understood the real reason behind her rapid departure. I felt like a New York bag lady in the Waldorf Astoria's main restaurant. As soon as humanly possible, I scuttled up to my room and stood under the shower for close on an hour. At any rate, from day four onward, my olfactory nerves seized up and I ceased being able to smell myself, Derek, or our guides, and this was a major improvement.

From then on, as I became used to my equipment, other things started to improve as well. I seemed to gain in strength and found my balance wading through the turbulent mountain streams, which, for the most part, were our pathways. Although I never mastered walking in the streams without the aid of a stick, something that even our guides resorted to from time to time, I became quicker and much more confident. I was able to keep up with my guide and began to take more notice of the beautiful surroundings in which I found myself. Even though the rain still poured down and I ended each day soaked to the skin, every now and then I would catch a glimpse of the snow-covered mountain peaks.

Then I spotted my first bear, a black bear high up against the snow line, which, by this stage, reached the tree line. I picked up the moving white dot of a mountain goat in my 10X pocket binoculars. I heard a bald eagle call and was amazed at the similarity between this bird and our own fish eagle. There were merganzers and swans and then my first brown bear in the bend of a river. She was a 7½-foot sow on a fishing expedition accompanied by two cubs. I watched, enthralled, as they fished for breakfast. Over the period of the hunt, I became aware of distinct fishing styles amongst the bears. There were the dippers, the flippers, and the subs. The amateurs (the dippers) were normally young bears who would rush dashing and splashing into the shallows after the shoals and usually emerge wet and bedraggled with a lost and bemused look, sans fish. The pros stood in or near rapids. I called these the flippers as they took the fish in midair with a deceptively fast flash of a paw or snap of a jaw. My favourite, however, was the sow and her two-year-old cub. Mom's whole head was under water as she searched for fish, looking for all the world like a scuba diver. When she stopped, for some reason she cocked and lifted her right back leg clear off the water. Her cub imitated her to perfection.

Compared with Africa, however, the number and variety of animals and birds were but a fraction and there was, therefore, less distraction, less to take my mind off the punishment that my body was undergoing.

Derek and I were determined not to shoot a young bear. We were both looking for old, mature boars who were no longer part of the breeding cycle. We were absolutely determined not to lower our standards, as apart from anything else, nonresidents are not permitted to return to Alaska to hunt brown bear within four years of shooting one.

After much plotting and planning, toward the end of the hunt, Ed and I decided to take a small rubber duck with a four-horsepower motor through the beaver ponds leading from Wolf Lake to the Gravina River and from there on down to the mud flats along the coast. This was far easier said than done as the beaver population had increased substantially since the previous hunting season. Every few hundred metres we had to stop, unpack the boat, drag it over, under, and across the beaver dams and then go back for the motor, fuel, and provisions that we packed for a three-day stay. Certainly not something I would have attempted in some of Africa's crocodile-infested waterways. Eventually we made it to the Gravina after battling for two-thirds of the day, but from there on, it was literally plain sailing as we sped silently downriver, only using the oars to negotiate the rapids and starting the motor when nasty eddies threatened to smash us into overhanging branches or the riverbank.

The weather had been getting steadily colder over the last few days. It stopped raining and regular snowfalls were bringing the snow line further and further down the mountain side. It was a bitingly cold day when we reached our camping spot. What little sun there had been now passed behind the mountain peaks. I was wearing everything that I possessed, which in this case consisted of two pairs of socks, thermal underwear, hunting pants, and hip boots. On top, I was wearing more thermal underwear, a T-shirt, shirt, jersey, two down-filled jackets (one over the other), a rain jacket, two pairs of gloves, and a thick, lined tweed hat with ear flaps. I was shaking like a country outhouse on a windy hill and could not hold the video camera steady as I filmed a glacier and snow-covered mountain on the opposite side of the mud flats.

Ed came to my rescue, and using an "old Indian trick" as he called it, turned one cold, wet, wretched African into something resembling a human being. A liberal dose of petrol from the fuel tank on the rubber duck poured over some sodden wood soon had it "whoofing" like a dog after he flicked one of his all-weather matches onto the pile.

And then Ed spotted him. Right up against the snow line, next to a diamond-shaped patch of snow on the mountain on the opposite shore, a bulldozer of a bear ambled around unconcernedly by on the 50-degree slope. He was absolutely gigantic. With the naked eye it was not possible to make out the front from the back. Looking through my 10X binoculars his head appeared deformed as it was so small compared with the rest of his body. This, Ed said, was one of the sure signs of a bruiser bear. He appeared to be eating rocks since our binoculars were not powerful enough to pick up the berries and frasses, which Ed was sure was keeping the bear up against the snow line. Ed was very excited about the bear and felt it would go at least 10½ feet. Soon the cold and wet were forgotten as we watched in awe and tried to plan a stalk. My .375 started to shrink in my hands and I thought longingly of my .460 at home. Why these magnificent animals are not part of the Big Five, I'll never know. As we watched, however, the bear turned around and took off diagonally upward and across the mountain face. As darkness fell, he disappeared into a steep ravine near the peak, moving at a pace that looked as if he was planning on emigrating to Canada by morning.

I was devastated, Ed philosophical. "That's bears for you," he said. "The most unpredictable animal on God's earth." I did not bother to tell him that leopards could teach bears a thing or two as I thought back on my nine-day leopard hunt in Mozambique the previous year. I was too despondent to even pick my head up.

We had a miserable night as we left our tent behind in order to save weight and make room for more provisions or "groceries" as Ed called them. We slung a tarpaulin over a tree branch and went to sleep, hoping that the weather would not change to wind and rain. I was up at dawn the next morning (although this a little misleading because it only gets light at about 7 A.M.) and I wandered down from our camp in the spruce to the lake shore to see whether I had calculated low tide correctly.

As I got to the shore, I flicked an involuntary glance up at the opposite mountain. My heart jumped. The bear was back. We watched for hours while he fiddled around on the snow line and then began wending his way lower and lower down the mountainside. We were starting to become just a tad excited again. He disappeared into a line of spruce about halfway down the mountainside, and quite simply, never appeared again. We sat, watched, and waited for him until my time ran out. On my eighteenth and last afternoon, we found an 8-footer fishing on a bend in Dead Creek. We tried to enlarge him in our binoculars without success and watched him eventually move off into the alders as dusk settled.

I had mixed emotions as the little Super Cub took off from Wolf Lake with Ed and Deb waving good-bye to me. It seemed only right and fair, what with having come so far and worked so hard, for a big brown bear to be the just reward. Half of me could not believe that I was returning empty-handed. The other half was pleased that I had kept my promise to myself. It had been the most demanding hunt from a physical and mental point of view that I had ever been on. I was chuffed with myself for having made it and come through in one piece and in good health. I had been awed by the solitude and sheer beauty of the surroundings. The Alaskans call it the "last frontier," and I truly believe that they are correct. I have already started saving up for my next trip to Alaska and hope to be back to try once again for a grown-up grizzly.

In retrospect, I learned a number of important lessons. No more sniggering inwardly at foreigners to Africa in their brand new, stiff khakis, noisy walking boots, and sombreros. No more simple sense of superiority based on the thought that if I could hunt big game in Africa on foot in an ethical manner, I could hunt anything, anywhere. No more facile assumptions that no one but an African could teach me anything about big-game hunting. Our guides were as tough and as expert as any top African professional hunter. They were as knowledgeable, resourceful, and hardworking, if not more so, in that they had no support from trackers, skinners, and other camp staff. I came away with a high regard for the country, the bears, and particularly, those who live in it and hunt the bruisers. A big brown bear seems as tough, quick, and dangerous as anything that Africa has to offer. Any ethical Alaskan hunter who hunts this spectacular animal on foot should be welcomed into the brethren of African big-game hunters with open arms—he deserves it.

I SURVIVED ABYSSINIA

Ethiopia is an extraordinary country. Like a landlocked island—asleep for years, it's a Rip van Winkle of a country. Midday is 6 A.M. Ethiopian time. The calendar has thirteen months and according to it, the year was 1990, although for the rest of us it was 1997. We arrived on flight ET876, which departed from Johannesburg via Harare in Zimbabwe (home of Menghistu Haile Mariam, the communist dictator who ruled Ethiopia with a titanium fist, calculatingly cruel heart, and a witless, baffled brain, for eighteen years) to Addis Ababa, on Sunday, 3 November. Ninety percent of the people speak Amharic, a 264-letter alphabet language spoken nowhere else and resembling no other. For instance, *"and, hulet, sost, arat"* (one, two, three, four). Not your run-of-the-mill African country.

Hunting in Ethiopia is an extraordinary experience. The country has undergone radical political, social, and cultural change over a twenty-year period, from an imperial dynasty to a communist dictatorship to a tentative democracy. Because of that, and because so little is known about modern-day mountain nyala hunting, one of the most popular safari companies, Rocky Valley Safaris, has run nine hunts in the two years prior to our hunt—of which only four have been successful. So I

Heart of an African Hunter

thought I would write a detailed article on hunting conditions in the country to help hunters prepare for the experience. As G. T., my hunting companion on the trip said, it was an adventure and an experience not to be missed, but the word "enjoyment" did not immediately spring to mind in the post-mortem discussions we held.

As such, many issues are raised that I would not normally mention. Many criticisms are highlighted that I would normally brush over, particularly when the hunt has been successful. I have, however, tried to be objective and informative, possibly concentrating a tad more on the negative aspects to help hunters in their preparation (after all, unexpected good news is never a problem). However, I do give praise where it is due.

Overall I would ask you to accept that this is not written out of a sense of "sour grapes"—been there, done that, got the T-shirt attItade. The proof of this, if you need it, is that both G. T. and I have agreed that should the opportunity arise and should we be convinced that there is a genuine opportunity to hunt mature mountain nyala bulls, we would both return.

So, back to the trip. Our flight left at 5 A.M. and is the only direct flight from Johannesburg to Addis Ababa. Why that early? Well, according to the airline, it is to enable passengers to connect with the lunchtime flight from Addis Ababa to London, although who in their right mind would fly from Johannesburg to London via Addis was a mystery to everyone. But that's the way it is in Ethiopia—an extraordinary place.

Bureaucracy and corruption were widespread. So much so that I began to suspect that it was genetic. Not so, said the older people with whom I spoke, many of whom had been incarcerated by the Communists. The bureaucracy and corruption were comparatively new phenomena created, nurtured, and fostered by a brutal and merciless regime. And it affected them more than us. For example, a citizen requires written permission to travel abroad. This permission requires a number of different ministries to grant clearance and takes anywhere from three to six weeks. And in Africa, wherever the cloven hoof of bureaucracy emerges beneath the cover of requiring ordinary people to obtain permits to do ordinary, everyday things, bribery is as sure to follow as night follows day.

So it was that, despite having paid for our safari and trophy licenses in full almost a month before arriving, it took until Thursday after our Sunday arrival before we managed to obtain our hunting licenses. I suspect they weren't even issued until Wednesday, and only after certain regional palms were greased, as by then, we had already obtained the requisite national permits. I also lost a full day at the end of the safari as I was obliged to deliver my two rifles to customs a full day before my departure. This was the time it would take to clear them. Not that it helped, mind you, as I was called from the airport departure lounge and confronted with my rifles and eventually a total of eight customs officials.

Now I have never paid a bribe in Africa. It is the thin end of the wedge. I had my rifle licenses, my export license from South Africa, my import license to Ethiopia, my customs clearance from Ethiopia. But where was "the other paper?" "What other paper?" "You know, the other paper. You can't take these rifles without the other paper."

I have a friend who says the more difficult it is to enter a country, the less likely you are to want to go there. Ethiopia is a country that makes it the most difficult to leave. The corollary is, of course, the less likely you are to want to return. Only after I asked the airline staff to call the police, as the custom officials were clearly trying to steal my rifles, did they crawl back into the holes from which they had emerged and I was able to leave.

Altogether I lost a total of seven full hunting days due to corruption and lies and a further day when we moved camp from the mountains to the Danakil Desert. In short, I planned to spend a week in Ethiopia after the end of my hunt to investigate the possibility of doing business in the country. Two of my colleagues were due to join me, and we had arranged a series of meetings with government officials as well as business contacts. I was sufficiently impressed by the extent of the deceit and corruption that I canceled all these meetings and returned home early.

What a pity, because the Ethiopians I had got to know on safari were intelligent, friendly, and hardworking. It's difficult to generalize, I know, because Ethiopia is made up of so many different types of people—predominantly fine-featured Tigreans in the north, dark Bantu-like Oromo people in the south, Kalashnikov-clad nomads in the east, and a strong Arabic influence in the west.

We eventually left Addis Ababa, midmorning on Tuesday, happy to leave a soulless city. Very much like Johannesburg. No real history, no real culture, dirty, dusty, noisy, packed with street vendors and beggars, and drivers with a death wish. The children all seem to know at least two words of English, "give money!"

The 220-kilometre drive south to our base camp in the Kakka Mountains, part of the Arusi Mountain Range, took more than ten hours. It was a tiring and often harrowing experience. Like many Ethiopian drivers, ours believed that the opposite side of the road was in a better condition than the side we were meant to drive on. The resulting near misses, perpetual hooting, two flat tyres (the jack didn't work), the throngs of people, goats, donkeys, cattle, and horses that stepped into traffic without a care or look, the wrong turns—it all became a bit much. Our chauffeur might not have been the worst driver in the world but he would certainly have made the grand final of the competition.

The next day at the base camp, some 9,000 feet up in the foothills of the Kakka Mountains, dawned crisp and clear. A brisk breeze blew and low, wispy clouds scudded overhead. The natural optimism inherent in and essential to all trophy hunters had reasserted itself, and we spent the day meeting the camp crew and repacking essential gear for our trip to our 13,400-foot-high fly camp the next day. We sighted in our rifles—spot on at 184 metres—and spent the afternoon playing with a Frisbee that G. T. dug out of somewhere. In the end, the whole camp staff—some thirty-four people in all, plus some curious local farmers— pitched in and made up for any lack of skill with boundless energy and enthusiasm. It was a great icebreaker.

Four in the morning our time, 10 P.M. Ethiopian time, we were up. A brief breakfast, and I met my constant companions for the next three weeks, Bora, a twelve-year-old palomino gelding, and Bulti, his fifty-something-year-old owner and my horse puller.

Three hours later, I sat on the edge of a rugged, rocky cliff at the head of a steep, green valley, covered wall to wall in the ever present, calf-length *Eritreana arboritica*, a most unusual green, bushy shrub, which can vary in height, depending on the conditions, from calf length to twenty feet high in the Kubsa Mountains. A cutting, cold wind chased rain, sleet, and thick, enveloping fog up the valley. Around me huddled the twelve members of my hunting team—Colonel Negussie Eshete (professional hunter), Mamou (chief tracker), Sufo (chief local tracker), six spotters, three horse pullers and Theo Pretorius and his camera crew of four.

Yes, I know it sounds a little crazy, but not only were we going to hunt mountain nyala, one of the most difficult trophy animals in Africa, but we were going to try to capture it on film. If we were successful, it might just be the first such film of its kind.

As usual, as part of my research into this hunt, I read everything I could lay my hands on regarding Ethiopia: Bahru Zewde's *History of Ethiopia*, Maydon's *Simien—Its Height and Abysses*, Powell-Cotton's *A Sporting Trip through Abyssinia*, Rey's *The Real Abyssinia*, Sanchez-Ariño's *Hunting in Ethiopia*, Thesiger's *Danakil Desert* and *A Life of My Own*, and Lesley Brown's book of research into mountain nyala, *Ethiopian Episode*. I also read reports filed with the *Hunting Report*, travel guides, coffee table books, and various magazine articles. Not even the book on mountain nyala had a picture of an adult male nyala bull. In fact, the only such pictures I had ever seen came from the Bale Mountain National Park. None from the wild.

As we sat surrounded by the remorseless mist, all feeling draining from my toes and fingers, I began to realize that, if this was what mountain nyala hunting was all about, our preparations, thorough as they seemed at the time, were barely adequate. And my premonition was right.

Over the next couple of days and nights, the three of us each settled on our own combination of clothing and gear. What I found best was an underlayer of expedition-weight Patagonia thermal underwear; 28-ounce, virgin wool Filson outerwear; heavy-weight cotton shirt (a woolen one would have been better); and a British army jersey on top. Also: two pairs of socks (one thin and one thick—both woolen); a pair of waterproof, insulated Italian hiking boots; waterproof. knee-length gaiters; woolen gloves that I could fold back leaving my fingertips exposed. A thermal balaclava and waterproof cap with ear flaps completed my clothing. One of the spotters carried my 35-litre backpack with a poncho, compact 35mm camera, spare film, flashlight (one that straps on your head would have been better), spare batteries, GPS, map, small medical aid pack, food, and water. I carried my own ammo, skinning knife, and Leatherman, and my gunbearer carried my rifle in a soft, waterproof gun bag with an extra waterproof scope-protector that fit snugly over the 2.5–10X42 Zeiss Diavari.

At night, all that G. T. removed were his boots as his thin sleeping bag and the one blanket he was provided (there were no more) gave little in the way of warmth. Theo and I were marginally better off but we both slept in two sets of thermal underwear plus balaclavas.

My .300 Winchester Magnum was made by Bill Ritchie and his assistant, Vince. It was built on a Brno action with a black synthetic stock and topped by a Zeiss scope with a Harris bipod attached to the reinforced front sling swivel. Lying on the gray foam inside the silvery aluminum gun case, with the silver cartridge cases and black bullet heads of the 180-grain Winchester Fail Safe ammo alongside, it looked mean and professional. Out loud, I agreed that it looked a little over the top. Inwardly, I was secretly pleased, and best of all, it was more than accurate enough for the task at hand.

Over the preceding months, I fired more than 300 rounds with it. First on my local shooting range—sitting, standing, and lying at 100 metres and then on the 300-metre range that Louis built for me down in the Karoo. The targets we used were lifesize colour photographs of springbok, an animal about a third of the size of a mountain nyala.

On a still day, when I am concentrating, I can group just on an inch at 100 metres, twice that at 200 metres, and within the size of a generous saucer at 300 metres. At 1½ inches high at 100 metres, I was 5 inches down at 300 metres. I know the ballistics tables say it should have been 7 inches down, but the facts must speak for themselves. On the 300-metre range, when the fine cross hairs of my scope obscured the front third of the springbok target, I would often think fondly of one of our local farmers who liked to tell about the time he shot a kudu bull at a much greater distance with his 7mm Remington Magnum. So far, in fact, that it was only once he got out of his *bakkie* (truck) that he heard the shot hit and saw the bull fall. After walking for 600 paces toward the dead kudu, which, of course, dropped in its tracks, the bull "*het nog wyd gelê*" (still lay a goodly distance away) and he called to one of his farmhands to drive over with the *bakkie*!

The next week fell into a steady hunting rhythm. Up around 5 A.M. (I say "around" because we never managed to train the camp staff to wake us at an agreed time and early morning tea, often promised, never materialized). A quick, very quick change—it was freezing cold and any water left out overnight was frozen solid in the morning; an egg of some kind (they were compulsory); and then the inevitable heated discussion/disagreement amongst the Ethiopians about the plans for the day before mounting up and heading out.

No matter how detailed the tactical discourse of the night before, plans were always rehashed at length the next morning with everyone participating and gesticulating in the loud and voluble discussions. A good sign, no doubt, for the newly emerging Ethiopian democracy but a big pain for those who did not want to waste the precious morning hunting time.

We would identify a spot somewhere on the mountain range, sometimes up in the peaks, sometimes midway up, other times down overlooking the farmers' barley fields, which afforded us a good field of vision. Once there we would disperse our spotting groups, leaving ourselves roughly in the middle of the group. Mamou would normally work between the various groups—all of whom were armed with binoculars, which supplemented their already acute vision. Sometimes we would move to a different spot in the middle of the day once the nyala bedded down, but we often spent the whole day just glassing and glassing and glassing.

Each day we would see, on average, five to fifteen mountain nyala cows and young ones. Every now and then we would surprise some of the biggest-bodied klipspringers I have ever seen (in this region, for some unknown reason, many of the females also carry horns, which is unheard of elsewhere). We also came across the odd ginger-coloured hyena, the bushy, tan-coloured bohor reedbuck, a sounder of warthog, and on three occasions, that rarest of Ethiopian animals, a red simien fox.

We also followed up leads brought in by the local farmers who hoped to earn the reward offered by the Colonel for sighting a mountain nyala bull. What can I say? They were, at best, figments of overactive imaginations. Not one supposed sighting could be corroborated by any track or sign on the ground. But they did waste a lot of our time.

The worst incident occurred when two of the Colonel's staff were sent to verify the sighting of two mountain nyala bulls at Kubsa, a forest-bedecked mountain range a day's ride away.

I Survived Abyssinia

I felt a little guilty that I was the one going. The two camp members, Sufo and Menayee, had seen the two bulls on the day after their arrival. One was 26 to 27 inches, the other about 34 inches.

"How far were you from them?" I asked.

"About 100 paces from the small one," said Menayee, his eyes shining with excitement. "The other one was running but from here to about there," he pointed to a rock on the mountain slope about 200 metres away. "Big, he was big," he emphasized with his hands.

Our little caravan of six horses and four donkeys arrived at Kubsa the next evening as the fog closed in and the rain began to fall. We hired a *tucul* (a thatch-roofed, mud-walled hut) from a local farmer and ate spaghetti and drank twelve-year-old Ballantine's scotch as we listened with mounting incredulity to the reformed local poacher, Gamou, tell us how easy it would be. The nyala in the morning, Menelik bushbuck in the afternoon, and, if we wanted a bohor reedbuck, no problem on the second morning. For some reason I could not contain my by now well-developed skepticism and everyone found it hilarious when I said: "Oh, as simple as that," and wiped my two hands against one another *chuff, chaff* as if they were cymbals.

Over the next three days we saw one female nyala, one female bushbuck, and the two nyala bulls. Only problem was that they must have shrunk a bit in the overnight rain. One was about fourteen inches and the other might just have made twenty. If there were other nyala bulls in the area, they must have perfected the art of walking on air.

I was much stronger now. The first two days of altItade sickness and the accompanying headaches and vomiting were a thing of the past. I could keep up with the locals as we led our horses up and down the tricky bits. I should mention here that, if you suffer from vertigo or have poor balance, you should give nyala hunting in the Kakka Mountains a miss. Even so, it was a weary, disheartened, and disillusioned hunter who returned to the fly camp under the crest of the topmost peaks of the Kakka Mountains.

There I found that Theo had left to film in the Bale Mountain National Park before returning home. G. T. had hunted hard in the interim and been rewarded with the sight of a young bull. "Not one, however, that you would want to hang on your wall," he explained.

We talked far into the night. What to do? Between the two of us, we had put in twenty man-days hunting. Each team had at least eight sets of eyes and binoculars. No one had sighted an adult male nyala bull. G. T. made the correct decision. With one week of his hunt left, he departed for Asela to look for Menelik bushbuck en route to the Danakil Desert for beisa oryx, northern gerenuk, and Soemmering gazelle. He succeeded and shot good representative specimens of each.

I had booked a twenty-eight-day hunt. At the outset I said that if all I shot was a representative specimen of a mountain nyala, I would be happy. After that, in order of preference, came Menelik bushbuck, lesser kudu, beisa oryx, Soemmering gazelle and Salt dik-dik. And those were the only licenses I originally applied for. In Ethiopia, you pay up-front for your licenses whether you are successful or not. At $4,000 for a nyala license and so on, the initial total came to a sizable amount However, encouraged by the suggestions and confidence of the safari company, I was persuaded to take out additional licenses for Abyssinian bushbuck, duiker, Haggard oribi, giant forest hog, and northern gerenuk. But for the last animal, I did not see any of the other species.

The next day the Colonel and G. T. left. I sat down with Sysay, my young professional hunter (with eighteen months experience) and had a heart-to-heart chat. If I was going to devote another two weeks to mountain nyala, I wanted to propose certain changes. Of these, the most important were the following:

1. I wanted a shower rigged up. The Colonel originally announced, "no shower—too cold to shower." He may have been right, but after two weeks of no washing, I was going to chance it.

2. I wanted the staff campfire moved from its position twenty paces in front of my tent to some place else as everyone congregated there and indulged in the Ethiopian National Sport—TALKING—until all hours of the night.

3. I wanted my tent swept daily, my washing done daily, and the camp area cleaned daily. Frankly, the camp was a pigsty; papers, plastic, and horse and donkey droppings littered the area.

4. I wanted to participate in the tactical discussions of the next day's hunt and the deployment of the spotters. Too often I found that after the spotters reported in at lunch time they were never redeployed. One ridiculous evening, we had sixteen men and six horses all congregated in one spot watching one small, tight valley.

Sysay and the Colonel are two of only fourteen professional hunters in Ethiopia. Their company, Rocky Valley Safaris, is one of only four internationally recognized safari companies in the country. They and their staff are keen to please, hard working, and enthusiastic but apart from the Colonel, who has sixtee,n years experience, the rest are unsophisticated, untrained, and desperately lacking in experience and knowledge. Questions as to what nyala eat, when nyala mate, what is the gestation period of a nyala cow, what is the name of that bird, insect, and plant are invariably met with a shrug or puzzled look—like why would you want to know that?

If we had hunted hard before, we now redoubled our efforts, choosing the best from the three teams to make up our new group. The weather continued to have its say and many mornings and evenings were interrupted by rain, sleet, mist, and fog, but we hunted every day from dark to dark. Still, the most common sight in the mountains remained Homo sapiens—cattle herders, donkey drovers, wood cutters, farmers, and travelers. During my entire hunt, I cannot remember a day when I was out of the sight and sound of people and their appendages.

On my thirteenth hunting day, at the confluence of two deep valleys, Sysay, Hassan (my new gunbearer), and I lay perfectly camouflaged on a rocky ledge fringed with *Eritreana arboritica* or *asta* (in Amharic) or *soto* (in Oromo) and were surrounded by great, lichen-covered granite boulders interspersed with more shrubs. To our right, two shepherd boys were whooping and screaming at one another and their mixed herd of sheep, goats, and cattle. We had already dispatched Fiaso to move them along when Hassan, pointing to our left, said "I see something."

Minutes ticked by until I eventually made out three shapes beneath the crest of the mountain on the horizon. Every so often they would disappear in a fold in the ground, but like an arrow in flight, they did not deviate from their course. They were heading straight toward us. From their size, they had to be three nyala, but although two were the minky brown colour of the cows, the third was a darker gray.

Could it be? As the minutes dragged I could sense the mounting excitement in my companions. "I can't see any horns," said Sysay. I flicked a glance over my right shoulder at the shepherds hooting and hollering at their herd. Where was Fiaso? I caught sight of movement on the ridge. There he was, still about half a kilometre to go. Turning back, I picked up three nyala cresting the valley wall to our front. Eight hundred forty-three metres according to the Leica Geovid, and yes, it was a bull! Probably a young one but a bull nevertheless.

With that, a series of piercing screams erupted from my right. The nyala immediately stopped their steady progress, turned on a tickey, and trotted off back up the mountainside. I lost it. I ranted and raved. Threw all my toys out of the cot. Pathetic, really. It did no good other than allow me to let off some of the pent-up steam from the preceding two weeks. Eventually Fiaso appeared, quieted the herders, and helped move them and their animals down the valley.

Sysay and Hassan were mortified, but when Fiaso returned, they put their heads together and proposed the following plan. Fiaso, Hassan, and Sufo would make a big detour and try to push the nyala toward me. I thought the chances were between slim and none—and Slim had recently emigrated—but it was better than any other idea we had.

I took a bite out of the peanut butter sandwich in my left hand and then a bite out of the jelly sandwich in my right hand as I watched them walk off. Somehow we could not persuade our new chef (Sysay fired his predecessor after he burnt the boiled eggs for lunch) to put the two in the same sandwich.

While all this had been going on, 600 metres away, six and then another three mountain nyala cows materialized out of the midmorning mist and were grazing on the green grass amongst the tufted hillocks along the valley bottom. Time ticked by. The nyala lay down, almost invisible amongst the tussocks. In the late afternoon light, a sounder of warthogs literally scampered down the mountainside to join them. Flights of olive pigeons were coursing up the valley from the barley fields below at full speed to avoid the lammergeiers hanging on the wind in ambush above.

I heard a gasp from Sysay.

"They've done it!"

And they had. One of the cows was missing but the young bull and the other cow were back on track, moving steadily and directly toward us. It was brilliant. Gradually I could make out his every detail. His predominantly gunmetal gray body. The dramatic black legs offset by white on their backs. The slashes of white across his chest, under his chin and the dash forming the chevron across his nose. He was magnificent. Absolutely outstanding.

We slid off the ledge and detoured some 400 metres in a shallow circle to our left. Crawling the last few metres, we slid on our bellies onto a broad, circular, flat rock overlooking the two nyala below. Settling into the classic Bisley shootist pose, I handed Sysay my binoculars. The cross hairs of my scope fixed unwaveringly on the bull's right shoulder as he stood broadside, gazing at nine cows to my right.

"How far?" I asked.

"248, 232, 221," Sysay replied, reading off the distance from the Leica Geovid. "Are you going to take him?" he asked anxiously.

Heart of an African Hunter

One voice answered in my head: *Of course you are. You've come so far, hunted so hard, you deserve it. You've paid your dues. More importantly, you've paid your $4000. So what if it's not a big one? You've still got a mountain nyala. If you don't take it, somebody else will. You won't get another one and what are your chances of ever coming back here?* The other voice argued back: *"What if this is the only young bull in the entire mountain range? How would you feel then? You came for an old bull out of the breeding cycle. This is not it. Any fool can kill a mountain nyala. You're a trophy hunter. Stick to your original resolution."*

Back and forth the arguments raged. Sysay was looking at me, a big question mark on his forehead. Eventually conservation won. Not without a battle, to be perfectly honest, but it did win. And I have no regrets.

As quietly as I could, I cocked the bolt over an empty chamber, checking with the tip of my little finger to be absolutely sure. Slowly I repositioned myself and settled into my sniper's role. My breathing steadied. I squeezed the trigger as the cross hairs settled in line with the front leg, midway up the body. The bull froze as the "click" of the firing pin broke the silence of the crisp, cold mountain air. I "shot" him twice more before he retraced his path gingerly up the valley with hesitant and faltering footsteps, unsure of what was making the foreign sound, unsure of where it came from or what it meant.

A sense of elation filled me as I watched him go. I was proud of our hunting team, proud of Sysay and proud of myself. We had all played our part, if not perfectly, then well enough to outwit and win the hunt for a mountain nyala bull.

I knew in my heart of hearts that it had been "my" bull, that there were no others in the mountain range. We did make one more dart in the direction of Kubsa and watched a promising series of valleys for a couple of days until a heavy, day-long downpour pushed us down the mountain to base camp and then on to Asela for Menelik bushbuck.

The three days in Asela were more of the same, except camp was the local hotel. Not one you would find in the Michelin guide. The Asela Ras Hotel was a holdover from the past and still owned and run by the government. Or so I was told, possibly to explain the dilapidated state of decay of the rooms, the poor service, and the barely edible food. The hotel had a lot of class—all low—but a lot of it.

Three days of glutinous spaghetti bolognese, hot chili omelettes, and malty Harar beer. Three days that produced one female bushbuck and one juvenile male with 8-inch horns. Three days of hunting with people, dogs, and domestic livestock all around, in fact, seldom more than a few metres away. Three days of glassing hillsides and valleys devoid of game but cluttered with cattle and their keepers. Not African hunting as you and I know it.

Off to the Danakil Desert. Home of the legendary Depression. Lowest natural point on earth and probably the hottest as well. Down the Awash River Valley we drove. Past a rusting Russian T54 tank. Over the Emperor Haile Selassie Bridge flanked by stone-sculpted lions. One Ethiopian soldier in a mustard-yellow tracksuit top, camouflage trousers, and white plastic sandals was directing traffic with his AK47. Six times we were literally driven off the road by trucks careening along around sharp corners and over blind rises. Never have I experienced such wanton recklessness and total disregard for the lives and safety of other road users. What prevented an accident was that none of these incidents occurred where the shoulder of the road dropped two to three feet below the level of the tar, which was frequently the case where the heavy rains in the region had washed away the earthen shoulder.

These rains transformed the arid Danakil Desert into a green and lush oasis, with knee-high grass and camels that were well-fed, sleek, and had what seemed suspiciously like ear-to-ear camel grins.

The area was alive with everything that could fly, slither, walk, or crawl. Dik-dik darted across the road, as numerous as rabbits in a carrot patch. Gerenuk gamboled amongst the thorn trees, able to browse without rearing up on their hind legs as the browse line barely reached above the backs of even the smallest one. The mosquitoes next to the springs where our camp was ill-advisedly pitched had their own air traffic controller as they attacked in billowing waves. My first unthinking trip to the toilet resulted in sixty-six bites on the exposed and unmentionable parts of my body while another thirty-two of the little buggers bit me clean through my socks.

But the Danakil was spectacularly beautiful. Pan-shaped pale green plains carpeted in delicate pink, trumpet-shaped blossoms, bordered by rocky rolling ridges, fringed with grass-green thorn trees and liberally sprinkled with the Afar and their camels.

The southeastern part of the Danakil is home to four distinct bands of nomads: the Keraway, Ita, Essa, and Afar—with the latter two groups engaged in a blood feud. Every Afar man I saw over the age of twelve carried a rifle, normally an AK47. I had been told about this before arriving in Ethiopia but had been assured that the firearms were merely decorative, part of the culture of the people but never used. Bull dust! The Afar are fanatical about firearms, and if my experience is anything to go by, become open and friendly if you can find a way to share this interest with them.

According to the two I befriended, they still need to kill in order to marry, and the Afar and Essa currently shoot one another on sight. "No negotiation," as one put it. Some of their other quaint customs include: shooting at anyone taking photos of them or their livestock without permission; shooting at any vehicle that may injure or kill any of their livestock that wander across the road at will; shooting at the next similar make and colour of vehicle if the first one gets away; shooting at this; shooting at that. Shooting seems to be the way the Afar resolve and create all their problems. All I can say is that all the firearms I inspected were well cared for, in good working order and loaded. Their ammunition and firearms are a storehouse of value. When times are good they buy more and then sell when they need cash.

I Survived Abyssinia

And I liked them despite their simple, one-stop solution to all their problems. They were straightforward and direct, and very different from the dishonest and deceitful Oromo farmers.

On the other hand, hunting in the Danakil was disappointing, and at times, downright embarrassing. The main tarred road from Port Assab to Addis Ababa divides the Awash National Park from the hunting concession, a fact emphasized by the many meat-drying racks on the side of the road in the hunting area. The only way to hunt, I was told, was from the truck. Despite my protests, I was assured that the moment you left the truck, the game fled. And so it was that we patrolled the tarred road looking for game en route to the one and only dirt road into and out of the concession, which began about 40 kilometres from our campsite. (Incidentally, this camp move cost an extra $1,500, which we only learnt about on arrival in Addis Ababa).

To compound my discomfort and embarrassment at hunting along a national highway, I discovered that the preferred way of hunting beisa oryx and Soemmering gazelle was to tallyho them in the vehicle across a wide, flat plain in the concession. This I flatly refused to do but I confess to shooting dik-dik, gazelle, and gerenuk from the vehicle on my second to last day in the Danakil. The first little beastie was close by but the other two were both at distances in excess of 250 metres. My practice paid off on this trip and I shot well. I missed nothing. I gave the bohor and Soemmering gazelle a second shot but only the reedbuck really needed it. I was particularly happy with the 321-metre shot on the gerenuk as it quartered away. Unfortunately, not one bullet remained in any of the bodies so I still don't know how the Fail Safe heads performed.

That night, the heavens opened and the rain bucketed down. The next morning, pools of water lay everywhere. The oryx would now leave the plains for the rocky ridges, as the soggy black turf of the flats stuck to and clogged their hoofs and made their footing uncertain. I was all for heading back up the Awash Valley to look for lesser kudu, but to his credit, Sysay insisted we try one last time for oryx.

Heart of an African Hunter

As we approached the last open plain before camp, I glimpsed a flash of brown and what I thought was a Soemmering gazelle in the tree line. No, not a gazelle but one, two . . . at least five oryx. There was nothing for it now but to walk. Despite my suggestion to circle around to the right and approach from downwind through the trees, Sysay and Mamou insisted on the full frontal approach. Of course the oryx ran, but the tracks were clear in the wet ground, which the rain had cleared of all other confusing signs. Off we went, line astern, in the time-honoured hunting tradition. For only the second time on this safari, I felt truly at home and in some sort of control of the hunt.

The first time was on a successful bohor reedbuck stalk in the Kakka Mountains. Sysay sighted the ram directly in front of us at about 350 metres. It had been a good bit of spotting as only the head and horns jutted between the white-flowered shrubs that made the mountainside look as if it were lightly dusted in snow. We dismounted, and behind the cover of a slight hillock, tried to close on the ram. As we crawled to its crest, I looked behind me to see two game guards nonchalantly walking toward us as if out on a Sunday afternoon stroll. Needless to say, the reedbuck was not where we last saw it.

We followed the ram down into a steep, deep valley and when it moved further down and to the right, we climbed back out in a lung-bursting effort to leapfrog the ram. Around the ragged peak, back down into the valley, now with the wind in our favour. I knew he had to be in front of us. He was. Only Sufo did not believe me and wandered off carelessly on his own and spooked the trophy-quality ram for the third and last time.

Sysay was philosophical and convinced we would find the ram again. After my second climb out of the valley, I was too knackered to speak, let alone to express my doubts. But he was right.

On our second to the last day in the mountains, Fiaso spotted him at the foot of a steep-sided, rocky ravine. As we completed our descent, we were frustratingly met by mist welling up from the barley fields below. When the cold, cotton-wool clouds lifted, the ram was long gone. Mamou, who remained in place on the peak, saw him on a plateau over a kilometre away. This ram clearly had a sense of humour.

Mounting our horses we circumscribed a huge semicircle and an hour later, Sysay, Koli (the national game guard), and I side-hilled our way to overlook where we last saw the bohor. Not there. Only one place left. Around Koli went and redeemed himself as the bohor bulleted from the tight ravine in which he sought refuge. Like a bat out of hell, the bohor flew over the golden grass of the plateau to our right.

When he skidded to a stop and looked back toward Koli, he was facing directly toward me, 341 metres away. The wind was gusting strongly from my right and I did not allow enough.

At the shot, the ram took off like a scalded cat directly away from me, around a rocky outcrop and disappeared. Something told me that he had moved up a fold of ground, out of sight and crossed into a neighbouring valley back from whence he had come. While the others fossicked around on the plateau, I pushed my weary body up the mountain once more.

I found him licking the bullet wound on his right rump in a sheltered nook in the next valley. The second shot from the .300 took him cleanly through the shoulders and he barely managed to spin on his heels before collapsing in midstride. A "never say die" determination by the whole hunting team had, at last, given me my first and last trophy in the Arusi Mountain Range.

But back to the beisa oryx. Mamou and I had our noses glued to the tracks and missed the fact that the bull detoured to the right. Sysay spotted him watching us approach at the end of an avenue formed by the thorn trees. His excited "shoot, shoot!" stopped me in midstride, but the antelope was out of the starter's block and thundering away before the .300 cleared my shoulder.

We had been on the tracks for more than an hour. Sysay proposed calling it a day. "You see, you can't hunt on foot; they won't stop running now," he complained. Only the silent, nodding encouragement of the young regional game scout at my lone suggestion to persevere helped me override Sysay's suggestions.

The ground became harder and drier. The tracks became fainter and fainter. We lost time unraveling them where the oryx had milled around grazing. Time stretched.

I caught the glances exchanged between Mamou and Sysay. But I was enjoying myself. I was hunting and I couldn't see why these oryx should behave all that differently from the fringe-eared oryx of Tanzania or the gemsbok of Namibia. I was sure they would stop again, particularly as there were a couple of youngsters in the small herd. And they did.

Sysay was again the one to spot them first. "Shoot, shoot," his explosive whisper erupts in my ear. Looking up from the tracks, I see the chest of a lone oryx through the thorn trees, the head obscured in the foliage. Mamou and the game scout plunge into the grass at my feet. Sysay jams his fingers in his ears. No time. A quick look through the scope. Too unsteady. Too far. I need a rest. Sysay jams the shooting sticks into the sticky, toffee turf. "Quick, quick," he urges. As the cross hairs reach the center of the chest, the shot thunders from the barrel and the oryx takes off at a dead gallop.

"You hit him!" shouts Mamou, heading off in the direction of the departing antelope. "Wait!" I yell. "Mark the spot where the oryx stood. I want to pick up the tracks from there."

We find a bone fragment and a dollop of bright red, foamy blood. Clearly the Winchester Fail Safe bullet had penetrated through the chest cavity, through the lungs, and exited, taking a chunk of rib with it. I feel better still as I pick up an increasingly clear blood trail and a few metres further see the rapier-straight horns of the beisa oryx protruding from a shrub. She is as dead as a doorpost.

Doom and gloom replace chattering, cheerful excitement in three nanoseconds. Eventually the silence is broken by Sysay, hesitantly trying to explain how the mishap happened. According to him there had been another oryx to the left.

I Survived Abyssinia

That was the bull. That was the one he wanted me to shoot. I look at the game scout. He shakes his head. "There was only one," we agree.

Sysay and Mamou propose leaving the oryx in the bush. How they propose to talk their way out of the sItaation, I don't know. I don't care either. I won't have it. We hunted on foot. Fairly and ethically. We made a mistake and must bear the consequences. The Colonel advises me that Sysay will be fined $1,000 and given a severe warning. I pay the fine for Sysay as he pleads poverty. He has no rifle, not even a hunting knife, and I believe him.

The hunt culminates on an even more sour note as we find their surefire lesser kudu area is inhabited, wall to wall, by nomads and their flocks. No one has bothered to check the area since last year. No matter where we try, we are greeted by bleating goats, bellowing cattle, barking dogs, and shouting sheepherders.

The long drive back to the Hilton hotel in Addis Ababa is a silent one as I sit alone with my thoughts. Of the six animals I sought, I had not seen an adult male specimen of any of the top three on my list. Of the remaining three, I shot a female oryx, a so-so Soemmering gazelle, and a disappointing dik-dik. The only other animals that I had seen and taken were a good bohor reedbuck, a decent northern gerenuk, and an ancient colobus monkey, which I wanted to mount above my bongo as a reminder of the monkey that had chased the bongo away in the closing phases of my hunt in the Central African rain forests.

The *coup de grace* was the export arrangements for my six trophies. There is only one taxidermist in the country and all trophies must be exported via this one company. They have the strangest tariff list: one trophy = $100; two to three trophies = $200; four to five trophies = $400; six to ten trophies = $1,300. It took a major debate to reduce the price from $1,300 for my six trophies to $600. The Colonel won the day by suggesting that he deliver them to the taxidermist, three per day, over the next two days in which case the price would be $400.

Heart of an African Hunter

As I said at the outset, hunting in Ethiopia is an extraordinary experience. Not for the fainthearted. Not for the novice. Not like any other hunt you will ever have in Africa. For those who have not tasted all that Africa has to offer, the $40,000 price tag can be better spent elsewhere and on other game. On the other hand, until you have survived Abyssinia, I am not sure you can say you have truly hunted Africa.

CROC AROUND THE ROCK

We lay behind an anthill, glassing one of the inlets leading off Lake Kariba. We were trying to trace the source of the echoing grunt of a large hippopotamus bull. I glanced at the opposite shore through my binoculars, and to my amazement, saw a large crocodile paddling leisurely along with the current, the scales on his back protruding above the water and showing almost his full length. He seemed totally unconcerned, and on reflection, I could see why. If I were that size, I'd probably also be relaxed.

What to do? At a distance of some 600 metres and in deep water, he was out of reach. I turned to my professional hunter, Lou Hallamore, with a questioning look.

"He's going somewhere and I think I know where," said Lou.

He beckoned to me, and we slipped backward through the long grass toward the tree line. As luck would have it, John and Derek drove up in Lou's Land Cruiser. We jumped aboard, and hidden in the tree line, bumped northward along the shore of the inlet.

It was the second day of our safari in the National Forestry Commission's concession surrounding Sijarira in Zimbabwe. The start had been anything but auspicious. Derek's pre-64 Winchester .300 H&H, which had been left in storage and hurriedly collected en route from London to Victoria Falls, suffered a broken scope and someone attacked the ring attaching the extractor to the bolt with a cold chisel, rendering it inoperable. The previous day we made a couple of abortive stalks on hippo, missed our vehicle at the rendezvous point, and hiked eight kilometres back to camp in the dark.

I did not believe we would intercept the crocodile and resigned myself to merely going through the motions. Thoughts of Derek's previous croc hunt in the Okavango Swamps went through my mind. I could still see his pale, drawn face in the firelight, a half-empty bottle of scotch at his elbow, as he told me in an unusually strained voice, "Bloody thing nearly ate me!"

It had been the last day of our hunt in the swamps. Our small aluminum dinghy towing a *mokoro* puttered slowly into a huge lily-pad-covered pool some 300 metres in diameter, with cold, crystal-clear water so deep we could not see the bottom. It was strangely quiet, almost eerie. No bird could be heard; no fish broke the surface of the pond. And then we saw the flattened area on the opposite bank. Huge claw-like footprints covered the area.

We left Derek, a tracker, and the mokoro wedged into a little floating papyrus island 150 metres opposite the spot and set off in the dinghy for pastures new. Some hours later we returned, empty-handed, to find Derek shaking his fist at us. Apparently a huge croc surfaced just as we made our approach but dived again at the sound of the outboard motor.

"He's an absolute monster, a submarine!" exclaimed Derek.

I told Derek I decided to go back for one last try at a leopard that ambled past our camp almost every evening.

"Well, I am not moving from here," he said.

"Are you sure?" I asked. "I'm going to have to take everyone with me to manhandle the boats through some of the overgrown hippo channels on the way back. I don't like the look of this place, and it will be a couple of hours before anyone can return to fetch you."

"I'm staying," he said firmly.

As soon as our boat was out of sight, my last statement started to nag at Derek. Maybe he made a mistake, a bad mistake. His thoughts were interrupted, however, by the intimidating sight of a huge croc heaving himself slowly onto the opposite bank.

It was a long shot, but Derek's an excellent marksman, and with a dead rest, had a lot of confidence in his .300 H&H. The 220-grain bullet struck, and the croc erupted like a Polaris missile, thudding back into the water with a huge splash. Then silence. Complete and utter silence. Where was the croc? Minutes ticked by as Derek gazed anxiously through the reeds. Suddenly, a mere 20 metres in front of him, was the croc, looking straight at him. It was swimming somewhat erratically, one foreleg hunched out of the water in a spasmodic, overhand crawl stroke. A quick second shot. The croc disappeared again.

Derek leapt to his feet to survey the surrounding area. He saw what he thought was movement among the lily pads and fired into them. The thought of this monster lurking beneath the water and preparing to launch itself onto his little island—no more than ten metres in diameter—really unnerved him. He fired again at a noise behind him. He worked the action. Pointed at the water. Pulled the trigger. *Click!* He found himself starting to tremble. In fact, his hands were shaking so much he had trouble reloading. He dropped a couple of cartridges but didn't want to risk bending to retrieve them.

As afternoon slowly changed to evening, all kinds of terrifying thoughts ran through his mind. Would we return? Had Bayete been lost on the way back? Worse still, had he been attacked by a hippo? Would he have to spend the night? When he finally heard the *mokoro* returning, his relief knew no bounds. To his credit, he went back with me before dawn the next day, but despite a diligent search of the area, we found nothing. I know the memory still troubles my friend to this day.

I came back to the present as Lou stopped the vehicle. The four of us slipped out and moved stealthily toward an anthill near the water's edge. A small island lay some 30 metres off-shore, and Derek's eagle eyes spotted the croc just south of it.

"Look for a small piece of dark driftwood that doesn't bob with the ripples," I remember him saying.

Something was worrying the croc. Perhaps he saw us or an eddy of wind carried our scent to him. He would not come out onto the bank but moved around the far side of the island, occasionally disappearing from view.

We held a whispered war counsel and decided that John and Lou would stand up, start talking, and walk openly up the bank and out of sight to the vehicle. In the meantime, Derek and I would leopard-crawl down the bank into a fold of ground closer to the water's edge.

The exercise completed, I lay there catching my breath, head on hands. Derek glassed the breeze-swept bay looking for his nonbobbing driftwood. For the first time since our arrival, my mind was clear of thoughts of rush hour traffic, telephones, business meetings, and so forth.

"He's easing onto the bank," whispered Derek.

We lay as still as stone.

"He seems more relaxed—he's opening his mouth."

I eased my way forward, ever so gently parting the long grass with the barrel of my .375 Brno. I was greeted by the sight of the croc's gaping mouth about 100 metres away. He lay almost head on to me, but at a slight angle to the left. Quite an impressive sight, gazing into the gaping, glistening, bright pink maw edged with a washing-powder-white neck-lace of razor sharp teeth. I felt an involuntary shiver tap dance across my shoulder blades.

Where to shoot him? I tried to work out where his brain was and decided to aim for the back of his palate, slightly to the left of center. I was conscious of how precisely the shot would have to be placed, for I did not relish the thought of paddling around in the murky waters of Lake Kariba looking for a croc that may or may not be dead. It is well known that unless the bullet strikes the brain or spinal column, crocs usually have the tenacity to get back into the water even though mortally wounded. And unlike hippo, they rarely surface again. I have heard of crocs surfacing quite some time after having been shot and killed, but it is difficult, if not impossible, to save the skin in those circumstances.

I gently eased back the safety, took careful, steady aim and squeezed the trigger. As I recovered from the recoil, I saw that the croc snapped its mouth shut tight, and its tail was furiously churning up water and mud. But it moved not an inch from the spot. Derek jumped to his feet.

"Brilliant shot!" he shouted.

The croc's tail slowed, then stopped. John and Lou came running toward us. Grinning happily, Derek and I pointed at the 13-foot, 4-inch croc.

With some trepidation and a great deal of care, we all waded across to the island to inspect the croc. He was the biggest Derek and I had ever seen. Angus van Jaarsveld, the son of a croc farmer at Binga, told me later that in all the years they've owned the farm (which currently houses some eight thousand crocs in captivity) the largest female they ever caught measured 10 feet 6 inches and the largest male 15 feet 6 inches. So we were all rather pleased with the way events turned out, especially as this was the first shot fired in earnest on our safari. Good spotting, followed by a careful and well planned stalk, and even if I say so myself, a pretty fair shot to conclude matters. Little did we know that subsequent events were to make the day's hunting pale into insignificance.

The next few days were spent hunting hippo—a far more elusive quarry than we anticipated, particularly trophy bulls in an area that is regularly hunted. We moved down-lake from Sijarira and hunted along the Gwaai, a tributary of the Zambezi, looking for Chobe bushbuck and klipspringer as well as croc and hippo. Churning upstream in our modern, 16-foot, red and cream power boat, John and I were facing the stern when, to our amazement, we simultaneously spotted a German U-boat beached on the bank. No, not a sub, but a gigantic, enormous crocodile sunning himself at the water's edge, partially screened by a lush patch of green grass. I grabbed hold of Lou who was piloting the boat, and almost speechless, pointed downstream. He instantly cut the motor and we drifted toward the bank. We were a good 300 metres away, yet as we nudged the bank, the croc slewed violently to his right and with a stunningly rapid, sinuous, squirming movement, disappeared under the green-gray greasy waters of the Gwaai.

Immediately a babble of comment broke out on the boat.

"He looked like a U-boat," I said.

"Absolutely incredible," said Lou, shaking his head. "But don't worry, we'll come back and get him tomorrow."

I thought the likelihood of such an old, experienced croc being caught out on the bank a second time in broad daylight was about as likely as Lou falling pregnant. I am glad I never said so.

We hunted the tributary the rest of the day and a most successful day it was. I shot a 16¾-inch Chobe bushbuck and a 5½-inch klipspringer, both ranking in the top twenty in Rowland Ward. The place absolutely abounded with these species, and we became quite blasé about rejecting trophy-size bushbuck to look for something bigger.

The following dawn found us speeding up the Zambezi, the water like glass, the crisp morning air biting through our jackets and bringing tears to our eyes. I felt good, fit, and delighted to be alive. Anticipation was palpable in the boat. A few kilometres from the spot where we'd seen the croc, Lou eased off the throttle and we burbled quietly forward.

Nearing the spot, we could see no sign of the croc and my thoughts of the previous day surfaced again, but I said nothing.

Croc Around the Rock

We spent the next couple of hours checking for bushbuck and hippo until Lou impatiently voiced everybody's thoughts.

"Let's go have another look if he's back. Maybe it was too early, not warm enough for him."

From 500 metres away, we could see the huge bulk of the croc sunning himself. He was even bigger than my memory served me. Our pulses quickened. We held a conference. The wind was wrong and we could not approach him from this direction. To climb off the boat and circle around the hills would probably take too long, would involve crossing another stream, and would bring Derek out in an area with very little cover. It was then that Lou's experience really told.

"If we zoom past him, not too fast, not too slow, he might think we haven't seen him and just lie there. The sun is ideal now; he's feeling nice and warm and won't want to get back into the cold water. Remember how he ignored us initially last time? Only when we stopped did he get a fright."

Holding thumbs, we put Lou's plan into action and it worked like a dream. Although we could hardly bear to look, the croc didn't move as we passed.

This time we powered upstream for some 1,500 metres before stopping. After some detailed plotting, Derek and John left on foot. The idea was that they would stalk close to the water's edge until they reached a big boulder jutting out from the riverbank. Then, behind the cover of the rock, they were to slip up into the tree line, climb up a steep slope and descend to the edge of the tree line above the croc. Derek took my .375, as he was more confident with it. We estimated that the closest he would get to the croc was about 150 metres, so pinpoint accuracy would be required.

Lou and I watched anxiously through the binoculars. Time dragged. The silence settled heavily on us. We could hear the odd fish breaking the surface of the water, while lily trotters paddled along the shoreline, splashing and disturbing the reeds. An air of expectancy seemed to hang over the place.

The shot came unexpectedly. My binoculars jerked involuntarily in my hands but I could clearly make out the pale green underbelly of the croc as it leapt vertically into the air. A huge splash followed, then the croc roared skyward again, then more spray, then croc. .

"We're going to lose him," shouted Lou, starting the motor.

We tore away from the bank and powered full throttle toward the spot. I could just see the croc as Lou slammed the motor into reverse. It was spinning in the water, snapping its huge jaws with branch-breaking cracks. Every now and then a limb would break the surface and then its awesome head would appear. It was gigantic, as long as our boat.

Simon and Lou tried to attach a noose to its back leg but it kept slithering off the slimy scales. I was trying to maneuver the boat, never having piloted one before. Forward, blip the throttle, too far. Neutral. Reverse. Turn, turn, turn. Stop. Frustrations were shouted back and forth from boat to shore. Just as we thought it was dead it would erupt, spinning violently like a high speed turbine. Thrash. Thrash. And disappear. As we gazed anxiously into the opaque water, it would float, pale green belly up to the surface, behind, in front, on the opposite side of the boat. And the process would begin again. We were making no progress. It was simply too dangerous to approach the business end of the croc. I could see that the bullet penetrated above the right eye but it was clearly not a fatal shot. We had to do something or else we were going to lose him. I was worried that he would sink and not surface, or get lodged under the thick mat of grass extending from the bank, or worse, recover his senses, nail one of us, and swim off.

Without thinking too clearly—make that not at all—I snatched up a rifle and chambered a round. As the thrashing head appeared, I shot it fair and square in the brain box, leaned over, grabbed its front left paw and heaved. As I did so, Simon slipped the noose over a back paw and tied it tight. We had it!

Croc Around the Rock

We towed the croc to shore. Even though we saw it through binoculars, nothing quite prepared us for the size of this monster—16 feet 1 inch long, and according to the 22nd edition of Rowland Ward, the largest Nile crocodile recorded! Clearly big enough to exorcise all of Derek's old nightmares. The original denizen of the deep.

Jaws the croc was simply too big to put into the boat and the seven of us could not lift him, so we rolled him onto the bank and skinned him there and then. The thing that amazed me most about the awesome prehistoric eating machine was his mouth. Having learnt from Peter Beard (of *Eyelids in the Morning* fame) not to climb into the croc's mouth—the stomach acid badly burnt his legs when he did it—I merely lay next to the beast. He could have inhaled my pale, puny body like an asparagus stalk.

I lifted his upper jaw. It was heavy, really heavy. I dropped it. It closed with a clang. A precise, neat, clunk of a sound. I found myself thinking involuntarily of the door of a large steel gun safe. Expecting to find evidence of past human meals in his stomach, we found nothing but the ever-present stones and a handful of fishing lures—bright, shiny, bronze spinners. Maybe he was still suffering from his winter appetite loss, or from some illness because his skin hung loosely on him, like a badly tailored suit. Nevertheless, despite all those fishermen's stories about 20-foot crocodiles, as far as I am aware, this is the largest croc, properly measured in front of witnesses, that has ever been shot.

'ill Stephens, my giant 6-foot, 5-inch guide and lifesaver in Alaska at base camp.

e and Derek Carstens alongside the amphibian, which took us from Cordova, Alaska, to eadwood Lake, to catch a Super Cub to an even smaller lake. In all, it took me three days d six flights to get from Johannesburg to the Gravina River, Alaska.

Gravina River, Alaska. The diamond of snow marks the spot where we saw the hu[...] 10-foot-plus bulldozer bear.

Bohor reedbuck—Arusi Mountains, Ethiopia. The only animal taken during twenty-o[...] days of mountain nyala hunting.

heo Pretorius, head of film production at VWV, me, and G.T. Ferreira, chairman of rst Rand Limited, at a fly camp at 13,400 feet in the Arusi Mountains, Ethiopia. The mperatures were below freezing.

e, Bora, and Bulti en route from the Arusi Mountains to Kubsa.

At 13,400 feet near a fly camp in the Arusi Mountains. The three of us abou to split up—Theo to the Bale Mountains and G. T. to the Danakil. retrospect, I should have left as well.

Our home for four days while hunting the area in vain for the two big bulls th turned out to be small juveniles—Tucul, Kubsa Mountains, Ethiopia.

lassing a valley for mountain nyala in the Arusi Mountains, Ethiopia.

My soemmerring gazelle—Danakil Desert, Ethiopia. Note that Hassan, the Afc tribesman on the far right has changed out of his traditional dress to avoi being recognized by Essa tribesmen since there is a blood feud raging betwee the two tribes.

Northern gerenuk—Danakil Desert, Ethiopia. The desert was lush and green afte unseasonal rains.

*maele, Afar tribesman and camp guard—Danakil Desert, Ethiopia. The Afar
ere intrigued by my rifle. After a lopsided shooting competition—their iron
ghts versus my telescopic sights—and a gift of ammunition, the tribesmen
came friendly, cooperative, and worked hard.*

Bora (my horse), Bulti (my horse puller), and his relatives on the way back from Kubs

Gamou, a local tribesman, Syfou, and colobus monkey—Kubsa Mountain Ethiopia. I wanted to place this monkey above my full-mount bongo to remir myself of the time I was stalking another bongo and a similar monkey scar it off—when I was only 40 paces away!

amou, me, Menayee, Koli, and Abebe in Tucul. Menayee claimed to have seen the *o big bulls at Kubsa that turned out to be juveniles.*

cal village chairman and villagers—Kubsa Mountains, Ethiopia. Gamou in front (middle) *as the local poacher-turned-guide who promised all and delivered nothing.*

My 13-foot, 4-inch croc—Lake Kariba, Zimbabwe.

Even though there were six of us, we could not lift the massive animal. We had to roll onto shore.

...ango, John Oosthuizen, Derek Carstens, Lou Hallamore, Simon Gwenzi, and world ...cord croc—Gwaai River, Zimbabwe.

...erb Kortof and gemsbok—Agtersneeuberg Nature Reserve, Karoo, Eastern Cape.

My 42½-inch lion bait—Rungwa River, Tanzania.

Gemsbok—Okakarara, Namibia.

My first sable bull—Elmboog Ranch, South African lowveld. That is grimace of reli rather than a smile of happiness.

...able—Matetsi, Zimbabwe. These are tough, proud, magnificent animals, and, except ...or the first bull, I have never used anything less than a .375.

...atal red duiker—Hluhluwe, Natal.

John McCullogh, Richard Flack, Mswele, and Richard's nyala—Hluhluwe, Natal.

A quality common reedbuck, my son, and me—Hluhluwe, Natal, South Africa.

iew from my bedroom—Zulu Nyala Hunting Lodge—Hluhluwe, Natal.

ulu Nyala Hunting Lodge—Hluhluwe, Natal.

Richard Flack and the two southern bush duiker referred to in the story.

Common reedbuck shot by Richard Flack—Hluhluwe, Natal.

My blue duiker—CAR.

Louis Marais and his oribi—Oribi Gorge, Natal. Louis is a top Bisley shot, degree farmer, and highly experienced professional hunter. I have hunted with Lou every year for the last eighteen years.

The Cape grysbok is a dainty and petite member of the Tiny Ten.

...al rhebok—Agtersneeuberg Nature Reserve, Karoo, Eastern Cape. In my opinion, ...is is one of the most challenging trophies in southern Africa and a wonderfully ...warding hunt.

...e, my son, and suni. Sometimes after bitter disappointments, missed opportunities, and ...lly mistakes, Diana smiles on you. This hunt was one of those times.

Danie van Rensburg and me with a chocolate brown southern bush duiker found at t
Agtersneeuberg Nature Reserve.

Mermaid carved out of soapstone by a policeman stationed in the area in the likeness
his daughter—Shlaralumi River, South African lowveld.

oribi.

*excellent 4⁷⁄₈-inch klipspringer—Gwaai River, Zimbabwe.   Proof yet again that
u should always take the animal your pro wants to shoot.*

A good quality Cape springbok. Kalahari springbok are longer, paler, bigger, and ha[far better horns—Agtersneeuberg Nature Reserve, Karoo, Eastern Cape.

Young Stephen Griffin at Karoo Safaris with a representative white springbok Agtersneeuberg Nature Reserve, Karoo, Eastern Cape. These springbok are a colo variation of ordinary springbok and not albinos.

THE PERFECT MODEL
OF A
MODERN MAJOR UNICORN

The Skeleton Coast, Namibia. December heat waves warp the air waves. Mythical moisture trembles in retreat in front of me. I drive the open, short-wheel-base Land Rover. Shirt off, elbow resting on the door. My hair and eyebrows are bleached white by the sun—my body so tanned my new girlfriend's mother asked, only half seriously, if I was an albino.

I was eighteen. Army training a month behind me. I was marking time. Sammy Collins—Mr. Collins to me—offered me a job on his diamond barges off the Namibian coast. Two weeks on, one week off in Cape Town. What a gas!

I was allocated to the land geological survey team. Our water came from Oranjemund some ninety kilometres to the east, so our boss decided to save costs. "Sink a well," he said. We did. Good, clean, hard, physical labour for the team of energetic youngsters he had under some sort of control some of the time.

I loved the Skeleton Coast. From the rolling morning mists seeping in over greasy, heaving, twenty-foot swells to the stark, pink-purpled, rock-shod mountains as the sun scorched its way down over the western horizon. The coast was a country of contrasts. The ice-cold ocean waters burnt when we dived for *kreef* (crayfish) among the sinister, slick, waving kelp. The sun burnt us biltong brown and dried us like *bokoms*—the sun-dried fish and staple food of the West Coast. The coast was barren, pure, unpolluted, and uninhabited. At times I felt like the man in the moon crossing the lunar landscape of dunes and rock-filled plains.

And yet I had seen *strandwolwe* (striped hyena) from the window of my cabin while on night duty. Black-backed jackal (mistakenly called silver-backed jackal by some) roamed the shore in the early mornings and I had seen baboon and ostrich.

I was thinking of none of these things as I drove in a total *dwaal* (daydream) toward our well-sinking site. George, our German shephard ex-guard dog, (ex because he had been fired for friendliness) panted, pink tongue lolling, over my left shoulder. Behind and to his left, Dezzi and Maxi, a pair of boxers in their prime, stared over the side of the vehicle. A startled woof in my ear woke me from my reverie, and before I knew what was what, the dogs bailed out of the moving Land Rover and were streaking across the sand like RPG7s. George was in the lead, the boxers chasing like greyhounds after a rabbit, their yelping cries fading into the veld.

As my eyes followed their line of advance, I felt as if someone had suddenly grabbed a handful of my heart. At the well stood a unicorn silhouetted against the cream-coloured dunes. The gemsbok bull stood like stone. Even as panic surged through me as the dogs closed the gap to the gemsbok, the thought flashed through my mind—*magnificent!* He was regal, royal, unflustered by the baying banshees howling for his hide. I thought he was transfixed. I hooted. Yelled. Waved my arms as I gunned the Land Rover through the thick, ponderous, powder sand. It was straight out of a nightmare. You know the one. The ghouls are coming. Slobbering, slavering for your blood. You run but your legs don't work. The harder you try the slower you go. And then you wake. I didn't.

The Perfect Model of a Modern Major Unicorn

But at last the gemsbok turned and nonchalantly trotted away like a quarter horse, angling away across the side of the dune. George ran to cut him off and then, inexplicably, stopped and sat down, wagging his tail. Not so the boxers. As Dezzi ranged alongside the bull, he stopped in a puff of dust, and with a flip of his head, so fast it made my eyes water, speared the dog in midair. One of the rapier horns penetrated clear through Dezzi's chest cavity. Maxi braked with all four legs, sat on her backside, bunched and turned to run, gathering her legs beneath her. Too late! The gemsbok killed her instantly with a thunderous thrust that traversed the length of her body.

He stood and surveyed the scene. The conqueror—cool, collected. Chaos everywhere else. As I closed the gap, he continued on his path up and over the edge of the dune. Gone. I was in a vacuum, a time warp. In retrospect, the whole sequence of events probably lasted no longer than sixty seconds.

Maxi was dead when I got to her. Dezzi was in very poor shape but alive. Although he miraculously recovered, he was never the same dog. And George—well, he was just confused. I mean, this was meant to be fun, a romp—not so? Like chasing jackal along the shoreline.

To say that the gemsbok bull made an impression on me would be an understatement of gigantic proportions. I was shattered. The death of a friend. The rapidity of events. The near fatal injury to Dezzi. The total ease and grace of the gemsbok. Awe is the word. I stood in awe as the desert closed around me and I began to come to grips with the reality of the situation.

Twelve years later. Still in Namibia. Hair still blond but thinning badly. No tan. I walked through the sandy Mariental soil behind the slender, overall-clad figure of a local Koranna tracker. I had shot the gemsbok bull in the throat with a 270-grain .375 Winchester Power Point as it peered over a bush at me. Distance about 120 paces.

To my absolute amazement, the bull took off running. We found him some 700 metres away, lying down and backed under a thorn bush. My tracker did not have to hold me back. I knew what those horns could do. I did not know that they could be used to bat away the stone my tracker threw at the sick animal.

Awe was the word again. I stood with head bowed next to the magnificent animal. His body stiffened, the hair on his hide stood upright, and he moved on to the great, green, grazing grounds in the sky. And he shrank. My first gemsbok bull shrank before my eyes. As I carefully examined the buck, I realized he was much smaller than he appeared on the hoof. *Just like the black wildebeest,* I thought. Tougher than titanium. Larger than life. An animal with presence. But, in reality, smaller than they appear.

I have always been careful with gemsbok, very careful. Maybe that's why I have never had any trouble with them. I have hunted them on a number of occasions, and although I always enjoyed the hunts, I never found gemsbok or their cousins, the sable and roan, as challenging as the spiral-horned antelope. It seems to me that I have found it easier to stalk and sneak closer to oryx than, for example, kudu.

My last hunt for gemsbok was in the Okakarara district of Namibia. It was a case in point. Late one afternoon I was slouching quietly through the bushveld, very reminiscent of the bushveld around the Warmbaths district in South Africa. I was walking more than hunting, but my .375 was loaded and slung over my shoulder and my compact 10X25 binoculars were safely housed in my shirt pocket. The fresh, heart-shaped tracks of a large gemsbok crossing my path immediately perked my interest. I cannot age tracks with any degree of certainty, but these were here and now, crisp and clear, free from dust and *gogga* (insect) tracks.

Right hand down and the game was on. The bull's tracks meandered, joined others, and it was clear they were grazing

The Perfect Model of a Modern Major Unicorn

and browsing. Gemsbok do both. Good. I would be moving and so would they. I lost the bull's tracks in the herd, but by following the herd, picked them up again. After an hour of walk, stop, look, listen, I picked up the horns of a gemsbok sticking out above the long grass. The horns were long, thin, and asymmetrical. *Cow,* I thought. A bull's horns are thicker, usually shorter; binoculars made out others. Eventually I spotted a bull standing off to one side, gazing into space. The sandy soil allowed me to leopard-crawl in a flanking move downwind of the dozing cow, my rifle resting across my forearms. The breeze was constant, but when I was some forty metres away, I had to stop for fear of giving the cow my wind. I rested, regained my breath and carefully rose to a kneeling position. The bull was about eighty paces away. He never knew what hit him. I used the shot taught to me by my hunting partner of many years, Derek Carstens. In line with the foreleg and nine to ten inches down from top of the shoulder. A devastating, killing spine shot.

The bull was a beauty. Two inches short of Mr. Ward's minimum trophy standards but thick, straight, black, symmetrical horns. A good representative of the species. But I doubt that a kudu bull of similar age and size or a kudu herd of similar number would have let me get as close. As I studied the bull, I thought, *Amazing animals, perfectly designed for dry, hot regions.*

In *Mammals of the Southern African Subregion,* the authors, J. Skinner and R. Smither, note:

> When gemsbok were subjected to high temperatures, their body temperatures increased. After three to four hours of exposure to high temperature, their evaporative processes accelerated to prevent a further rise in temperature. . . . This meant that they could get past the hottest hours of the day before expending moisture for cooling, thus saving large amounts of water, even when under severe heat load. . . . In

addition, they have mechanisms to ensure that the blood circulating to the brain remains substantially cooler than it does to other parts of the body. The carotid artery, which supplies most of the blood to the brain, divides into retia in the head where it is cooled by venous blood from the nasal passages before passing to the brain. Panting increases the air flow over the capillaries of the veins to achieve this cooling process. . . . When gemsbok were deprived of water, they did not sweat at all in response to heat, but began to pant when their body temperature exceeded 4 degrees Celsius.

And so it was that my partner, Louis Marais, introduced them to our game ranch in the arid Karoo of the Eastern Cape. They are the logo on the letterhead of our company, and our breeding herds, after a period of adaptation, are going from strength to strength. Only problem is, Louis likes them so much no one is allowed to hunt them!

THE BLACK-WHITE BELLY,
OR
HIPPOTRAGUS NIGER TO YOU

I suppose everybody has their favourite animal, and I would be the last to argue with someone who chose a statuesque kudu bull, an arrogant nyala ram, or a dainty Chobe bushbuck. For me, however, a sable bull is what it's all about. Its pride, its power, its colour contrasts, its courage, its majestic sweeping horns. It is one of the most mythical, magical, beautiful creatures on this planet. Rowland Ward's *Records of Big Game* has this to say:

> This animal, with its stately bearing and magnificent colouration, is one of the most beautiful of all antelope. Its courage is proverbial, and Selous relates how a pack of strong dogs were either killed or wounded within seconds after attacking a wounded bull. It has a majestic head and massive, heavily ringed horns rising vertically from the skull and sweeping back in a semicircular curve. It is somewhat smaller than its close relative the roan.
>
> The upper body of an adult bull sable is covered with black hair, presenting a satin-like sheen, while the cows have a lighter body colour. The underparts are white (hence the Afrikaans name *swartwitpens* meaning 'black-white belly'), and the tail is tufted.

Heart of an African Hunter

The *SCI Record Book of Trophy Animals* states:

> A good sable is a spectacular trophy that is essential to any African collection. As it tends to be belligerent rather than wary, a sable bull is usually approachable. Shot placement is very important, as is the calibre used, because sable are 'hard' animals. May be dangerous when wounded.

Pity that I only bought the book later, much later. I could have used the advice, as you will see.

And here I was in Gravelotte, just south of Phalaborwa, Transvaal, South Africa, on the last day of my third hunt, to try to outwit one particular sable bull. Why one? Well, for reasons known only to the game rancher, he only had two sable bulls—no cows—and was prepared to let me have the bigger of the two at an affordable price.

The first hunt had been more of a reconnaissance than a hunt. The second was an unmitigated disaster from start to finish. It had been a last minute decision, and in the rush to pack and leave, I took my .458 instead of my .375—a mistake not too difficult to make as they were both identical Brno rifles topped by identical 1.5–4X compact variables. In fact, I only discovered the error when, on sighting in, the bullet hit the ground some twenty feet in front of the target. A bit like those nightmares when, on being confronted by a slobbering, slavering, blood-dripping burglar, you fire your potent, man-stopping pistol only to find that the bullet trickles down the barrel and falls with a hollow plop onto the ground. Terrifying! They tell me that such dreams have Freudian connotations, but what the hell, I've had them and it's no good denying it.

From there, things went from bad to worse. I borrowed a .375 with a trigger pull like the elastic in a very old and thoroughly perished pair of pyjama bottoms. Not by a long shot the crisp, 2½-pound pull on the Timney triggers I used. Shots seemed to be released by random selection. To make things even more frustrating, I managed to track the sable and sneak within shooting range twice. A feat that was not as easy as it sounds, given the rocky, ridge-like terrain, the cornflake crackling of dry mopane leaves underfoot, and the sparseness of cover in the stark, gray, Gravelotte area in midwinter.

The first time we came upon one another quite by accident. It was an overcast, gusty midmorning. I was out in the open—so was the sable. He was in a small dip some 200 metres away. I could see his head and horns but no other part of him when I knelt or sat to steady the rifle amongst the bobbing, bowing, golden grass. It was more than double the distance that I would normally attempt an offhand shot and I could get no closer. So we stood and looked at one another, both of us equally bemused, before the bull trotted away through the arthritic, twisted fingers of the leafless mopane branches.

We let him settle down and then took up the tracks once again. I began moving through thick, noisy, intertwined scrub, and knowing the sable's habit of watching his backtracks once disturbed, decided to take a chance. He seemed to be moving steadily in a southwesterly direction and I jogged off downwind and to the right, hoping to hit a farm track where I could make better time and possibly pick up his tracks crossing the road.

My plan worked almost too well, and walking around a 90-degree left-hand bend in the road, I caught a movement through the ghostly, gray trees on my left. Without hesitating, I flung myself down in the dry, brittle grass on the side of the track. I reached for the thick webbing sling of my .375 to wrap around my left arm to steady myself, only to realize that Bertha (my .375) was at home in my gun safe. My breathing started to settle as the huge, lone bull eased his way across the road, quartering away from me. I gave a short, high-pitched whistle. He stopped in his tracks, turned and looked back and down his nose at me from some 270 paces away. I flicked down the Mauser flag-type safety and settled the cross hairs behind the front leg, two-thirds of the way up from the bottom of the sable's stark, bright, white-washed belly, aiming to drive the bullet through the offside foreleg. I breathed in and then out and gently squeezed the trigger. I squeezed and squeezed and squeezed– the cross hairs acquired a life of their own and began to bobble around. I was beginning to wonder whether something was wrong with the rifle, whether the safety was properly off and started slackening my grip on the stock. As I started to lift my head, the gun went off and I had a superb view of the shot striking the ground between the sable's feet. The sable was like a lighthouse at night– now you see it, now you don't! I cannot begin to describe the language that bubbled through my brain. I did not know who to be angry with–myself for leaving my favourite rifle behind, with the borrowed weapon, or the weapon's owner. In the end, honesty won. I had only myself to blame.

It was a long, dismal, 6½-hour drive back to Johannesburg in the Land Cruiser and yet, toward the end of the trip, I was planning my hunt for the following year, already hoping that no one else would get a chance at "my" sable bull.

People tried and people failed, and I was back again a year later, older and wiser, and definitely more organized. It hadn't helped all that much though, as I spent the best part of a week tracking the sable. The closest I came was a brief blur of black through some mopane scrub. I was fast running out of time. In fact, it was midmorning on our last day. To make matters worse, I lodged the Land Cruiser firmly in a dry riverbed while trying to recover my hunting partner's Rowland Ward red hartebeest. The riverbank over which I drove caved in and left us well and truly stuck. The hitch and back bumper hung from the riverbank, leaving the rear wheels suspended in midair. Jogging back to camp to fetch the tractor–hot, sweaty, and frustrated–the last thing on my mind was sable. As I bumbled through the entrance to the camp, I saw the ranch owner's vehicle. He had decided to pay us a visit on our last day to say good-bye before we left. As he saw me, he started waving and came walking toward me.

"Come quickly", he said, "I've been waiting for you. Your sable is in the bush just off the road to the gate." With that, a friend of his arrived and confirmed the news.

Based on the experience of my last trip, where the only possible shots at the sable were at distances of more than 200 metres, I brought along my 7mm Remington Magnum as well as my .375. Hesitating for a moment, I made a bad mistake, picked up the 7mm and some 176-grain, spire, pointed Hornady softs and ran to the friend's open Jeep. Derek, my hunting partner, jumped into the back and we shot off in a cloud of dust. As we approached the spot where the friend had seen the sable, we slowed down, and with the motor barely ticking over, approached the spot. We all saw him at the same time, standing in thick bush facing directly toward us. In his excitement, our driver missed the brakes and we rolled past the sable. He had been standing to the left of a large, dark tree trunk, which now obscured him totally. Our driver was beside himself with excitement.

He started mumbling to himself, "Oh my God, he's going to get away—shoot, shoot, shoot!"

I had never seen "buck fever" in a driver before, but if this wasn't it, it was the next best thing. Before I could get out, he jammed the Jeep into reverse and we hiccuped backward. The tree now obscured the left side and foreleg of the sable. By now our driver was incoherent. I could see the sable was tense, looking to its right and ready to run. I had to make a decision and quickly. Various thoughts flashed through my mind as the Jeep rocked around as our driver squirmed in his seat, no longer mumbling but almost shouting to me to shoot the animal.

Now I hunt on foot and mostly on my own or with the help of a tracker. I had spent days hunting this sable on foot, and at last, here he was. I did not want to shoot him from the Jeep and yet I did not want to lose him. The whole situation seemed surreal to me. I swiveled in my seat, rested my elbows on my knees, and looked through the sights at the sable, the cross hairs bobbing around the chest area. At 150 metres, I knew I could not miss but I was scared of the tree. In one of my worst hunting decisions, I let the shot go. The sable bolted frantically through the bush and I could hear the brush crashing. I aimed for the heart and the frantic burst from the sable seemed to confirm it. Our driver was now out of the vehicle, running after the disappearing sable bull, shouting that I should shoot again, that I had missed it, that it was going to get away.

Derek ran up behind our driver and grabbed him by the shoulder. I could see anger written all over his normally amiable and friendly face.

"Shut up, just shut up!" he said. "Go back to the vehicle and wait."

I thought he was going to hit him.

Turning to me he said, "Come on, Pete, let's see what has happened."

After about 500 metres, we caught sight of the bull walking slowly away from us. I knew I hit the bull. My only thought was to make up for the previous shot and kill the magnificent animal as quickly and cleanly as possible. I took the only shot available to me, and from a standing position, aimed at the base of the spine and fired. The sable staggered, half fell, and was up and running as I fired a quick second shot. The situation had reached nightmarish proportions.

"How was the shot?" Derek asked.

"Good," I said.

"Listen, I think that rifle is just too light for the sable. I am going back to camp to get your .375 and I'm going to take this fellow with me," Derek said, jerking a thumb over his shoulder at our driver. "You stay on the tracks and just mark your trail. I'll find you."

Quiet descended over the bush as the sound of the Jeep faded away. The sun baked down and the heavy midday silence settled. I was thoroughly shaken by the whole experience, and with a conscious effort, dragging a stick behind me, I took up the tracks. At times I had to cast around but, fortunately, there was enough blood for me to pick up the tracks again.

The tracks went on and on. My shirt was soaked through with perspiration. The tracks became confused, and at times, the blood spoor seemed to dry up. Afterward, we worked out that the sable had joined up with the other bull. Much later, Derek and Alfred, an excellent tracker, caught up with me and handed me my .375.

"I'm going up ahead to check the cutline in the direction that the bull is moving," Derek said.

"Fine," I answered. "If he comes that way, please put him down."

In the end, I nearly walked right into the sable as it lay in the shade of some wilting *vaalbos*. The bull struggled to its feet. I dropped to my knees, cradled my favourite rifle to my cheek and immediately squeezed off a shot aimed at the point of the shoulder. The sable crumpled. To my absolute horror, he started to struggle to his feet again. *What does it take?* I asked myself in desperation. My old habit of rechambering my rifle immediately after a shot saved the day as I put a second bullet within an inch of the first. At last! It was all over.

Afterward, I asked myself how I could have made so many elementary mistakes. How, after years of hunting, I had allowed myself to be chivied into the folly in which I had become involved. And never again did I hunt anything the size and toughness of a sable with my 7mm Remington Magnum, although the rifle still plays an important role in my battery. Whether it was poor shot placement, too much velocity from too close, the bullet striking a bone, poor bullet construction, or whatever, the 7mm bullets failed to hold together and penetrate sufficiently to hit a vital spot. Only the 270-grain Winchester Power Points from my .375 held together and penetrated in a straight line through the heart and chest cavity, stopping under the skin of the off foreleg.

While that sable hunt has haunted me for years, it also served to reinforce so many basic lessons that I have learnt over forty years of hunting—to hunt ethically on foot, to hunt on my own or only with close, tried and trusted friends, to use the right calibre weapon and the right bullets, to only take a shot once and be totally convinced that it will result in a humane and immediate kill.

Over the years, although the hard-learnt lessons remained, the unhappy memories faded. I became, I believe, a better hunter, more thorough, more careful, and when I was offered the opportunity to hunt sable in the Matetsi area of Zimbabwe, one of the best sable areas in the world, I decided it was time to try to put the bad memories to bed.

After the scarcity of sable in South Africa, it was an absolute delight to walk and drive through the Singuja Hills and along the Bingwa Loop and see herd upon herd of these magnificent animals. I took my time. I studied the difference between herd bulls and .erritorial bulls. I saw how the biggest bulls staked out the best territories. I watched and watched; the little ones, still brown with spiky horns, nudging their mothers—the herd bulls standing with their forelegs on a termite mound to make themselves look even bigger and more imposing. It was truly a wonderful experience. The big 45-inch bulls for which Matetsi is renowned eluded me, however, and the days started to slip into one another. I climbed the hills, walked along the watercourses and drove kilometres looking for fresh tracks. Nothing in the 42-inch-plus Rowland Ward class.

It was midday. We were picking our way through a sterile area of impenetrable bush, which the locals call *gussu*. The sun was pounding. My head was hanging. My blood sugar level was low. I was hot, sweaty, sticky, and tired. I hadn't eaten since 5 A.M. and my thoughts were centered on an ice cold drink and not my surroundings. The thick, soft, red Kalahari sand was cramping my calves.

The Black-White Belly, or *Hippotragus niger* to You

Suddenly James, my tracker, grabbed my arm and pointed. My professional hunter, John Oosthuizen, not exactly known for becoming excitable in any hunting environment, pointed and in an animated way exclaimed, "Take him!" At first I could only see a vague, black form through the bush ahead, but as the animal turned to the left to pass behind the trunk of a midsize baobab, I caught the briefest glimpse of the elegant sweep of a sable bull's horns. He did not seem aware of our presence, although we were only some seventy paces away. He too had the plods.

Moving out from behind the tree, the bull had a mere five or six paces to travel before he disappeared into the *gussu*. I had only a few seconds to aim and fire before the sable disappeared. Quickly, but without haste, I cradled my faithful old .375 to my cheek, found the spot on the bull's shoulder and squeezed the trigger. The bull collapsed instantly, killed as quickly and cleanly as could be by the devastating spinal shot that Derek taught me—nine to ten inches down from the top of the shoulder and in line with foreleg. And that was that!

The bull was a beauty—pitch black and long, sweeping horns. Just not quite high enough in the front to beat Mr. Ward's minimum standard but close enough to make no difference. And, in time, two more bulls fell to Bertha—one in Zimbabwe, one in Tanzania, both killed with the first shot. The larger of the two hangs on my study wall to this day, opposite the third largest roan ever shot in South Africa (but that's another story). The other stands on a pedestal mount in our lounge. I have laid the nightmare to rest, in my own mind at least.

OF SUNI AND SONS

My cup was overflowing. That familiar "school's out" exhilaration was coursing through my veins as we sped southward to the rolling green hills of Natal, South Africa. The lanky sixteen-year-old at my side, whose profile I glimpsed out of the corner of my eye, calmly watched the golden grass of the Transvaal flash past.

"You must always have something to look forward to—no matter how big or small," is a favourite saying of my old hunting companion, Derek. And I had been looking forward to this hunt with my son for almost a year.

Richard first fired a rifle at the age of four—a .22 Brno fitted with a silencer and loaded with subsonic rounds. I still carry the picture in my mind's eye of an overall-clad Dennis the Menace, with hair sprouting like spiky pineapple leaves, and a rifle butt tucked under his armpit, trying to sight with his left eye while shooting right-handed. To me, it is a most endearing, if not eccentric, portrait of my son as a very young boy.

I remember his first dassie (rock hyrax). I remember his first buck—a fallow deer shot with Louis in the Karoo. I had been too nervous to take my son out myself. Too keen for him to want to hunt. Too keen to share my passion, and ultimately, too afraid that my enthusiasm might put him off. And so, after weeks on the rifle range and days on the farm dassie hunting, Louis took him out. He shot perfectly. A clean neck shot as the deer gazed away into the wind. He used his mother's 7x57mm Brno. He was twelve, already showing signs that he was going to be as tall as my 6 feet 3 inches but still not really suited to the rifle. In fact, I even remember the startled, stunned mullet look on his face as he turned to me after squeezing off the first shot on the rifle range. "Yoh! Dad!" But it got better; it also got worse.

There was the wild goat that we had to cull in the mountains. A long, leopard crawl over the rock-strewn, sandstone ledges, through the spiky Karoo bushes and then another clean shot. My ego nearly crippled me. When Richie could not help carry the goat any farther, I hoisted it onto my shoulders and carried it the remaining two kilometres. I almost burst a valve, but the look of admiration on my son's face was compensation enough. Until I awoke the next morning, that is. Stiff as a board. Unable to hunt for the next two days.

Then there was the old stub-horned blesbok that needed culling. He was too clever for us. I blew it. For the first and last time I put pressure on the young man to take the shot on a cold, overcast, blustery day at a distance with which he was not yet comfortable. I rue that mistake to this day. It took us two days to find and kill the wounded animal and years to repair the damage to my son's confidence.

But a wonderful hunt followed a couple of years later. Just the two of us. Mountain reedbuck. Up hill and down dale.

"Don't let me shoot anything that's not a trophy, Dad. . . . That's too far for me. . . . I'm not steady enough." And so on.

We ran the roller coaster of a trophy hunter's hopes, despairs, and doubts. I was the pro, tracker, driver, chief cook and bottle washer. And on our last evening, as the colours brightened and then faded to gray, my client spotted and shot a trophy mountain reedbuck. We carried that ram down the mountainside together, stumbling in the dark over Karoo shrubs that became rocks and vice versa. The framed photograph of Richie with his one-shot trophy stands behind my office desk to this day. I am very proud of him.

And here we were. Both a little nervous, I suspect. Me, because the bumpy road through adolescence is full of people-eating potholes. I wasn't always "cool," (pronounced as if it has at least three *O*s). We knocked heads. The old bull-young bull syndrome, no doubt. And I am not always the easiest person to live with: stubborn; irritable at times; my-way-is-the-right-way; trust me, I know; that kind of thing. And this hunt was to be a week with the old man in the bush. How "cool" was that? But I had given him plenty of opportunity to change his mind. To my surprise and joy, he remained steadfast in his decision to go.

At his request, I was also breaking what has become one of my golden rules, "never hunt two-on-one." By this I mean never fall into the tempting trap set by shrewd safari outfitters of accepting a relatively small discount on the normal daily rate if two hunters agree to combine and together use the services of one professional hunter. For a start, assuming each hunter gets his fair share, he will only be hunting half the time, and for the rest, he will merely be a passive participant. I am not into spectator sports, for starters, and the concept of "fair share" can change in a flash—a blinding rifle barrel flash that is, if an animal is wounded. Ethics dictate that such an animal must be followed until found and put out of its misery. This might take moments and it might take days, and I know of instances where "friendships" have not withstood the resulting pressure. I have also heard of cases, admittedly from hunters hailing from countries bordering the Mediterranean, where competition to outdo their companion has eliminated all the fun of hunting with a friend. The result was that the two hunters finished the trip in strained and stony silence.

But it can be fun. *If* the two of you are compatible. *If* this is combined with a genuine wish on the part of both hunters to see the other do well—to help the other in every way possible to achieve success—then it can also be very rewarding. Some of my best hunts have been with my old friend, Derek, on precisely this basis. Never a cross word. The triumphs shared meant pleasure was doubled. The troubles shared meant pain was halved. But, on balance, as the amount of my free time diminished and the trophies I chased became more elusive, I have tended to hunt on my own.

But this was not a pressure hunt. It was part of my ongoing, decade-long quest to complete my search for the Southern African Tiny Ten: blue duiker, Natal red duiker, gray duiker, steenbok, oribi, klipspringer, mountain reedbuck, gray rhebok, grysbok (Cape or Sharpe), and of course, that most difficult and elusive of all South African game—suni. I had become intrigued by the little fellows. By their different habits and habitats. I had, long ago, concluded that they were much more difficult to hunt than the Big Five.

As such, I thought my chances of completing the collection in the sand forests of Hluhluwe were slim. All I needed were the suni and a Natal red duiker, and I had high hopes for the latter. But the former? I knew what I was in for. I had hunted there once before for nyala and really enjoyed the experience of sneaking through the dark, damp forests. Look, listen, sneak forward, whisper-quiet over the sandy soil and stop, look, and listen again. So it would be fun. Fun to hunt, share the experience with my son, and fun to just see what the hunting goddess, Diana, had in store for us.

It was the bewitching half-hour before dark, the time when spiral horns believe they are invisible. The colours had faded and the guinea fowl started *chur-churring* from the trees—the bush was preparing for bed. I was sitting on my haunches, watching a bright red patch of colour emerge cautiously, daintily, from the undergrowth and enlarge into a perky, young Natal red duiker. Then, a nyala bull made an unannounced entry into our little theatre in the round from my right. Having already seen me, he advanced on stiff legs, with ruff raised and neck arched. He was set on "stealing the show" from the duiker, who was instantly reduced to a minor character. *And now?* I remember thinking. Well, whatever *he* was thinking, my .375 changed his mind. No duiker that time. But a very nice nyala.

When the hunt was over, I decided to concentrate on the suni. I contacted my taxidermist, Rodney Kretzschmar. Taxidermists in South Africa are an excellent source of information. They receive trophies from all around the country and are in constant touch with hunters, pros, and other taxidermists, and Rodney is a particularly good and generous source of information. "Where do I go for a Livingstone suni?" I asked. He told me that all the top suni trophies come from either Mozambique or Natal. In fact, seventy out of the top one hundred came from Mozambique, and fifteen out of the first one hundred came from Zululand, according to Rowland Ward's *Records of Big Game* (23rd edition).

After casting around, I booked with John McCullogh of Zulu Nyala, who had a concession to take a few suni on the Phinda game reserve. Now Zulu Nyala is the most luxurious lodge from which I have ever hunted: a magnificent, air-conditioned room; bathroom *en-suite* (no long drop and shower in a bucket on this trip); and spectacular, uninterrupted views over the green, undulating hills and ravines of the Zululand lowveld.

I found the integration of my modern, elegant quarters and the age-old hunting practices disconcerting, however. One minute stalking quietly, focused on the environment and the task at hand: walking, stopping, listening, glassing; worn khakis, perspiration soaking through an old baseball cap, the weight of Bertha, my sixteen-year-old .375 Brno bearing down through the broad webbing strap over my shoulder; the tracker bending and peering through the gloom, holding a branch aside, moving the tiny, black pearls of suni droppings with his foot.

The next moment, back at the lodge: hustle, bustle, electric lights, snooker table, bar, tablecloths and table napkins; young game rangers buzzing in and out with photographic safari guests; the busy bee waiters; the hubbub of foreign accents. I hankered for flickering firelight, night sounds, and quiet, companionable conversation covering the day's events. This paradox was jarring to me—but my son loved it.

Our first morning started on an inauspicious note. No tracker. Nor the allocated area in Phinda that we wanted. We were late. The sun was up. The cicadas were buzzing and burring when we stopped the venerable Land Cruiser. We wasted no time. A quick equipment check. Solids in the .375, water, and we're off.

Slow pace. No noise. We move along an overgrown vehicle track winding through the trees. The sand forests were magnificent. Not as impressive or as massive as the Central African rain forests with their sense of brooding, dark menace, but certainly more user-friendly. Trees not as tall, undergrowth not as matted, therefore, easier to move quietly. Also lighter, and therefore, easier to see.

Suddenly Mswele stops. We freeze. Look! Concentrate! Ah! An ear twitches. A mature, dark nyala bull materializes like a TV image fade-out in reverse. He stands erect, like a statue, the ruff on his back raised. Dark, brown, serious eyes fixed gravely on mine. As I pick my pocket-size 10X25 binos from my shirt pocket, he stalks stiffly away to the right on rigid legs. I can still see his ivory-tipped, lyre-shaped horns, but in a few paces, he is lost from view. Fantastic! We stand dead still for a few seconds longer, held captive by the magic of the moment. "Amazing," whispers Richie from behind me. I turn and grin as I see the look on his face. Would he like to hunt a trophy bull later? Would he! Would he!

John sinks to his knees. Binoculars fixed to his face. Some eighty metres away through a lattice-work of light twigs, I make out movement. Resting on my knee, I peer through Bertha's 1.5–6X

Of Suni and Sons

Zeiss Diavari low-light scope cranked down to 2X. I make out the body of a small brown animal shuffling and scuffling to and fro in the undergrowth. I cannot see which end is which. All I know is that one end, the bigger end, is a darker brown than the other.

"He's a good one," whispers John. *How can he tell?* flashes through my mind. I switch off my thoughts. I focus through the scope, steady myself, breathe out, squeeze, and the .375 solid glues the little animal to the ground. John and Mswele rush forward. Later I ask them not to do this again. What if the animal is wounded? No follow up shot would be possible. And tracking a tiny animal like a suni with its inch-long hooves in thick undergrowth must be a nightmare. I half forgive them, however, when John proudly holds up a beautiful—no, magnificent—suni. Well up in the book. Mswele shakes my hand as if he is pumping water from a deep well. Richie hugs me around the shoulders. "Well done, Dad!" No more elaborate praise could make me feel better.

Our species of suni is slightly larger than *Neotragus moschatus moschatus*, found in isolated areas of East Africa around Mount Kenya and along a coastal strip in Tanzania. It is still tiny, however, and weighs 10 to 15 pounds (4½ to 7 kilograms) and has a height at the shoulder of 14 to 15 inches (35 to 38 centimetres). According to Rowland Ward, it inhabits the densest bush and may slink away or leap off if disturbed. The minimum trophy standard is 3 inches for the longest horn. The world record is 5¼ inches, shot by H. A. Luebermann in Mozambique in 1971, although I am reasonably sure that this record was broken in Natal in the last year or so.

The *SCI Record Book of Trophy Animals* says:

> The suni is a good game animal. The usual hunting method is by slow, silent stalking in thick cover with frequent glassing ... that calls for agility, the ability to move silently and sharp eyesight ... Suni are usually taken with a shotgun using small shot; however, if the range is

short, this can damage the fragile skin or even blow the horns off. A case can be made for using a very small calibre rifle, or a large one with solids. Any scope should be of low power.

Interestingly enough, and probably a sign of the times, seventy-nine out of the top one hundred in this record book came from Zululand in South Africa and only fourteen from Mozambique. The minimum trophy standard is nine inches, combining the length and circumference of both horns. The longest horn of my suni measured $3^4/_8$ inches and the SCI score came to $10^1/_3$ inches, so the little ram qualified well under both systems.

The SCI advice is sound, however. Everyone I spoke to argued against the use of a shotgun for the reasons given, and as I shot my suni through cover from about eighty paces, I would probably not have made the shot if armed with a shotgun or a small calibre rifle. No, I would opt again for my old .375 Brno with solids.

On reflection, I could not believe my luck. The first hour of the first morning! It never works out like that for me. I am the original Peter Perseverance. In fact, if you gave me a dollar for every mile I have walked after trophy animals, it would pay for an excellent overseas holiday.

And it got better. A Rowland Ward Natal red duiker followed, also within one hour of leaving the vehicle, and then a gray duiker. The gray duiker taught me yet another hunting lesson. It was early morning as we rounded a corner on the bone-jarringly bumpy dirt road. "Stop the car!" A choking haze of red-brown dust enveloped me as I sat on the back of the vehicle and obscured whatever I had seen out of the corner of my eye. Through the clearing murk, I made out knitting-needle straight horns extending way above the ears of the little gray animal nibbling a knee-high shrub to my right.

The sight pattern was still and clear in my mind's eye as the sharp recoil of the .375 obliterated my view of the little buck.

Of Suni and Sons

As I instinctively rechambered and looked up simultaneously, there was no expected still, gray form next to the bush some ninety paces away. "You missed," said John in answer to my questioning look. "I saw dust puff on the far side of the duiker." Before I could express my absolute amazement and embarrassment at missing such a sitter, Mswele confirmed John's statement. "Yes, he ran off to the right." I could not believe it and insisted we check. "He was standing here and ran off there." I couldn't make out the tiny duiker tracks but knew from past experience that, even with solids, a .375 hit would leave a clear blood trail. No matter how much I looked and shook my head, I could not find a thing.

Late that afternoon I asked to revisit the scene. I noticed the silent "let's humour him" look pass between tracker and pro. But I was right. We started at the wrong shrub. The shot had been 105 paces, not 90, and just as I expected, there was a conspicuous blood trail. Even so, with a .375 solid through the middle of its heart, the little animal had run more than 100 paces in a wide arc. Talk about the toughness of African animals!

At any rate, I learned yet again how important, vital really, it is to accurately mark the spot where the animal stood when the hammer dropped. As a younger man I may have lacked the confidence to override the skepticism of my companions. I might not have suspected that the puff of dust seen by the others could have been made after the bullet passed through the buck's body. Still, all's well that ends well, and I had a third Rowland Ward trophy to add to my collection of the Tiny Ten.

Richie had also come to hunt. An impala and a warthog were on the agenda and maybe, just maybe, if he was up to it, a nyala. But man proposes and God disposes, and quoting one of my favourite hunting sayings, he said, "Dad, hunting's not like shopping at Pick 'n Pay. You must take the opportunity that presents itself." And so, on the second day of the hunt, we set off on a brief stalk that culminated in a clean neck shot on a very acceptable 14-inch common reedbuck.

We spotted his nyala from afar on an overcast afternoon with the sweet smell of rain in the air. Through the binoculars, he looked a good representative animal, but what Richard liked was that he was in a clearing some one hundred metres from the forest fringe with the breeze blowing from the bull to the bush. Off he went with John and Mswele on a long stalk. It was going to be his stalk and his decision. I grew old waiting. The nyala started to feed away from the forest. "What are they doing? Hurry up! The shot's lengthened to at least 170 paces!" The agony of a long-distance dad. My binoculars started to suck my eyeballs out of their sockets. The nyala vanished suddenly, as if it had been a figment of my imagination, before the flat bark of the rifle and the echoed thud of a solid hit reached my ears and explained the disappearance.

My car was a happy place as we winged our way back to Johannesburg. Six excellent trophies. All killed outright with one shot each. We even played some of Richard's music. Surprisingly, I tolerated it. It had been that kind of week and that kind of hunt. A hunt that we'd recall time and gain as the years passed. And, so, long after, Richie and I have listened to one another's stories for the umpteenth time. Long after we have reminded one another of the good, the bad, and the ugly. Long after the trophies have gathered dust on the walls, we will remember and hold on to the shared experiences, and they will bind us, not just as father and son, but as friends.

THE TINY TEN

It's taken me years to get there. Decades in fact. Decades spent learning to shoot at targets; then culling springbok; then hunting whatever I was allowed to hunt; then trophy hunting; then, at long, long last, big game—the Big Five—the dream, the aim, the goal of every serious hunter. Not so? Not so. Well, at least not so for me.

I won't pretend to be blasé about the Big Five, because I'm not. I loved it. All of it. From the marches after elephant, to hanging smelly bits of meat for cats, to the heart thumping, adrenaline rush of the final moments of a buffalo stalk. But possibly because these animals loom so large, both physically and mentally in a hunter's world, they obscure much else that is at least as important for the hunter as he grows and develops.

Looking back on my own hunting career, such as it has been, it was almost as if a shroud was lifted from my mind once I hunted big game. Not immediately. I mean it was no "road to Damascus conversion," but more a gradual thing. A personal thing. For example, I began to actively dislike hunting lion and leopard. The whole business of baiting began to pall. From culling bait animals (as if suddenly they weren't important anymore), to the ritual of hanging the meat, inspecting it, building blinds, and the endless waiting. It all began to seem somehow less desirable. In those long hours of waiting, I found myself asking more and more frequently, *Why am I doing this? Is this hunting? Is this what I want to hunt? Is this how I want to hunt?* And more and more frequently, the answer to the latter question was *No*—muted at first, but then louder and louder until I could no longer ignore it.

I know there will be some who say—and correctly I think—"Well, it's all right for him; he's shot his lions and leopards." But that's the point I make, that's part of the natural progression of hunting. Just like your first impala led you to your first kudu, so the Big Five also lead the serious hunter onward.

The "onward" in my case was, first, to try for the more difficult animals like bongo, giant eland, and mountain nyala, and second, to hunt the exact opposite of the Big Five, the small animals, the tiny animals—the Tiny Ten.

Looking back, I feel distinctly uncomfortable at the nonchalant way I often used to dismiss these beautiful little creatures. Have you ever done it? You know the time when you were acting as a guide on a game drive/horse ride/walk because you, the serious hunter, knew the bush and the others bowed to your greater knowledge and experience. There was a burst of sound, a small animal darted across an open space and dived into a dense bush. What was that? "Only a duiker," you replied dismissively, "only a duiker."

I didn't even bother to shoot them for camp meat. Too small. Too much P.T. for too little meat. I barely paid them a second glance. They were more an irritant. Would their dashing, darting run disturb something worthwhile? At best, I would wonder and watch as some turbo-charged tick streaked toward the horizon. *What possesses such a little thing?* I would sometimes think.

I wasn't a total "big and hairy" freak. Looking back, I can remember admiring a wonderful Sharpe grysbok that tripped into the dappled light of a tree-shrouded hillside in Zimbabwe while I sat on an overturned tree trunk waiting for the trackers to sort out the spoor of the elephant bull we were following from the tracks of the matriarchal herd that had enveloped them. He looked at me curiously from a distance of about thirty paces. Unafraid. His nose twitched. He stretched his right rear leg languidly backward, shivered briefly as he retracted it (as if someone had walked over his grave), bustled forward a few steps, and stopped. Compared with the Sharpe grysbuck, which I eventually managed to shoot last year, he must have been close to, if not better than, the world record. At the time, I was quite content to watch the little fellow and view him as a pleasant interlude before getting on with the real business. I did not even lift my binoculars, let alone my rifle. In fact, the thought never entered my head, not then nor later when I saw a second one, a few days later, on the banks of the Deka, that I would want to shoot one, let alone hunt one. So I didn't even belong to that group of hunters who would occasionally collect a duiker or steenbok during the course of a hunt for some other animal merely because it was there, because it happened to stand too long, because there was nothing else. I simply had no interest.

The first member of the Tiny Ten in my collection was a real winner and was one of the first full mounts my taxidermist, Rodney Kretzschmar, ever did for me. I often watched a pair of the little creatures as they levitated up a sheer rock face in the bend of the Shlaralumi River. It was a magical, calm, and peaceful spot. Across a broad reach of white river sand, at the foot of gray, granite cliffs scoured out by the river over the ages, was a life-size figure of a mermaid carved into a ledge of soapstone. Legend has it that there were originally two figures, carved by a policeman stationed in the area in the likeness of his wife and daughter. He obtained permission to remove one as a gravestone on the death of his wife, but the other remained. I loved the spot and spent hours there. I saw buffalo there. I saw elephant there, including one of the Kruger National Park giants with his special radio collar and 100-pound tusks. And I got to know the ever-present klipspringers.

No, I didn't shoot one. But I did become interested enough to do a little research. Rowland Ward minimum $4^1/_8$ inches. Hoof structure designed to fit the end of the limb, like an extension of the leg itself. Coat more bristle than hair. Used to stuff saddles in the old days. Greenish gray in colour. Only males have horns except in and around Ethiopia, where the females often also carry horns.

In other words, perfectly designed for their environment. Their coats blend in perfectly with the rocks, lichen, and moss of their habitat and provide a good cushion in the unlikely event of a slip. Unlikely because the hooves do not extend past the circumference of the leg they join. In other words, the klipspringer walks on tip-toe and the likelihood of a hoof slipping off a rock or ledge is largely negated.

Even so, I probably would not have shot my first of two klipspringers but for a certain "dog in the manger" attitude to which I uncharacteristically succumbed.

We were up. We were more than up. We were hot. We had been hunting a 10-kilometre stretch of the Gwaai from its point of entry into Lake Kariba. Apart from an average hippo and a decent Chobe bushbuck, my hunting partner had taken what is still the world-record croc and I shot a Top Twenty Chobe bushbuck . . . but that's another story.

"Yoh!" exclaimed the pro. "What? What?" I asked in a whisper, more breath than sound, as I followed my leader into a slow motion crouch under cover of the drooping leaves of a large no-name shrub on the banks of the Gwaai. "It's a monster," he said with his head cocked to the right (just like an old English pointer called Miller that still hunts gray wing in the Bankberge of the Karoo). He was gazing steadfastly up at the bush-bedecked cliffs edging the river bank.

Seeing nothing, I said nothing. "That's a super klippie," he murmured. Taking my silence for disinterest, he said, "Look, if you don't want it, do you mind if I take it?" That got my attention. I love hunting with pros who still enjoy hunting for themselves, but it is rare for any of them to allow you to see past their carefully crafted veneer of "been there, done that." Normally there's no story you can tell that they can't cap. Their animals are always bigger, the horns larger, the shots further, the situation more dangerous.

The Tiny Ten

So you must know, when they ask a question like that, I pay attention! My attention, my whole being, was now focused on the cliff facing me. Near the very top I made out a klipspringer. The needlepoints of his horns just broke the skyline. I hadn't seen enough of them to know whether this was a particularly big one, but the pro's question had rendered all of mine superfluous. Without a word I gave him a *Do you think I'm one sandwich short of a picnic?* sideward glance and eased my .375, fortunately loaded with solids, to my shoulder.

At the shot, the little beast tumbled, bounced, and juddered down the cliff face. Aghast at the thought of the damage that had been wrought by the brutal fall, I rushed forward with the pro. What saved the pro was the broad, webbing cartridge belt around his waist, which housed the fat, fountain-pen-size .470 cartridges. As he knelt over to pick up the "dead" animal, it slammed its horns into his midriff with a sharp *clack* as they made contact with the cartridges. But for them, he would have had his innards perforated to a depth of more than four inches—the horns actually measured $4^7/8$ inches—by the deadly little daggers.

And the thick, bristle-like coat met the manufacturer's warranty. But for the substantial holes behind the shoulders of the little buck, we found no bruising, let alone broken bones, when we skinned him out for the full mount that now resides in my study.

So, that's how it started. Back in the Karoo the following year, I sat down with my partner and drew up a list of all the littlies in southern Africa—they came to fifteen in total—Kirk dik-dik, Damara dik-dik, Sharpe grysbok, Cape grysbok, klipspringer, Natal red duiker, blue duiker, gray or common duiker (also called southern bush duiker), mountain reedbuck, Chanler mountain reedbuck, vaal rhebok, steenbok, Livingstone suni (*Neotragus moschatus livingstonianus*), suni (*Neotragus moschatus moschatus*), and oribi. To arrive at the Tiny Ten for South Africa, we eliminated some of the animals on the list. Damara dik-dik because it is found in Namibia, Kirk dik-dik, and Chanler mountain reedbuck because they are found essentially in Tanzania, and Sharpe grysbok because the little beast has only limited distribution in the old Transvaal. But I suppose a good case could be made to include the Sharpe and leave out oribi or even mountain reedbuck, and possibly include the springbok. What do you think?

Right, I thought. I've made a start. Little was I to realize then that it would take eight years for me to complete the collection. At the time, the next step seemed easy—gray or common duiker as they were then called (southern bush duiker as they are now known in the latest edition of Rowland Ward) were plentiful, in fact, really common in the riverine bush that borders the Great Fish River, which flows through my ranch. Except they are brown. Chocolate brown. Not gray at all.

Piece of cake, I thought. Nice gentle sneak along the bank at dawn and Bob's your aunty. Well, I won't bore you with all the gory detail. Suffice it to say, I walked. I stalked. I rode. I ambushed. I beat. In the end, my neighbour took pity on me and I shot a nice, neat male from a ridge of rocks overlooking his *mielie* (corn) fields. Nice but no cigar. The duiker did not make the book, and somehow, I never received the skin. How I regret this now, for I still don't have a full mount of one of our local Karoo versions of the common or gray duiker. Like many animals, it's not that difficult to shoot a duiker, any duiker, but it's another thing to find a good one, on foot, on equal terms, so to speak. I have aimed at more than one from my truck returning from the veld in the late evening as the duiker gazed curiously at me from the cover of a thicket. But whatever shooting from a truck happens to be, one thing it's not and that's hunting. On foot, in my part of the world, "arses and elbows" are the bits I know best as the little blighters burn a blue streak through the Karoo bush en route to Botswana.

In the end, I shot two very gray, gray duiker (after all these years I can't bring myself to suddenly call them southern bush duiker) in one day near Hluhluwe in Zululand. On the same hunt, I took a good Natal red duiker and an excellent suni and none of the hunts, although all were on foot, lasted more than half a day. It only goes to show.

I was particularly nervous about the suni. In fact, when I drew up the original list, the three animals that gave me the most pause for thought were the oribi, the suni, and the vaal rhebok.

And then I had a lucky break. The Natal Hunters and Game Conservation Association, to which I belong, sends out forms to members each year asking them to indicate the species they are interested in hunting during the course of the forthcoming hunting season. Pat Ogram, the executive in charge of the program at the time, put a tremendous amount of work into trying to meet member's needs.

Part of his role involved regular liaison with the Natal Parks Board. In my opinion, they run the most efficient and effective conservation effort in Africa—bar nothing. Now it so happened that the Natal Parks Board decided to make two mature oribi rams available to members of Natal Hunters at the Oribi Gorge Conservancy. The first since 1953. To be fair, Pat put them out to tender and I and my partner, Louis, made the highest bid.

Louis's flight arrived late at Johannesburg International Airport. It was a good nine-hour drive down to the Conservancy near the Transkei border in Natal. The two speeding fines en route upped the cost of the hunt substantially. Weary and disgruntled, I piled into bed that night without supper and put the day behind me.

A good night's sleep. A clean, crisp, cloudless dawn. An aromatic cup of steaming, black, bittersweet coffee and the first cigarette of the day (I still smoked then) put a totally different complexion on things.

The object of the exercise was twofold, the warden said. The first was to promote Ourebia Ourebi and Oribi Gorge, draw attention to the plight of the animal and the devastating effects of poaching in the area, and the second was to derive revenue for the conservancy by removing old rams who were out of the breeding cycle. I was aghast at the warden's tale of poaching.

The poachers came from all cross sections of the populace, used every underhanded, dirty trick—from dogs to spotlights to vehicles—and had no scruples in using violence to avoid arrest.

My heart still sinks when I think of the area, and much as I would like to think that our hunt contributed to conservation in the Conservancy, I could not but help wonder whether the warden's valiant efforts were not doomed to an unavailing fight against failure.

At any rate, with the warden and two of his staff as guides, we meandered through the gorge after which the Conservancy is named. Only one word for it. Beautiful. Staggeringly beautiful. Worth a visit for the view alone.

But enough. Up onto and into the golden sea of grass in the hills surrounding the gorge. Because oribi are territorial, it did not take our expert guides long to identify an excellent ram. Old, they said he was. Very old. Right—Carl Lewis old. Like a tan anti-tank projectile, he streaked across the rim of the ridge-ringed basin in which we found him. His forelegs barely skimmed the grass tops, defying gravity. His legs stretched parallel to his body. His back arched like an elfin Olympic gymnast on the run up to the ramp before a vault. Perky and proud at the same time. I know tsessebe are reputed to be the fastest antelope on earth, but this little pocket rocket, fast as a speeding bullet against the blond background grass in the basin, would certainly give them a go over the first fifty metres or so. I gave the little ram a perfect ten for technical merit and a nine for artistic expression.

Eventually we spotted one before it spotted us as it lay in the long grass, only the tips of its horns telltale still among the gently waving stems. Patience paid off, and as the ram rose to stretch in the late afternoon sun, the .375 solid killed it cleanly and quickly. The next morning, Louis took an identical ram in an identical manner but not before we had surprised the father of all oribi as he basked in a sugarcane clearing. The ram did not wait on his leaving and I lost sight of

The Tiny Ten

him through my binoculars as he cleared the second set of hills on the horizon. No wonder he had grown so large.

In the end, however, as much as I enjoyed the experience, it was more of a collection exercise than a hunt, and I would guess that's what most oribi hunting is about.

My research into suni ultimately led me to the sand forests of Zululand and a cursory glance at the latest entries in Rowland Ward will tell you that, in recent years, this region has surpassed Mozambique as the most prolific producer of quality specimens of Livingstone suni or *Neotragus moschatus livingstonianus* as opposed to the smaller *Neotragus moschatus moschatus,* which is most easily found on the slopes of Mount Meru in Tanzania.

Looking back over the last eight years and the different types of hunts for the Tiny Ten—from culling blue duiker in the forests, to climbing and glassing the windswept mountains for vaal rhebok—I enjoyed my suni hunt the most. First, I was hunting with my son, which is always a treat and something special for me. Second, it brought back fond memories of a successful nyala hunt in the same area with two old friends years before. Third, I have always enjoyed the "sneaky" hunts. And that's what is required when hunting an animal barely the size of a rabbit in thick forest with the overhead canopy dappling the sandy ground in surreal shadow.

I expected the hunt to last for days. I was prepared to go back empty-handed. In retrospect, I felt half amazed and half hard done by that the whole hunt was over so quickly. But I will always treasure the time we had. The soft shoe shuffle for a few paces. Glass. Look. Listen. Shuffle a few paces more. It was exciting—really exciting. The place, the people, the prey combined to make it almost mystical. The coucal that swooped silently through the thicket. The rippling, water-tinkling call, eerie in the early morning silence. A lone nyala bull, big brown eyes soulful but alert, on stiff, stilted legs, ruff raised, ghosting into the gloom.

Heart of an African Hunter

And then the scurry, rustle, and bustle of suni oblivious to our presence. The quivering intensity and excitement of pro and tracker. Thumbs up. My job now. I move from kneeling to sitting. I sit behind my trusty .375 loaded with solids, bipod extended and resting on the tops of my soft, khaki-coloured boots. I settle into the shot. In and out of the dappled dimness moves the tiny tot. In and out of the deflecting twigs and *takke* (branches). Cross hairs steady. Imprint of the buck in the scope clear and still as the recoil wrenches it away. I know the hunt is over before I hear the whoop of delight from the pro or feel the hug from my son. For a moment, the silence and customary sadness is all I hear or feel.

The tiny ones have an ability to test and humble a hunter to a far greater extent than any of the Big Five. Yes, the big ones can chew you and tramp on you, but it is the little ones that bruise bits the big ones can't reach—your ego.

My worst moments as a hunter were not when the green mamba fell across my bare arms in a *mokoro* in Botswana, nor when I found myself accidentally within twenty paces of a tail-lashing lioness with a .22 for protection, but on my first vaal rhebok hunt. After I missed the Rowland Ward buck for the fourth consecutive time in an open, windswept basin high in the Eastern Cape mountains, my previously unshakable belief in my shooting skills evaporated like sea spray on a boiling hot Clifton boulder. One more shot to put it down. Still another to kill it. And all this in full view of my partner, my neighbour, and two of his sons. And all this because, after many years, I had somehow convinced my neighbour that I was a serious and responsible trophy hunter who would not stress or injure any of his precious vaal rhebok. I have never felt so ashamed or embarrassed. 'Nuff said!

The member of the Tiny Ten that I have consistently enjoyed hunting most is the mountain reedbuck. Each time I return to the Karoo, they draw me like a magnet into the mountains. I know it's not only the buck. Behind my house, a pair of black eagles make their home. From a vantage point in a neck above their cliff nest, I can see down into an oxbow carved into the mountains by the Great Fish River. I can look over the *Sprinbokvlakte* (Springbok Plains), across into Waterbank and up the slopes of *Kapteinskop* (Chief's Head) and *Boesmanskop* (Bushman's Head). I can watch the sun set behind the *Wapadsberge* (Wagon Road Mountains). More often than not, this is where I like to start and end my hunting day.

In recent months I have been preparing for a mountain nyala hunt in Ethiopia. My gunsmith, Mr. W. J. C. Ritchie (better known as Silver Bill), and his right-hand man, Vince, built me a .300 Winchester Magnum, on a Brno action, with a synthetic stock topped by a Zeiss Diavari 2.5–10X, 42mm. It looks awesome, even sinister, like something from a movie about assassins and snipers. The whole effect is enhanced by the Winchester Supreme 180-grain Fail Safe ammo—silver cartridge cases and black bullet heads. I know it looks a little over the top, but secretly, I am quite pleased with the way it has turned out. It certainly looks the part as it nestles in the gray foam of my aluminum gun case. And it shoots!

My partner built a 300-metre range on the ranch, and for the last two weeks, I have been practicing every second day. Although I have been working with the rifle for more than six months, this concentrated practice has done wonders for my confidence in the weapon. We fit. At 100 metres, I consistently group the barest tad over an inch. I sight in two inches high. At 200 metres I am spot on, and when the wind is still and I concentrate, I can plant four shots from the magazine within a generous two-inch diameter. At 300 metres, my shots scatter over a saucer-sized area with their center of gravity some five inches below the bull. I know the ballistics tables say that the drop should be seven inches but what can I do? After 200 rounds, practical reality and tables part.

"Enough," says Louis. "What you must do is copy the conditions in Ethiopia. See if you can find a mountain reedbuck across a kloof (ravine) at about 300 metres. See if you can do in the field what you've been practicing on the range." Good advice. Bert

Klineburger, the booking agent for my hunt, has done his best to prepare me for the forthcoming safari, and according to him, 300-metre shots across steep valleys are par for the course. Of course, mountain nyala, although similar in colour to mountain reedbuck, are much bigger, and therefore, my mountain reedbuck hunt is theoretically more difficult. But I am on familiar territory and at 4,000 feet above sea level, a good 9,000 to 10,000 feet lower than I will be in the Kakka and Kubsa Mountains of Ethiopia.

At 4:30 P.M. I am at the top of the *Rooiberge* (Red Mountains) behind my house. I have clumsily spooked two ewes and two young ones. They sprint across the hillside before slowing down as they reach a neck that splits the range. With my new Leica Geovid binoculars, I press the range-finding button, place the red square that appears in the center of my field of vision on the rear of the departing female, press again and read off the distance—424 metres. Too far. Much too far.

People often ask me how these gentle creatures manage to charge blindly, hell for leather, across the rock-strewn mountains, without the hint of a stumble or sign of unsure footing. Even with sturdy-soled, proper mountaineering boots, it is difficult enough to walk briskly, let alone jog. Then I show them the runways made by these clever animals through regular use. Barely two inches across, these runways (to call them paths is to dignify them with a name they don't deserve), crisscross the mountain sides. The reedbuck know them well and what can appear like haphazard, helter-skelter panic is, more often than not, a brisk trot on a well-trodden track. Reedbuck are territorial and follow regular if not predetermined habits. The ones in the *Rooiberge*, more often than not, start moving downhill in the late afternoon on the west-facing slopes (to catch the last of the sun), to the valleys below, where they graze. They reverse the process the next morning, this time seeking out the warmth of the east-facing slopes to drive out the nighttime chills. By about 10 A.M., most are bedded down in some warm, sheltered nook and if you are not above them well beforehand and have watched their progress, you will need an awful lot of luck to spot them before they spot you, and a whole season's full of luck to approach within shooting distance. The only other alternative is to bring along a farmer. You know the type. The ones who shoots running springbok in the head at 600 metres with an iron-sighted .303.

Over the years, having made more stalking mistakes than I care to remember in these mountains, it gradually dawned on me that buck on a particular part of the mountain often seem to follow a regular route when running away. With time, I have discovered a number of these runways, and they have helped me predict the direction of departure and how best to make a follow-up stalk.

So I felt sure that, on crossing the neck, the reedbuck would stay on the left-hand ridge and gradually work their way down against the skyline to the valley below. I set off to the right, knowing that the mountain would split into two ridges with a deep, steep kloof in between. I set off, parallel to the course of the reedbuck, walking at a leisurely pace, glassing ahead of myself at regular intervals—more concerned to be quiet over the rock-strewn terrain and avoid spooking another group of reedbuck than to make up time. Walking directly after spooked reedbuck is usually a waste of time as they carefully watch their back trail. Although terrain and weather conditions can sometimes conspire to allow a successful, direct follow-up stalk, it is a low percentage tactic, particularly as the spooked buck will typically put a good few hundred metres between you and him just for starters. In addition, the open nature of our Karoo mountains provides little in the way of stalking cover, and you need to use your knowledge of the terrain and geographic features to bring you within shooting distance.

At first I didn't see them on the opposite side of the valley. Then one, a mature ram, moved into a diminishing patch of late afternoon sunlight. *Got you!* I say to myself.

Wonderful when a plan comes together, flashed through my mind, mimicking the words of the hero of one of our interminable TV action dramas. Press once. The small red square appears on command in the sight picture. Steady on the buck. Press again— 308 yards. Unwrap the jersey from my waist. Jersey on rock, rifle on jersey. I lie with my front half on the lichen-bedecked stone slab, legs splayed behind in the red dirt of the *Rooiberge*. Breathing slows, steadies. At this distance, the beat of my heart bumps the cross hairs on my scope up and off the back of the buck and back again. I wait patiently for the ram to turn sideways. Ewes and young ones fossick around him. First in front, then behind, then he turns directly away.

Patience. "Patience is a virtue, virtue is a grace. Grace is a little girl who doesn't wash her face." The nursery rhyme torments me. But I wait. So much of my shooting skill, such as it is, rests on confidence. Confidence in my equipment. Confidence in me, in my judgment. I want to be sure that I don't wound the animal at this distance and I want to be sure that this first practical test of my new rifle works well.

Time works in my favour. I check the range again. What little breeze there is flows slightly to my right. I check that there is no grass, twig, or other obstruction in front of my barrel. I make myself more comfortable. The cross hairs settle to a more stable heartbeating bob. *Level with the back, just behind the shoulder.* The words turn up in my mind, unannounced, as the ram turns to my right. Gentle, steady squeeeeeze. Crisp, 2½-pound trigger break. The shot flows down the barrel, smooth as mopane silk. As the recoil dissipates and I rock back into position, I catch the merest hint of a horned head flopping into the welcoming arms of a *besembos* (broom bush).

The rest of the little herd takes "just a jump to the right" and disappears over the rim of the ravine. I check the "last known whereabouts" of the buck through my scope, reconfirm with my naked eye and triple check with my binoculars. It is too easy in these mountains with their gray, granite-like rocks to lose one small, gray mountain reedbuck in all the clutter.

I walk to fetch my *bakkie* (truck). I toy with calling my son on the radio to give me a hand. Pride wins. I don't. I walk down into the kloof and up the other side. I gut the buck, leave my jacket, rifle, and binos behind and do the reverse trip with the buck over my shoulders.

The Tiny Ten

Sweat burns my eyes. Not enough hair to trap the perspiration. Correct that. No hair. My breath rasps like a pornographic phone caller. My thighs are on fire. Two hundred paces to go. I know if I drop the buck, I will never pick it up again. My heart jackhammers. "181, 182, 183," I count each pace. I heave the buck into the back of the *bakkie* with one last convulsive surge of energy. Done it! At forty-nine, the heroics of mountain hunting become harder and harder each year and I still have to return to fetch my kit!

But I'm happy, very happy. So happy that, on my way down the mountain, I stop before the last rise, peek over, and spot a decent quality, lone red hartebeest bull. More the size of a mountain nyala, I tell myself. At 215 yards, I kill him with a single shot placed precisely through the heart. It has been about ten years since I last shot a red hartebeest and I have forgotten how big they are. None of my euphoria or loading tricks help.

Fortunately, by the time Richard, Thomas, and Louis arrive, my knees have stopped the worst trembling. The stabbing pain in my lower back has abated sufficiently that I can at least stand straight and assume a nonchalant pose against the *bakkie*. I don't fool my son.

"Dad," he says, with that perfect mix of youthful pity and condescension—"Dad, who do you think you are, Rambo? You're covered in blood! Why didn't you call us earlier?"

Why indeed!

Within two shakes of a Karoo lamb's tail, they load the hartebeest while I pretend to help. On the way down, he looks over at me, nudges me with his elbow. "Far?" He questions.

"308 and 215," I reply.

He purses his lips. "You must be pleased," he says with a friendly smile.

I am. Not quite up to the "seven with one blow," you know the fairy tale about the little man who killed seven flies with one swat, but two buck with two shots is all right with me, especially as both are good trophies and even better eating.

The Tiny Ten opened a new page for me in the Book of Hunting. They took me to new and different places. They taught me new and different things. They expanded my hunting experience.

They can never replace the Big Five. Hunting them can never be a substitute for hunting the Big Five. No layman is ever going to "ooh" and "ah" at a 6-inch steenbok. No layman is ever going to hold his breath while you relate the story of a close encounter with a duiker. And that, maybe, is the nub of the issue. The little ones simply lack the charisma of the big and hairy.

In my opinion, however, the Tiny Ten represent a far greater hunting challenge than the Big Five. They are more difficult to hunt and require greater levels of skill, patience, and perseverance. Possibly, as hunting becomes ever more expensive, more hunters may turn to the Tiny Ten, and in time, they might get the recognition they deserve.

THE SPRINGBOK SLAM

The farm owner had a round, ruddy face topped by thinning, sandy hair with reddish tints. His narrow, pale blue eyes were buried in his fleshy face to either side of a heavily pockmarked, bulbous nose. Speaking Afrikaans, he looked first at Derek, then at me and said:

"In the ten years that I have possessed this farm, we have hunted fallow deer every year but with very little success. If we have shot ten altogether it is a lot. They are wild as wild can be. They take just a little look at you and they take the gap. You can still see them running over the third set of hills," and he pointed at the horizon to the west. "Man, they don't just run away; they emigrate! You *stadsjapies* (city dwellers) will never get near one. I tell you what, you can keep whatever fallow deer you can shoot; you don't even have to pay me. It's your time you're wasting."

With that, his Michelin Man body started shaking, his little eyes disappeared completely, and he began wheezing and chuckling simultaneously.

I didn't like him but said nothing. We were guests and he had just made us an offer we certainly couldn't afford to refuse. Free fallow deer? Who could turn that down, no matter how difficult the old man made it sound.

He summoned one of the farmhands to accompany us, "so that you don't get lost or hurt yourselves." After delivering this last salvo, which emerged from his remarkably small, goldfish mouth, amidst much mirth, the Michelin Man wobbled indoors and returned to his coffee and TV.

"So, how does the boss hunt fallow deer?" I asked Klaas.

"*Ja*, no well, they ride after them in the veld with their *bakkie* and try and shoot them," he replied in Afrikaans, lisping through the gap where his front teeth should have been.

"What happens then?" I queried.

"Listen," said Klaas, "the buck are wild, very wild. They see a *bakkie* and they run like the gray hell back up against the kopje (hills)."

His wrinkled, wizened, yellow-brown skin puckered, almost in pain, at the memory.

"Do they ever get any?" I persisted.

"Every now and then with one of those 'goobye' shots," he said.

Until then, the only fallow deer I'd ever seen were scattered around Rhodes's Memorial on the slopes of Table Mountain, Cape Town. They were so tame you could almost pet them. They were the European subspecies, *Dama dama dama*, and I was told by the Memorial caretaker that they had been introduced by Lord Charles Somerset, governor of the Cape, in 1822. Quite how they had proliferated from there to the Karoo and been joined by the Persian subspecies, *Dama dama mesopotamia*, is a mystery to me. They have spread both north and east from the Cape and have adjusted remarkably well to the semi-arid regions they now so successfully inhabit—aided no doubt by their ability to jump the low sheep fences in the region, migrate to better grazing in times of hardship, and feed on most types of indigenous vegetation.

Sean Ryan, in his interesting article, "Fallow Deer," in the 1993 edition of *Pelea,* the East Cape Game Management Association magazine, states:

The Springbok Slam

Fossil remains found at Clacton in 1868 indicate that there was a larger but very similar deer to the Fallow extant in Britain 250,000 years ago. . . . The species has represented a highly desirable and easily transportable source of food throughout recorded history. They have also had great religious and hunting significance for many of the various people who have invaded the British Isles. . . . It is now the most widely distributed . . . deer species in the U.K., and populations drawn from British stocks have been established in North West Africa, Australia, New Zealand, and, presumably, South Africa.

After a brief team talk, the two of us decided on tactics exactly opposite to those applied by the Michelin Man. We would climb up into the hills, away from all farm tracks, and hunt on foot. We had almost immediate success. Peeking through the leaves of a *besembos* (broom brush—so called because the old timers tied their branches together and used them to sweep their houses) on the crest of a ridge, we spied two fallow deer about 250 metres below us, nibbling on the high protein Karoo shrubs on the plain. One was the tan variety, the other a gunmetal gray. Both of them were good stags with complete, broad, palmed antlers not yet damaged by the imminent rut.

We wiggled our way over the ridge, ending up next to one another in a prone position.

"OK," I said, "when you're ready, I'll count to three, and on three we shoot together."

After a bit of fidgeting, we settled down. The vertical cross hairs of my 3–9X Bushnell mounted on top of my 7x64mm Brno, which Bill Ritchie customized to a 7mm Remington Magnum, rested between the stag's horns with the horizontal cross hair level with the top of his head. (At that stage, I hadn't learnt that gravity acts over the horizontal distance the bullet travels, and if aiming at an animal at a steep angle beneath you, it is necessary to aim a little lower than you would if the animal was on the same plane as you are, albeit at the same distance from barrel to target).

Come on, Derek, I remember thinking, *my first aim is normally my best.*

"Ready," he said, reading my mind. "Right—one and two and three!"

The sound of his Pre-64 Winchester 7x57mm loaded with 135-grain bullets in Norma cartridges merged with the 7mm. As I rocked back into place from the recoil, I could see the white belly of my stag. (We later found that the bullet shattered his skull and the antlers lay crossing one another on top of his head.) Derek's stag was busy running up the kopje toward us at great speed. "Shot over him, muttered Derek as he chambered another round. With kamikaze intent, the fallow deer barreled directly toward us. We were both dumbstruck. At about fifty paces, Derek snapped out of his reverie and the 7x57mm took the stag in the middle of the chest. The deer turned sharply to our right and died some twenty-odd paces away.

In those days, we hunted for the meat. Some we turned into biltong (jerky) and dried sausage, the rest went into the deep freeze. We wasted nothing, even cutting up the shin bones for soup and the ribs for our dogs. Trophy hunting was something we'd heard about, and while shooting good-sized mature bulls was the name of the game, the real reason was that they were better value. More meat for your money.

If you think this is the preamble to an excuse, you're correct. I'm afraid we took the farmer literally and made pigs of ourselves. The next day we shot another eight. The kopjes and the narrow, rock-strewn valleys and ravines in between were crawling with fallow deer. The trick was to get above them. If they were in range we would take turns. (We decided that shooting together was too risky. If one of us wounded an animal, the other would be too preoccupied to help and heaven forbid that we should both shoot badly). If they were out of range, we would shoot over their backs. More often than not, the bullets striking the rocks in front of them caused the deer to run up hill toward their traditional place of safety. Instead they found us. Of course, the sound of the shots reverberating in the steep, narrow confines of the ravines gave no hint as to their direction and that probably helped as well, although this region is no stranger to thunderstorms and lightening and the deer may have paid no mind, confusing the shots with the noise of summer storms.

Older and wiser now, we would not be as greedy or selfish, although from a conservation point of view, the eight were a drop in the bucket if not the ocean. But I confess that the farmer's attitude also had something to do with the fact that we shot ten in all. We could, in fact, have shot more.

At any rate, as we sat on the crest of a hill in the late afternoon sun, having a last soft drink and a smoke before heading down to break the happy news to the Michelin Man, I saw some white dots on the horizon. Something about the washing-powder whiteness and the way they moved made me look again through my binos. Then the penny dropped. It was too early for shearing. They couldn't be sheep, which at this time of the year, were a dull, woolly gray. And they weren't. They were white springbok. The first time I had seen or heard of such an animal.

A year later, I was at Frank Bowker's farm. There were hundreds of them. Hundreds of white springbok. And they all sprouted from two original rams. Or that's what Frank said. His grandfather found two white rams amongst a group of wild *trekbokke* (traveling buck that, in those days still somehow found their way through farm fences and followed the grazing from farm to farm) and decided to try to breed them. He succeeded. In fact, as Frank proudly told us with a twinkle in his eye, his grandfather eventually moved the two old rams across the river as they were inhibiting breeding by fighting with the young up and coming white rams. "And you know what, Peter, they turned that whole herd white!"

It was a long time ago and all I really remember was that it was a simple hunt. By that afternoon, I'd shot two. They seemed good representative specimens but small, even by Eastern Cape standards where springbok are, on average, about two-thirds the size of Namibian or Kalahari springbok. The next person who shoots a Rowland Ward springbok in the Eastern Cape will be the first I have heard of.

I remember much more clearly how well Frank Bowker treated us youngsters. How friendly and hospitable he was. And the two paintings in his beautiful old farmhouse by one of his relatives, Barber. An old mining town in the north of our country was named after him—Barberton. The paintings included species of virtually every wild animal in South Africa.

That particular hunt coincided with a culling expedition to Hofmeyr—a small Eastern Cape village. We stayed in the little, white-washed local hotel. Eight bedrooms in all—none with a lock on the door. It was the week that I first tasted scotch whiskey. Derek said I should start with Tullamore Dew, a gentle Irish drink, because it was on the extreme left-hand side behind the bar. I did and then gradually, over the rest of the week, moved my way to the right. At any rate, to complete the expedition we ended up at a farm called Langkloof (Long Ravine) owned by Louis Marais. We were looking for blesbok, my wife's favourite venison.

I shot twelve that day (some for myself and some for friends) and it was when we were sitting around afterward, settling up and drinking a welcome ice cold Castle Lager that, somehow, the topic of white springbok came up. "Oh, yes," said Louis, as calm as you please, "I have a small herd of white springbok but a much bigger herd of black springbok."

"Black springbok! Where? Can we see them? How much? Can we hunt them?" The questions tumbled from my mouth. Louis set aside five to be hunted that year and all five were

The Springbok Slam

spoken for. No matter how I cajoled, persuaded, pleaded, or begged, he was adamant. "Next year you can have first choice," was his final decision. And so it was that I booked to hunt with him in the first week in May the following year and came back for the next seventeen consecutive years thereafter.

I remember that first black springbok hunt to this day for three very good reasons. I arrived a day early to give myself time to settle down and sight in. Louis had a party of meat hunters in camp so I stayed with him in his house, which also became a custom for many years. At least until I bought the neighbouring ranch.

That night friends came to visit, and during the course of the evening, I found three curious kids lying next to my customized 7mm Remington Magnum, one of them cuddling the stock to his shoulder with the bipod extended. Showing them from the room, I locked the door and thought nothing more of it until sitting next to Louis the next morning on the broad bench seat of his venerable, old Ford F250 culling truck, complete with meat hooks and conveyor-belt-covered sides.

The morning began inauspiciously. On arriving to pick up the meat hunters, one walked to the truck drinking from a beer can. Without raising his voice, Louis pointed and asked, "Where are you going with that?"

"Onto the *bakkie* and then into the veld," the man replied.

"No, you're not." said Louis. "You're going to pack up, get into your car, and leave. And anyone else who has been drinking can join you."

Said mildly but firmly, his manner clearly brooked no contradiction, but I was still amazed at the lack of protest from the beer drinker and his mates. They obviously knew more about Louis than I did. Over the years, of course, that has changed and I too have come to understand that this degreed farmer, ethical professional hunter, champion shootist in many disciplines, and ardent conservationist means what he says and says what he means.

Heart of an African Hunter

At any rate, as I sat in the truck with the barrel of my rifle resting on my boot, it occurred to me that I should check to see if the kids had fiddled with my rifle. I pulled the bolt up and back and peered down at the chubby, bright brass of the necked down .375 cartridges. All seemed to be in order and I crimped the cartridges in the magazine with the fingers of my left hand while sliding the bolt over them with my right hand. As I closed the bolt, concentrating more on the conversation in the back of the truck than on a task I had performed thousands of times, the fact that the closing bolt felt a trifle stiff hardly registered. I moved the barrel off my foot and pulled the trigger. *Ka-blam!*

I felt as much as heard the painful, ear-destroying noise inside the confines of the cab. Louis, his eyes starting from his head, wide as a raped owl, gawped at me through the dust storm unleashed inside the *bakkie*. Heaven knows what I must have looked like, but it must have taken a while for me to close my mouth. When I did, it was all gritty inside. Moments passed, stretched into seconds. Complete silence settled over us along with the dust. Not a sound from the back of the *bakkie*. Maybe they thought Louis was trying to encourage their dismissed and disgraced mate to get a move on. Maybe they thought it was a backfire—a serious backfire. Eventually, reverting to Afrikaans, his home language, Louis asked, "Did you hit anything important?" Looking around me, like the fool I was, I eventually noted the clean, round hole through the floorboards. "N-n-no," I eventually stuttered. With that, Louis started the truck and we moved off. We have never discussed the incident again.

I can only assume that somehow when I pulled the bolt back, the top round in the magazine must have come loose and slipped into the chamber. It had never happened before and has never happened since. Not the least because now I never close the bolt on an empty chamber without first feeling with the point of my pinkie to make doubly sure.

The Springbok Slam

The third reason for remembering the hunt after all these years is even more painful. I still wince at the thought. By midmorning the next day, the sun had already burnt off the frost that whitened the golden brown grass of the veld and made it scrunch beneath my boots. A bushy, dark green shrub behind me broke my outline and the grass in front of me was short, giving me a clear field of fire through nearly a full half circle. I had already shrugged out of my big down jacket and lay warm and comfortable facing downhill in an easterly direction toward the false crest as it dropped steeply into a rock-strewn ravine.

Somewhere down there, two farmhands on horseback were slowly moving through the riverine bush. Louis was on the plateau opposite me in the F250, a white speck in the distance. Unlike ordinary springbok, which coalesce into bigger and bigger herds as they are stressed, black springbok do the reverse and bombshell individually in different directions.

I heard them before I saw them. The clatter of stone on stone as they trotted out of the kloof. They were truly beautiful. Shiny dark brown black. In the bright sun I could see a darker, blacker stripe along their flanks beneath the glossy sheen of their coats. They were all dark except for a snow-white patch on their nose, which develops in their seventh month. They were all females and youngsters.

Many people believe that the black springbok is merely "a chocolate brown colour phase of South African springbok that was developed through selective breeding on private ranches in South Africa," to quote from the *SCI Record Book of Trophy Animals*, Edition VIII, volume I.

In an absolutely fascinating article by Alex McDonald, "The Black Springbuck–Crown Prince of the Karoo," in the 1994 edition of *Pelea,* he debunks the theory. He writes that:

> Dr. Courtney-Latimer, the then curator of the East London Museum . . . together with Boeta van der Merwe . . .

Heart of an African Hunter

carried out a number of scientific and breeding tests. It was established that the black springbuck differs from the common springbuck in several respects. They have a white blaze on their faces. The bottom jaw is stronger and carries an additional one to three molars on each side. The hooves are longer (an adaptation that nature uses for swampy conditions). Horn formation is bolder . . . [and] the breeding tests proved the black springbuck game to be dominant, both from black ram to common ewe and common ram to black ewe. . . . The fact that the progeny from black parents is always black is typical of the true breeding species and dispels any speculation of a random melanistic variation.

[McDonald's conclusion is that] the differences between the black and common springbuck are greater than the differences between blesbok and bontebok, which are discerned as being two totally different species, originating from totally different habitat types. Perhaps therein lies the key—different habitat types. The upper central Karoo might, at some time in ancient history, have been totally different from the surrounding territory, a vast inland sea perhaps.

As I said, fascinating, and I agree with him. From my own observations, although I cannot prove it scientifically, black springbok behave differently; they are bigger and I believe they are stronger and more vigorous.

As I lay watching, off to the left—far off—I spotted a ram. Cocky from years of Karoo culling, I took the long shot and stood up as the ram dropped. I strolled the 273 paces to the ram. The 7mm Remington Magnum nailed the buck so convincingly to the ground I didn't bother to rechamber a round. I certainly didn't screw my 3–9X Bushnell down from its highest magnification. And why should I? The buck lay on its back in a small but slowly spreading pool of blood. After a cursory glance to confirm it was as big as I originally thought, I called Louis on my handheld radio.

"I can see you. I'm on my way," he replied.

As I looked up to see where he was, I heard a scrabbling sound at my feet. In utter disbelief I watched the ram struggle to its feet and with a hop, skip, and a jump disappear over the cliff edge, never to be seen again. Oh yes, we looked for it all right. All that day and the next. All four of us. Unfortunately, tracking over the stony hillsides is impossible, but even so, you would have thought that the four of us on foot and horseback would have turned up something. But no, nary a thing. It was a bitter, bitter blow and still ranks as one of only four wounded animals I have not been able to find in forty years of hunting. Every now and then one of them takes a turn to trek through my mind in the still, dark, early morning hours. As if to mock me. To remind me of the responsibility of our passion, our sport.

The next May I was back. Again. On the same hillside. Overlooking the same ravine. This time the ram was on his own. Only bigger. Much bigger. A quarter-inch bigger than 15 inches, to be precise. This time, instead of falling and running, the buck hunched at the heart shot, jet propelled itself across some sixty paces, stumbled, caught itself and fell ploughing along, pushed by his hind legs. Sometime after that, I can no longer remember when, I made up a rhyme: "If the animal falls and runs, the 'fun' has just begun. If the animal runs and falls, then the animal is all yours."

It was a great, big, beautiful, black springbok. Sleek, smooth, shiny. He made the book. Any book. No matter how you measured him. No matter under which class of springbok you entered him. He completed the grand slam of springbok for me. And was the biggest of them all.

I have had chances to shoot others, many others. Somehow since I became Louis's partner and neighbour, the animals . . . well, all I know is that my attitude toward them changed. The temptations are there. But I have only succumbed once. The rest of the time we leave the big, old rams for the overseas trophy hunters—we need the money. It helps expand what, over the last many years, has become the biggest, private registered nature reserve proclaimed by an act of Parliment.

KENMEKAAR FORUM
(Getting to Know One Another Forum)

This article was reproduced from S.A. Hunter, journal of the South African Hunters and Game Conservation Association.

The Grand Champion Trophy winner of 1993, Mr. P. Flack, was born in Fish Hoek in 1948. He attended the universities of Cape Town, Cambridge, and Wits, and practiced law for twelve years, whereafter he accepted a management position with one of his clients, Fraser Alexander Limited.

Peter shot his first buck, a vaal rhebok, at the age of nine on a farm near Bredasdorp and has, since then, hunted in Namibia, Botswana, Zimbabwe, Mozambique, Central African Republic, the United Kingdom, and the United States of America. He confesses that hunting to him remains somewhere between a passion and an obsession and that he hopes to hunt intensively for many more years to come.

Question:

This year you came back from a hunt in Central Africa where you hunted a magnificent bongo. Can you please give us details on the area where this hunt took place, the type of weather, how you managed to get there, where you stayed, did you make use of a fly camp, infrastructure there, etc.

Answer:

I hunted the Oubangui Safaris concession area in the eastern corner of the Central African Republic. The southern border of the concession extends for some 206 kilometres, from Mboki in the east to Zemio in the west, along the Mbamou River, which flows into the Ubangi and then into the Congo River. The concession is roughly U-shaped and from Mboki heads north toward Ouagou and then northwest toward Djema for approximately 190 kilometres before heading south toward Zemio. In total, the concession area comprises almost two million acres and is largely uninhabited but for a small village at Ouagou in the north. The area comprises a combination of equatorial rain forests and open savanna areas. This part of Africa has a high rainfall and the hunting season begins in January and ends in May when torrential rain, swollen rivers, and tall grass make hunting impossible. I chose to hunt during the month of April, which is the beginning of the rainy season, as the bongo that I was searching for inhabit the equatorial rain forests and it is difficult, if not impossible, to move through the forest without making a lot of noise when it is dry. It is important to hunt at the beginning of the rainy season and hope that it does not become too wet too soon. In order to meet my scheduled hunting dates, I was obliged to fly via Paris to Bangui (the capital of CAR) and from Bangui to Mboki via private air charter and then a six-hour drive from Mboki to the main camp on the Bouye river. All in all, it took some four days to reach the main camp. The area is so vast and the roads so poor that extensive use is made of fly camps as well as two semi-permanent camps, one near Ouagou in the north and the other along the Pabou River in the west.

Question:

Is bongo hunting really as difficult as hunters have been told or did you depend on a good portion of luck also?

Answer:

Bongo hunting is certainly the most difficult type of hunting that I have ever experienced. Not only is a high degree of physical fitness required but also mental stamina as long periods of intense concentration are required. The conditions in which the hunt takes place, i.e. equatorial rain forests, seems to place all the odds in favour of the bongo. The forests are extremely dense and it is usually difficult to see farther than 25 to 30 paces. The undergrowth is thick and the hunting party is armed with garden clippers to cut a silent path through the creepers, shrubs, branches, and bushes that impede progress. When the forests are dry, the undergrowth is too noisy to stalk, and due to the terrain, it is pointless to hunt other than off fresh tracks, which are usually picked up on the fringes of the forests and at water holes and salt licks inside the forests. Once tracks are discovered, you obviously follow the biggest and best bull track, and as has often been said before, animals like that do not grow that size by accident. Bongo seem to possess the same senses as a large kudu bull. In addition, before he beds down in the middle of the day, he starts to meander backward and forward, often crossing his own tracks, which can give the game away as he often ends up downwind of the hunting party. I found the terrain tremendously difficult in that at 6 foot 3 inches, I was continually bending, ducking and crawling in order to move through the undergrowth. Then again, as there is not a whole lot to see in the jungle, it requires a lot of mental stamina to retain concentration, which is necessary both if you want to walk quietly, and at the same time, be ready to take the shot. From my brief experience and listening to André Roux, my professional hunter, and the trackers, bongo bulls give you very little time for the shot, and this is where, I believe, luck plays a substantial part.

Question:

Being a nimrod, are there any other specific species in Africa on your list to hunt, and if so, please name them and tell us why?

Answer:

I would very much like to complete my collection of spiral horned antelope, namely, Lord Derby eland, mountain nyala, and lesser kudu. In this regard, I have booked to return to the CAR in

Heart of an African Hunter

January 1995 as, at this time, the eland still retain their winter ruff. Unfortunately, Ethiopia has closed hunting and I am not sure whether I will ever have the opportunity to hunt for mountain nyala. Tanzania still retains healthy populations of lesser kudu, and God willing, I would like to try for this superb and dainty animal some time in 1996 or 1997. On the local front, I intend to devote next year to the only animals that I have not hunted in our own country, namely, Natal red duiker, suni, and bushpig with a possible trip to Namibia for a black-faced impala and a quality springbok.

Question:

A hunter in Africa is totally dependent on his professional hunter and this person must therefore have certain special qualities that you as a client look for. Please give us some guidelines.

Answer:

While I do not believe that an amateur hunter is or should be totally dependent on his professional hunter, there is certainly a degree of dependence and interdependence, and it is equally true that the two must be compatible. Personally I look for a fit, keen, and young professional hunter with a good few years experience in the area that I wish to hunt and with the species that I am looking for. I try to avoid the sex-drugs-and-rock-and-roll type of professional hunter whose conversation is confined to those topics and the number of times he was charged while hunting. I try to avoid the professional hunter who is tired of hunting, who sees his job as something of a chore or who wants to complete the list of animals I am looking for as soon as possible and who has no respect for the game. I also try to steer clear of those professional hunters who want to make their own holes in the animals I hunt. Hunting with a professional hunter invariably involves you spending more time with him during a period of a three-week hunt than you do with your best friend during the course of a year. Therefore, it is important to ensure that your two personalities are compatible as well as your hunting ethics, hunting style, and to a lesser degree, your relative degrees of fitness.

Kenmekaar Forum

Question
What type of hunting do you prefer—i.e. plains, jungle bush, etc.—and why?

Answer:
I cannot say that I prefer a particular type of hunting. I like all kinds of hunting. Variety is the spice of life and the same applies to hunting. However, I do like hunting in certain places more than others, for example, the Eastern Karoo, the Okavango Swamps, the Zambezi Valley, and lately, the CAR.

Question:
As owner of a hunting farm in the Karoo, will you tell us why you chose that specific area of our country to intensively relocate game as you are doing at the moment?

Answer:
The decision to establish a game reserve and safari company in the Karoo is, clearly, not a decision one makes lightly. There were a number of reasons for the decision, for example:

I have hunted the Karoo since I was a boy, and more recently, every year since 1980. Quite simply, I love the area, its peace, open spaces, weather, terrain, and game.

There is no malaria.

The area of Agter-Sneeuberg, which I chose, is some sixty-five kilometres from the nearest town (Cradock), eight kilometres from the nearest tarred road, and combines three particular ecosystems—namely, riverine, plains, and mountains.

This allows us to keep a wide variety of species, some twenty-four in all, excluding primates and predators.

We have no veterinary restrictions on the transport of meat.

Owing to the drought, the downturn in the economy and the collapse in wool and angora prices, land became more affordable.

Given the terrain and the twenty-four species of game that are now present, the area offers a wide variety of hunts, including outstanding gray-wing shooting.

Heart of an African Hunter

The area is some forty kilometres as the crow flies from the Mountain Zebra National Park and we were able to purchase game that were acclimated to the region relatively inexpensively and with the minimum of transport and translocation problems.

The area is zoned for buffalo and rhino and we could in due course, as the children grow older, possibly incorporate these species.

The people in the Karoo are extremely friendly and helpful and I knew and liked my neighbours prior to acquiring land in the area. In fact, my neighbour, Louis Marais, is both my partner and manager of the reserve and safari company.

A tributary of the Fish River runs through the area which also has a number of perennial springs.

My wife and children feel secure and at ease in the area and can hunt, walk and drive around the area unaccompanied.

Question:

Most hunters prefer not to hunt plains game because of distances of more than 500 metres to shoot a trophy. Is this true of hunting in the Karoo and if not, could you give advice on calibre of rifles, etc., on your farm in particular?

Answer:

I have never shot at any animal at a distance of 500 metres. Apart from the high risk of wounding the animal in these circumstances, it is simply not necessary. Even during culling exercises, which we conduct each year, I mark out, by means of toilet paper tied to bushes, 200 and 300 metres on the four points of the compass. I have never found it necessary to take a shot of more than 300 metres in the Karoo. Then again, because of the variety of terrain, it is easily possible to stalk within acceptable shooting distances and, particularly, along the riverine areas or in the kopjes and mountains it is rare to have to take a shot of more than 150 to 200 metres. Of course, even shots at these distances can be tricky. My accuracy is greatly helped by planning the stalk properly, using a rest in the form of bushes or rocks, or a walking stick, or as I prefer, a bipod attached to the front swivel of my rifle. I would hesitate to give advice on calibres or rifles, but I can say that, after trying many different calibres, I have mostly used a 7mm Remington Magnum firing 176-grain bullets with a Harris bipod mounted on the front swivel. My partner in Karoo Safaris, Louis Marais, uses a .300 Winchester Magnum and there seems little to choose between the two, although neither of us would make this admission to the other of course. I have used. .222s, .223s, .243s, .244s, 7x57s, .270s, .30-06s, .300 H&Hs, and .375s, but I have consistently returned to the 7mm Remington Magnum. I must admit, however, that I do keep a .222 for trophy hunting the smaller game such as steenbok and duiker, and have used my .375 on bigger game such as eland, zebra, blue wildebeest, and kudu.

Question:

Conservation is a big effort for owners of game farms. Much time and money is spent on this. Do you think that this will be the trend in the future and that governments will put a bigger portion of conservation on the shoulders of game farmers? Your views please.

Answer:

Certainly the trend highlighted by Professor Eloff in his articles and speeches would seem to indicate that for some time, the expansion of private game farms and the conservation efforts involved therein have exceeded similar efforts by the public sector. Given the priorities of the new government, I have no doubt that this gap will widen even if the private sector were not to increase its conservation efforts.

Question:

You have hunted extensively both here and overseas. Can you tell us which animal gave you the biggest thrill to hunt, why, and where you hunted this?

Answer:

This is a hard question to answer. After forty-nine days of elephant hunting spread over four years, I thought that the big, lone bull I shot high in the Chewore Hills would not be superseded as the biggest thrill that I have had while hunting. This hunt, however, was surpassed by an unforgettable three weeks in the Chugach Mountains of Alaska, despite the fact that I did not once pull the trigger apart from sighting in. Both of these unforgettable hunts paled into insignificance, however, when compared with my recent hunt for bongo in the CAR and I suppose there are many reasons for this, namely:

The lush, green beauty of the area, its birds, game, orchids, butterflies, and so on.

The amount of training and preparation that went into the hunt. I do not think I have ever been fitter or better prepared.

The fact that bongo is recognized as the top African trophy and the most difficult to hunt.

The relative difficulty of hunting bongo and the fact that I shot it on the fifteenth day of the hunt and the tenth day of hunting that particular animal.

The quality of the animal (No. 9 in the world).

Finally, if this does not sound too boastful, I was proud of the fact that I pulled off a difficult shot and killed the animal cleanly with my first effort. In a sense, I felt that the hunt and the shot encapsulated my entire hunting career. The hunt tested all my skills and experience and it was a tremendously satisfying experience to know that when the opportunity was offered, I was not found wanting.

Question:

Every hunter has a special hunting rifle, please tell us about yours.

Answer:

My favourite hunting rifle is an old .375 Brno I call Bertha, topped by a Zeiss Diavari 1.5–6X scope. I would be guessing at how many rounds Bertha has fired, but it must run into the thousands. She has been reblued twice and has just returned from the gunsmith after a complete overhaul and having had her stock redone and rechequered. Quite a bit of work has gone into Bertha over the years. For example, the trigger has been replaced, the bolt polished, the ramp smoothed, the lugs lapped, and so on. She fits me like a glove, has never let me down, and I suppose, most importantly, I have tremendous faith in the gun. I take extremely good care of her and the gunsmith assures me that if I continue to look after her as I have, my grandchildren will one day be able to use her. After her service last year, and off a dead rest at the rifle range, I put three consecutive rounds through the bull, cutting one another, at 100 metres. If I were to choose one rifle and one calibre to use for the rest of my life, I would not change.

Question:

Like housewives need household tips, so do hunters need hunting tips. Please supply some to our readers.

Answer:

I am, at best, only an average hunter and average shot. As such, I feel it would be arrogant of me to hand out hunting tips as if I were some top professional hunter. What I do try to do is make up for my lack of natural talent by intensive preparation. I exercise every day of my life and try to run or cycle every second day. I spend many hours on the rifle range, starting each year in January with my .22 and progressively working up to my .475. Apart from shooting off a bench rest, I practice lying, sitting, kneeling, and standing and before the start of the hunting season will have fired somewhere between 300 and 400 rounds on the practice range. I read extensively about the hunting experiences of others and try to learn from every hunter I meet. I believe that there is no substitute for preparation and practice. After that, it is up to Diana, the goddess of hunting, and taking the opportunities as they present themselves.

Question:

As our Grand Champion for 1993, you have mixed feelings about "winning" the trophy. Please explain your views on competitions of this sort.

Answer:

I do have very mixed feelings about any form of competition in the field of hunting. On one hand, I enjoy having a reference such as Rowland Ward in order to be able to measure myself and my trophies against these standards, although I have never entered any of my animals in any record book. On the other hand, I am extremely concerned that competition, particularly if it becomes unhealthy, could lead to the transgression of ethical standards such as hunting at night with a spotlight, cornering animals with dogs, shooting from helicopters, and the whole contentious aspect of canned hunts. Our sport comes in for ever-increasing amounts of criticism and I believe most sincerely that we should strive for higher ethical standards. Having said that, I am extremely honoured and humbled by the awards I received, particularly when I think of the great hunters who have previously won them and in whose footsteps I now tread. As I said at the annual dinner, I can only hope that as many people succeed me in winning the trophies as those who have preceded me.

It has been a sheer pleasure interviewing such a modest and honest man as Peter Flack. The lesson in all this seems to me—if you want to hunt bongo, you should not be 6 foot, 3 inches or taller, but rather be a *stofpoepertjie* (half-pint) like me.